CW00747541

MARCHING
WITH
MAO

By the same author

Alone on the Great Wall

William Lindesay

MARCHING WITH MAO

A biographical journey

Hodder & Stoughton

LONDON SYDNEY AUCKLAND

British Library Cataloguing in Publication Data

Lindesay, William
Marching with Mao: Biographical Journey
I. Title
915.104

ISBN 0-340-55664-1

Copyright © William Lindesay 1993

First published in Great Britain 1993

Map by ML Design

All rights reserved. No part of this publication may be reproduced or transmitted in any form or by any means, electronic or mechanical, including photocopying, recording, or any information storage and retrieval system, without either prior permission in writing from the publisher or a licence permitting restricted copying. In the United Kingdom such licences are issued by the Copyright Licensing Agency, 90 Tottenham Court Road, London WIP 9HE. The right of William Lindesay to be identified as the author of this work has been asserted by him in accordance with the Copyright, Designs and Patents Act 1988.

Published by Hodder and Stoughton,
a division of Hodder and Stoughton Ltd,
Mill Road, Dunton Green, Sevenoaks, Kent TN13 2YA.
Editorial Office: 47 Bedford Square, London WC1B 3DP.

Photoset by Rowland Phototypesetting Ltd,
Bury St Edmunds, Suffolk

Printed in Great Britain by Mackays of Chatham plc,
Chatham, Kent.

To the scores of peasants, nomads and workers
who fed and sheltered me as I footslogged
through closed China.
They opened their doors to reveal China's heart.

Foreword

Mao Zedong welcoming Edward Heath to Beijing, 1974.

I first visited China in 1974. The warmth of the welcome I received from the Chinese people, on this and my many subsequent visits to China, made a powerful and lasting impression upon me.

During my visit in 1974 and again in 1976, I had long discussions with Chairman Mao Zedong. I was the first and the only British Prime Minister ever to do so. I found in him many of the same qualities that I had seen in Churchill, Adenauer, de Gaulle and Tito. They all possessed the ability to go to the heart of the matter, to sort out the important from the insignificant, and to see their policies through to the end.

I remember asking Mao what motivated the Chinese people today. "Ah," he replied, "that's a long story. There's no point going back over the past. You must think about the future. That's what you have got to do." I have always believed, however, that China's past is as fascinating as her future and itself offers an unique insight into this remarkable country and people.

Marching With Mao recounts William Lindesay's experiences whilst retracing the route of the Long March of 1934. His account of this six-thousand-mile journey, from the south to the north of China, provides an intriguing history of the Long March and its impact on modern Chinese society.

China is a huge country, with over one billion inhabitants. However, it is a land little understood by those outside it. As this true giant among nations looks ever-increasingly outwards, so we must endeavour to improve our understanding of China; its history, its people and its future. *Marching With Mao* is an interesting personal introduction to China and I was delighted to be asked to contribute a foreword to it.

The Rt. Hon. Sir Edward Heath, K.G., M.B.E., M.P.

Contents

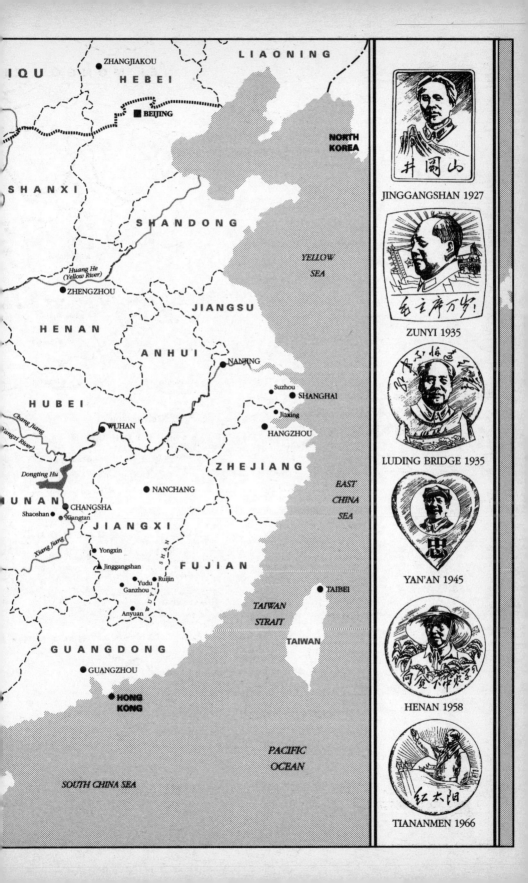

ZHANGJIAKOU

LIAONING

HEBEI

IQU

BEIJING

NORTH
KOREA

SHANXI

SHANDONG

YELLOW
SEA

*Huang He
(Yellow River)*

ZHENGZHOU

JIANGSU

HENAN

ANHUI

NANJING

Suzhou

SHANGHAI

HUBEI

*Chang Jiang
(Yangzi River)*

WUHAN

Jiaxing

HANGZHOU

Dongting Hu

ZHEJIANG

NANCHANG

EAST
CHINA
SEA

HUNAN

CHANGSHA

Shaoshan   Xiangtan

JIANGXI

Yongxin

Xiang Jiang

Jinggangshan

FUJIAN

Yudu   Ruijin
Ganzhou

TAIBEI

Anyuan

TAIWAN
STRAIT

TAIWAN

GUANGDONG

GUANGZHOU

HONG
KONG

PACIFIC
OCEAN

SOUTH CHINA SEA

JINGGANGSHAN 1927

ZUNYI 1935

LUDING BRIDGE 1935

YAN'AN 1945

HENAN 1958

TIANANMEN 1966

Author's Note

The travels recounted here form a personally selected, but chronologically continuous, narrative of what can be called a biographical
journey through the life and times of Mao Zedong. Specifically, I
have focused on Mao's birth and his formative years after the turn
of the century; the origins of the Communist Party and the roots
of the embryonic Red Army in the 1920s; and most importantly, by
way of feet-on experience, the Long March of the mid-1930s. The
period after the so-called Xi'an Incident of December 1936 until the
foundation of New China in October 1949, although cataclysmic in
witnessing the Sino-Japanese War followed by the ensuing War of
Liberation between Mao and Chiang, does not concern the book
and receives only brief mention for the sake of historical linkage.
From Liberation in 1949, when Mao founded the People's Republic
of China, I begin to draw on the reminiscences of my wife's family
in terms of the Great Leap Forward (late Fifties) and Cultural Revol-

ution (mid-Sixties to mid-Seventies). But since my actual travels were in the early Nineties, over fourteen years after Mao's death, then the observations recorded in this book span a whole century 1893–1992 of both Mao's life and his posthumous influence.

On a practical note, I was alone on my own Long March, although my wife saw me off, met me at the finish and halfway through to relieve heartache. At other times she accompanied me, acting as interpreter. These arrangements are not always referred to nor obvious in the text since I use the first person singular. During our extended stay in China we made ends meet by both teaching English and photo-journalism. The entire book was written in China.

All place names and Chinese dialogue are transcripted using the Pinyin system. So there is no Peking, only Beijing, and no Mao Tsetung, only Mao Zedong. There are three Wade-Giles rebels, namely Sun Yat-sen, Chiang Kai-shek and the Kuomintang. The Communists replaced the 'ping' of Beiping with 'jing' – meaning capital – in 1949. So Beiping refers to the old city, pre-1949.

Although my journey was entirely self-financed, I have many people to thank for opportunity, help, encouragement and services. First and foremost must come my wife Qi. Quite apart from her practical help, she gave me the motivation to achieve a better understanding of China. My sister-in-law, Wu Xiaoping, is not only the focus of attention in the chapters on the Cultural Revolution but she had the laborious task of typing my manuscript. I was fortunate in finding a cross-section of veteran revolutionaries, men and women of advanced years with emancipated minds to recall their roles in New China's birth. Special thanks and wishes for long life to Ma Xiaji, Gu Yiping, Xu Youwan, Bao Zhong, Zhang Chaoman, Zhong Ling, Tan Bing, and Luo Shaoqing. They not only provided eyewitness testimonies but considerable motivation when difficulty and dangers were encountered to press on and tell their magnificent story in the following pages. On the Long March in particular many peasants and nomads offered their homes, larders and wells to me, and I broke the Red Army's rule of discipline by not paying them.

Other providers of valuable information were Tang Ruiren of Shaoshan, Wang Anting of Chengdu, Dr Ma Yanlong of Beijing and the Sichuan Exhibition Centre. I owe special thanks also to artist Zhang Da who sketched from impressions in my mind and historical source materials images that my camera could not capture.

Back in Britain, before my departure for China and for the duration of my stay, my brothers Nicholas and David Lindesay have been of enormous help. Nicholas has managed my affairs and given valuable encouragement and advice. David, together with his wife Hilary, has sorted through hundreds of transparencies and printed copies in association with Merseyside photo specialists Max Spielmann. Thanks also to Mountain Equipment for Ultrafleece clothing and a Lightline sleeping-bag, and to Timberland for sturdy boots. I am also indebted to Charles Phelps-Penry of British Airways, Beijing, for generous flight assistance.

Finally, because a book is not written but rewritten, I thank my manuscript editor David Blomfield, and Margaret Body who has overseen the project. Apologies to them for my combative attitude, a trait inherent from the trials and tribulations of adventure travel in China.

William Lindesay   Xi'an, Shaanxi, P.R. China
                                    December 26th 1992

PROLOGUE   *Seize The Year!*

Mao's statue in the entrance hall of his mausoleum, Tiananmen Square, surrounded by floral tributes.

It was as if our future was destined to be inextricably linked with China when my wife-to-be, Wu Qi, and I spent New Year's Day 1988 walking upon the nation's dramatic stage of revolutionary history – Tiananmen Square. Eighteen months later the world would be shocked by very different images of this place. But on this auspicious day a holiday atmosphere prevailed. Moreover, it was the first opportunity for the public to visit the balcony on the Gate of Heavenly Peace, which forms an historical hinge between the myriad of buildings known as the Forbidden City and the contrasting socialist-style architecture bordering the Square.

We were given metal badges instead of tickets in return for our entrance fees, which triggered the first of Wu Qi's many family memories. 'As a little girl, twenty years ago,' she said, 'I collected Chairman Mao badges just like this – some as big as saucers!'

Standing on the balcony we looked out across the Square as the portrait of Mao still does, our backs turned on the feudal past of his birth, facing the New China that he created. On my recent 2,500-kilometre journey along the Great Wall, I had been inspired by Mao Zedong's legendary Long March and for me this visit to the very place where the 'Great Helmsman' had stood to proclaim the founding of the People's Republic of China (the PRC) was something of a pilgrimage. I had identified closely with the Red Army's struggle against all odds, whilst some of my hosts had pedestalled me – quite undeservedly – by likening my revolutionary spirit to that of their father comrades.

It would, however, have been sheer idolatry to regard Mao in that single light, and Wu Qi's vivid recollections of her own family's fate gave me a personalised insight into the traits of his alter ego.

'When Chairman Mao stood here on October 1st 1949,' she said, 'my father, as a Beijing student, cheered from the avenue below – but in 1966 he was sent to the "cowsheds" for being an intellectual, the stinking ninth category of society.'

Along the balcony her memories were being prompted further as echoes of the Cultural Revolution were being given an impromptu airing by other first-footing Chinese who were coaxed into shaking their red plastic-covered identity cards aloft by a foreign TV-news crew. 'They're mimicking the Red Guards saluting Chairman Mao with *Little Red Books*,' Wu Qi explained, 'just as my sister Wu Xiaoping did when she saw him from below during the Fourth Red Guard rally in 1966.'

I suggested we should capture this moment on film to post to her sister. Hurrying down into the Square I focused on Wu Qi, speck-like, peering out from above the gargantuan portrait of Mao.

Later, walking south across the Square I remarked that in the peasant communities I had visited along the Great Wall Mao continued to be highly respected, if his omnipresent portrait was anything to go by. Some eleven years after his death he still held pride of place on the walls of the rural populace – who make up eighty per cent of China's billion-plus population. Wu Qi assured me this loyalty had not survived in the towns, but pointing east to the crest of red flags billowing like flames atop the entrance to the Museum of Revolutionary History, she added, 'Still, no matter what you might think of Chairman Mao, he was the genius, the spark who started the prairie fire.'

Mao had, from the conception of Communism in China, been adamant that the key to achieving lasting revolutionary change rested with winning the peasantry's support. This was in contrast to the model of the Soviet Union where the revolution had been centred on urban workers. Mao, himself from a peasant family, likened the Chinese people to 'blank sheets of paper on which any message could be written' – and it was he, together with his Red Army who wrote their message on some 200 million people along the route of the Long March. It was arguably the most influential of political campaigns, giving later life to the dreams of tens of thousands who fell along its 9,000 kilometres.

Appropriately we now stood beside the obelisk which is the Monument to the People's Heroes, a pillar of glistening crystalline granite incised with golden calligraphic eulogies of Mao and Zhou Enlai. It is not only a memorial to the Long Marchers, for the ten reliefs on the plinth tell the whole story of the Revolution.

Chronologically, beginning with the Opium War, Wu Qi interpreted the long and bloody path which had led the People's Liberation Army (the PLA) into Tiananmen. Several reliefs depicted the misery and death suffered by the Chinese at the hands of empire-building foreign powers like the British and the Japanese. Wu Qi recalled the emphasis placed on these episodes of history at school when she was taught to despise imperialists. But there was also the internal question of the correct course of the Chinese Revolution, resolved by the waging of a civil war against the Kuomintang (the KMT) – on and off for twenty-two years. That ended when Chiang Kai-shek fled to Taiwan in 1949. The cost in human life was millions – so many, in fact, that each hero shared a crystal of this Shandong granite memorial with a thousand other comrades.

A man who could be embalmed and laid to rest in a giant mausoleum must by comparison have been a god. We joined the snaking queue waiting to file past Mao's body and entered the Memorial Hall to see, in the annexe, a giant white marble statue of Mao seated amidst a sea of wreaths garlanded with eulogies from Party, State, Army, relatives and staff, in remembrance of his recent birthday. Qi knew that date well, for it was used, along with the birthdates of

Lenin and Marx, for teaching middle-school students the date in English.

'Chairman Mao's birthday is December 26th; he was born almost a century ago now, in 1893,' she said.

Now, seventeen years after his death, Mao's reputation is as remarkable as ever. China could have banished the cursed memories of the Cultural Revolution both symbolically and literally by putting Mao six feet under. Instead, they have put him on show six feet above, for all to see through a crystal sarcophagus. The most prominent leader of the post-Mao era, Deng Xiaoping, along with his family, had experiences that typified the suffering and humiliation endured by many in the wasted decade. But Deng, far from taking vengeance and removing Mao from Tiananmen Square, eulogised him on the tenth anniversary of his death, praising 'an illustrious life and immortal contributions to the people, towering above errors and defects'.

This verbal benefit of the doubt is often translated into numerical terms of seventy per cent correct and thirty per cent incorrect, and, this figure-fudging is sometimes reinforced by finger-fudging. Some Chinese hold up five fingers when mentioning the Gang of Four – damning sign-language, and tantamount to a posthumous sentencing of Mao in the Communists' equivalent of purgatory alongside the clique exposed to the nation by televised trials for their crimes during the Cultural Revolution.

Almost all Chinese born before the mid-Sixties have some mementos of Mao. My wife Qi is no exception. Despite her family's suffering, it has never occurred to her to throw away her personal relics from the Cultural Revolution. Indeed, when emigrating to England after our marriage in 1988, she packed some of these red memories which telescoped thirty years of life into her two suitcases.

Clothing apart, almost all her chattels retained the aura of revolution. She had eschewed the opportunity of selling her *Little Red Book* for waste paper and her Mao badges for scrap metal. With an attachment borne from years of loyalty they were forever keepsakes, just as love letters are between separated partners, reminders of the climaxes of a turbulent affair that was endured despite the pain of it all. Photographs too showed the withering of the peony silk and the rise of the red-starred cap, a fashion revolution depicted by her mother wearing an elegant *cheongsam* dress before Liberation and an army uniform after. Photographs of Qi and her two sisters completed a full circle by tracing the progress from the sexless Mao suit back to the dress. The first one Qi ever owned was bought in the mid-Eighties.

Other insights into those reactionary days were somewhat latent, illustrating the comprehensiveness of propagandists who sought to exploit every opportunity of spreading the revolutionary message. In a weighty English–Chinese dictionary all contextual definitions were seized to wage a war of words. Propaganda came before useful application as one-liner examples traced the rise, and rise, of Communism:

BEFORE:

⎰ Liberation

We will never bow ⎱ difficulties

Put the study of Marxism, Leninism and Mao Zedong Thought ⎰ anything

It won't be long ⎱ imperialism comes to an end

⎰ long the whole world will be red.

Kept flat within this mighty tome were postage stamps. An issue to wish 'A Long Life to Chairman Mao' was followed just two months later by another to wish him 'A Long, Long Life'. A further set gave unnecessary publicity to his *Little Red Book of Quotations* which, during its decade-long print run was churned out 6.5 billion times overtaking the 4 billion Bibles published over the previous half-millennium, to become, and remain to this day and for the foreseeable future, the world's number one bestseller ever. To show that the weapons of foreign languages were being successfully harnessed, another large stamp depicted Chairman Mao surrounded by the people of the world: Blacks, Whites, Arabs, Indians and others, all bathing in his nourishing sunlight smile as they upheld their own *Little Red Books* which had been translated and exported to 148 countries. Like Jesus Christ Our Lord, God the Almighty Father, His Holiness the Great Prophet Muhammad, Mao Zhu Xi too now had his god-like suffix previously the reserve of emperors: *Mao Zhu Xi Wan Sui* (A life of ten thousand years to Chairman Mao).

Yet Mao died aged 83, a mortal. I had gleaned much during my initial China years about his character, but the more I had travelled, often crossing the route of the Long March, the more I yearned to embrace the full picture of Mao's life and his fight to create the new China which, for better or for worse, had shaped Qi's life and that of her family.

Mao's early life was especially peripatetic and hence ideally suited to retracing; so to make a biographical pilgrimage seemed the perfect way of retracing the last century of China's history. Mao would escort me from the feudal, twilight years of the Qing Dynasty into the mid-Seventies. Beyond then, what better way was there of taking stock of the New Long March (to use Deng's time-honoured metaphor for China's modernisation) than to travel to the sites of the principal events and episodes in Mao's life which were quintessential elements of the Chinese Revolution?

'Seize the day, seize the hour,' urged Mao in one of his poems. I would now seize the year. In Tiananmen Square, Qi had fortuitously prompted me with her reference to Mao's birth. I would grasp this chance opportunity provided by history to make a biographical journey to celebrate the centenary of Mao Zedong's birth.

The Wind Veers

Stalin and Mao sealing the Sino-Soviet Treaty of Friendship, Alliance and Mutual Assistance, in 1950

The word for crisis in Chinese is *wei ji*, which is made up from the characters for danger and opportunity. The death of Mao in 1976 was a *wei ji* which China survived and it did not encounter another until 1989 – with the nightmare of nationwide chaos and martial law.

At the time, Wu Qi and I were in England preparing for my own Long March, and for us the images of those distressing days were indelible: a solitary man blocking the path of a mighty column of tanks in the middle of the inappropriately named Chang'an (Forever Peaceful) Avenue; mangled bicycles, burnt-out buses and the face of Party Secretary Zhao Ziyang pleading with the students to vacate the Square. Yet, as Beijing was paralysed by the marching masses, it was the portraits and slogans of Chairman Mao which were upheld and chanted as being symbolic of the ideological purity lost by corruption within the Communist Party of the day. As law and order began to break down, one element, presumably subscribers to the five-fingers assessment of Mao, defaced his portrait with ink bombs. The culprits were duly arrested by students and handed over to the Public Security Bureau. In spite of the mayhem, public works officials were assisted by the protesters in reverently covering a defaced Mao with a canopy whilst a replacement portrait was sought and repositioned. The portrait of Mao Zedong was not the last thing to leave Tiananmen draped with a shroud.

Having my China experience set during the comparatively liberal years of 1986–8 when economic reform flourished had made me sceptical of those who glanced backwards in fear of further political upheavals. In 1989 at the sight of open dissent throughout China I had to eat my words. At the same time I knew from my own dealings with security officials that the law was always implemented, whatever the opinions of the individual official. I recalled police officers – with their hats on the table – praising my determination and revolutionary spirit one minute, then literally putting their official hats on to fine me for my repeated trespass into closed areas.

The most striking thing one notices on arrival in China – after the droves of bicycles – are the masses of people in uniform. Brought up on the notion that the army and people are one and united it is understandable why most Chinese never expected military intervention from an army prefixed 'The People's'. But the veterans of the Long March who still hold sway called in their Great Wall of Iron and Steel to write the latest instalment of the ongoing Revolution. The official terminology to be used by Government chroniclers would be Counter Revolution. The Western press dubbed it the Tiananmen massacre. The Chinese, rightly fearing further upheavals, call it 'the event'.

The Draconian measures of the crackdown were followed by purges, round-ups of the so-called black hands, and an intense barrage of propaganda. Chairman Mao's good student, Lei Feng, was resurrected as a model from whom to learn. (It was no coincidence that Lei Feng was a dead PLA soldier who had devoted himself to serving the people.) At the same time gory photographic displays of decapitated soldiers, charred corpses, gutted tanks and APCs were posted in the street and broadcast on TV. Economic reform had made China the biggest TV audience in the world; so it was a powerful tool to persuade the country's increasingly square-eyed populace that there had been a counter-revolutionary plot.

In such a climate, I calculated, my planned biographical journey could provide welcome propaganda for a China now shunned by the West – in 1987 the New China News Agency (Xinhua) had hailed me as the only foreigner to have completed a traverse of the Great Wall – but I decided to steer as clear as possible of all government patronage. I wanted to remain the lone traveller, free to journey at will, wherever I dared, to see for myself. Chinese involvement might have meant my biographical journey being promoted as an idolatrous pilgrimage rather than an objective quest to understand the man, his policies and his country. Furthermore, because I was an independent, with no paymaster nor host, neither a Communist nor an anti-Communist, my observations and conclusions would be accepted as more even-keeled.

I made my journey back to China overland, and a stopover in Moscow gave me a glimpse of the other great Communist giant now teetering on the brink of catastrophe.

For months the news from Moscow had resembled a Punch and Judy show played out by Gorbachev and Yeltsin bashing each other in the Congress of Deputies. Gorbachev, preaching the gospel of *glasnost* and *perestroika* had become the darling of the West, but the hopes of the hungry Russian people were pinned on the maverick poster smile of Boris Yeltsin.

Krushchev had said decades before that Communism would be judged a success when all Soviets could eat beef and potatoes. Perhaps Gorky Street provided a vision of the future, where the queue for McDonald's Big Macs and French fries was comparable in length to the one at Lenin's tomb.

Artists and craftsmen on Arbat Prospekt exercised their new freedom by venting the frustration of the Soviet people on the entire leadership, past and present. Lenin was depicted as a horned devil, Krushchev as a knobbly-kneed boxer-shorted military commander who had been over-generous in awarding himself military honours. Still more critical were the protesters from the Soviet Central Asian republics squatting in their camp of boxes outside the gargantuan

Hotel Rossiya in the shadow of the Kremlin, and the nests of painted wooden dolls caricatured as the tenants of the Kremlin, fitting inside one another and all ultimately in Lenin.

This was dissidence that would not be tolerated in China. Even the smashing of small bottles by Chinese students, which was a play on words for the downfall of Deng Xiaoping – *xiaoping* sounds like 'small bottle' although the characters are not alike – had been viewed as a counter-revolutionary act. Strangely, the Chinese students had championed 'Gorby' for his political reforms during that historic Beijing summit upstaged by the unrest gripping the capital – but they could choose to go on hunger strike. Deng's economic reforms had given them fully stocked state shops, mountains of fresh produce in the free markets, smatterings of imported goods and – the modern opium of the people – beer and cigarettes everywhere. Muscovites had no such choice: there was hardly any food at all.

Despite an Asian chill which lasted for over three decades, in the Lenin Museum close to Red Square one can still see copies of Lenin's works published in Chinese, for the man primarily responsible for adapting Leninism to meet Chinese needs came to Moscow just two weeks after founding the People's Republic. It was Mao's first overseas trip, travelling overland by train from Beijing on the Trans-Siberian railway (on the advice of the Central Committee he was never to travel by air) to arrive at Moscow's Yaraslavl Station.

Over forty years later I now stood in the hall of the same station about to depart on the Rossiya for Beijing. From the alien din in Russian I could imagine the tone of Stalin's welcoming address echoing beneath the arched ceiling. From the notices and advertisements in the Cyrillic script I could picture the banners exhorting Sino-Soviet friendship draped between pillars. And from the familiar tones of Mandarin chattered by my fellow passengers came to me the voice of Mao Zedong. It was past midnight. Train No 4 was about to depart on its 7,800-kilometre haul to Beijing.

2

A Route of Badges

1893·12·26

红日出韶山

A badge commemorating Mao's birth on December 26th, 1893 in Shaoshan, Hunan Province.

With my geographer's mind and the most vivid of armchair traveller imaginations, maps had hitherto been the catalysts for many of my tickets to adventure, but for this journey the steers on my intended route were provided not by maps but by a box-full of Mao badges. Qi had not exaggerated – some were as big as saucers. Regardless of size, all showed Mao's head in silver or bronze relief on a deep red background etched with the characters and images relating to their issue.

At best they seemed no more than a hotch-potch of revolutionary relics; at worst the graven images from a decade of worship. Yet, placed at their relevant locations on an outline map of China, these badges, produced during the Cultural Revolution to commemorate every event and enshrine each revolutionary site, linked up a comprehensive route through all the sites concerned with the conception, genesis and evolution of the Chinese Revolution. For me, they were no mere nostalgic miscellany but a jigsaw that pieced together Mao's story, the metallic annals of New China, a political gazetteer and an historical map combined, showing the mountains and rivers, real and metaphorical, that the Communists had crossed.

My plan was to follow as closely as I could in Mao's own footsteps, retracing his life from cradle to mausoleum. Some of the journey would be straightforward. Mao's early life was well-documented and I would certainly be welcomed at the various shrines to the birth of Chinese Communism. Other parts, though, would be extremely hazardous, for my pilgrimage would include feet-on experience of Mao's great Long March – and most of that, I knew, was out-of-bounds to foreigners. It would also be fearsomely hard travelling through some of the most inhospitable regions of this sub-continent. From the mid-Thirties onward, the journeying would be less hard work, though I would find the authorities progressively less co-operative, for I would be exploring the most sensitive area of all – the years when Mao held power.

My base for the journey was Xi'an, the capital of Shaanxi Province. This was selected for several reasons. Firstly, it is Qi's home town, and I needed somewhere to stay between trips – for it was clear I could not pack Mao's long life into one year – also I could gain frequent access to her family's reminiscences. I was well aware at this stage that although the route of badges seemed complete it might well exhibit the fault of many a jigsaw and have a piece or two missing. Once Mao had achieved leadership, the events and episodes that history was to generate were not inextricably linked to specific locations. So I would focus, post-1949, on the consequences of Mao's policies on the lives of individual Chinese in general, and of my own relatives in particular.

Subsidiary reasons for temporary settlement in Xi'an concerned the city's geographical location. Administrators classify Xi'an as a northwestern city. That went against my innate sense of direction. Xi'an is bang in the middle of China so I preferred to describe it as a central city. How could one travel 1,000 kilometres southwest from Beijing and be in northwestern China? With regard to my proposed route of badges Xi'an was centrally located too, and as such was a hub of rail and road communications. Finally – climate is always a major consideration in China – though Xi'an's winters are bitterly cold and dry, and its summers searing hot, far worse extremities of weather are to be found elsewhere.

With a hesitant recognition of Chinese characters, supplemented by a fair instinct for reading between them, I picked out the badge of Shaoshan. The numerals 1893. 12. 26 etched on the front reassured me that this was Mao Zedong's birthplace and therefore the logical starting point for my biographical journey. So first, I must head south of the Yangzi River, for Shaoshan was in Hunan Province.

In Xi'an I boarded a train for Changsha, capital of Hunan. Catching sight of that city's name on the destination plates of the carriages gave me the feeling of truly being on my way. This sense of melodrama was enhanced as I glanced at my watch, and with the reassuring punctuality I had come to expect from China Railways sensed the train edge forward, heard the first chords of 'Auld Lang Syne' and, as we picked up speed, saw the station guards standing to attention flash past the window.

As we rolled east towards Zhengzhou, the exchange of personal histories, so much the expected norm of travel chat especially with a foreigner, soon began. Many of my fellow travellers were heading further south than Changsha to the resort of Guilin amongst a landscape of pinnacled limestone mountains. Few Chinese can personally afford the time and money to take a holiday, and so have learned to use the system. Since the cadre class of most state enterprises are Communist Party members, holding their meetings in such resorts is regarded as a Party perk. How anybody could pass up the opportunity of visiting Guilin and prefer Shaoshan baffled them.

Yet twenty years ago the opposite was true, for all of those around me themselves had headed for Shaoshan during their revolutionary educations. All then carried the standard text of the day, their *Little Red Book*s. In the preface, Lin Biao, at that time Mao's chosen successor, advised all students to, 'study Chairman Mao's writings, follow his teachings and act according to his instructions'. It is a quote not easily forgotten, coming as it did from a would-be traitor.

For Mao's own thoughts on these Party fringe benefits at the exclusion of the broad masses I consulted my own copy of the *Little*

Red Book. Its appearance, or rather reappearance, in the carriage caused quite a stir. Predictably I found some relevant words of wisdom under a section subtitled 'Building Our Country Through Diligence and Frugality'. As I read the English version of Mao's advice to Party members on 'enforcing strict economies, combating waste and extravagance whilst shunning personal gain and reward', my bunkmates mouthed the translation, printed character-form on the facing pages.

Action had spoken louder than words in 1989 when the masses held Beijing and the Party by the throat, warning against the same Party perks and corruption; so I prepared a question on the root cause of the students' discontent. I got no further than the mere mention of the toxic cocktail – June 1989 and Beijing's Tiananmen Square – before my companions retreated with the excuse of being unable to comprehend my Chinese.

Next morning, around six o'clock, the lights flickered on and the *Fu wu yuan* (carriage attendant) announced, 'Comrades, it's time to get up, have a wash and tidy up your bed!' After a gentle introduction of melodic music peppered with chirping birdsong the volume and tempo intensified, and some 120 passengers sprang to life busying themselves with the preparation of instant noodle breakfasts in the most enormous enamel mugs in the world, minimum capacity one and a half pints, decorated with cats, cocks and camellias.

This music-while-you-work atmosphere was suddenly deflated by the unmistakably mournful drone of a requiem. It produced a hush throughout the carriage, as we speculated on the front runners for Babaoshan's cremation ovens and an audience with Marx beyond. Was it Deng Xiaoping? Ever since the Beijing Spring of 1989 there had been regular rumours concerning the health of the grandfather figure of Chinese politics. Every couple of months, however, he reappeared, resurrected by the wonder of traditional Chinese medicine to confound the rumour-mongers.

Soon the uncertainty was answered: Comrade Xu Xiangqian had died, aged 88, in Beijing. He was, we were told, remembered as a Great Proletarian Revolutionary and devoted Communist fighter, a founder comrade of the People's Liberation Army who held high and important positions and gave his life to the Party, Army and country. It was only the slow and deliberate tone of the eulogy, interspersed by the fading-in of the background requiem, that allowed my inadequate ear to grasp the highlights of Commander Xu's glorious life. As a youth he was influenced by the May 4th Movement and attended the Whampao Military Academy, a hotbed of political activism, where he plunged into revolutionary struggle against imperialism and feudalism . . .

The fact that another Long March veteran had passed away awakened my hitherto subconscious concern that men of this ilk were indeed a dying breed; seeking out their testimonies was becoming a more difficult task by the day. Of the four thousand survivors of the March in 1935 perhaps only a few hundred were still alive. Of those, a large percentage were occupying high positions in Beijing despite their advanced age. How many veterans still lived in the revolutionary base areas to which I was heading? How many could I track down? Would these octogenarians be of sound enough mind and body to talk? Not all Long Marchers were as privileged as Deng Xiaoping in having a team of doctors to revitalise them.

For me, these men were the top of the mountain, for they had been led by Mao. The next level were those who felt Mao's policies, a generation later, and were therefore two score years or more younger, ubiquitous in comparison, like those around me heading south. They all knew the biographical facts as part of their education. Emphasising this, a chorus broke out as the train crossed the Wuhan bridge spanning the Yangzi. 'In July 1966 Chairman Mao swam for twelve kilometres here!' It gave me hope. Mental arithmetic told me Mao must have been in his seventies then. His generation were made of revolutionary stuff.

*　　*　　*

Twenty years ago the village of Shaoshan was deluged with visitors, but now it was as if the climate had changed from wet to dry, leaving a deep and wide river valley gouged by powerful torrents in a bygone era to be host to a present day trickle. Today, the only clue to the influx is Shaoshan's fossil-like transport infrastructure – a purpose-built highway and railroad. I took a bus along the former which stretched 104 kilometres west from Changsha.

As I stepped down from the bus, my ears still humming from the constant blaring of the klaxon horn, Shaoshan at first seemed indistinctive. But as I entered the bus station and my eyes accommodated to its dim interior I realised that this was indeed the Mecca, the Bethlehem of Maoism. A ten-metre chrome statue of Mao rose up from a litter of orange peel, sugar-cane shavings, sunflower seeds, spit and other debris, while on the benches sat, stood, slept and squatted a handful of small and swarthy Hunanese: the children, grandchildren and great grandchildren of Mao's county fellows.

Perhaps it looked like this during the Sixties and Seventies – minus the garbage which would have been an anti-revolutionary slur under Chairman Mao's nose. People then had converged on Shaoshan from all China, and with the village bursting at the seams the bus station was used as a dormitory. Every square metre was sleeping space, though carpeting the floor with newspapers was a dangerous thing then: almost all carried Chairman Mao's photographs and quotations, and throwing them away or even putting them on the floor was inviting criticism.

In the main, the occupants of this station would have been Red Guards on their *Da chuanlian* (exchanges of revolutionary experiences). Two hundred could lodge here. Their chatter would have told of 'New Long Marches' – the more hardships endured en route the more revolutionary the experience. Blisters and injuries were trophies of the trip. Sunstroke, dehydration and soakings were elements Chairman Mao had taught his students to endure. Some had even walked barefoot, their plimsolls in their knapsacks. But it was surely worthwhile, just to reach Shaoshan and sleep under the eyes of their Father, and to receive Shaoshan Mao badges to add to their already expanding collection. In all, it was such an inspiration that the Red Guards were likely to continue New Long Marching, perhaps east to Changsha to see Chairman Mao's school, with some good soldiers trekking into Jiangxi province to the first revolutionary base of the Red Army – the very route I was about to take.

Peasants along the way would have willingly provided food and lodging for the New Long Marchers, who in return were keen to learn the skills of farm labour. Some such peasants were depicted in an art-gallery size painting inside the bus station, though they looked a different breed to the matchstick men of Hunan today. The masterpiece in question commemorated Chairman Mao's return to Shaoshan in 1959. Striding forth along a road, Mao is flanked by muscular peasantfolk, their shoulders broad, biceps bulging, their faces eager with bright eyes all focused on the Chairman.

Since artists then painted the message of the propaganda team, interpretation calls for the acquired skill of revolutionary art appreciation. Qi had taught me its intricacies. The peasants were well nourished and developed as a result of reaping the benefits of long days in the fields. They were not fat – as landlords are traditionally depicted – through the lack of work and exploitation of others. Food production was high because the latest Five-Year Plan had been victoriously fulfilled. In other words, the Party's, and therefore Mao's, policies were correct and successful.

This was the revolutionary artist's licence – misleading by definition, and in 1959 especially so. Politically disastrous policies had combined with natural calamities of floods in the south and drought in the north to cause a Great Famine. During that time, for instance, Qi had been sent as a baby to her grandmother in Anhui Province. She returned the following year malnourished, her limbs thin and belly swollen with hunger. Some twenty million did not escape as superficially, perishing in the famine.

Perhaps it was because of these very setbacks that Mao made his nostalgic journey back to Shaoshan. The problems, however, did not stunt his intellectual powers. In the Shaoshan Guest House, built especially for his visit, in which I too was now lodging, Mao stayed up until the early hours, writing a poem entitled *Shaoshan Revisited*:

> Like a dim dream recalled, I curse the long-fled past –
> My native soil two and thirty years gone by.
> The red flag roused the serf, halberd in hand,
> While the despot's black talons held his whip aloft.
> Bitter sacrifice strengthens bold resolve,
> Which dares to make sun and moon shine in new skies.
> Happy, I see wave upon wave of paddy and beans,
> And all around heroes homebound in the evening mist.

Next morning, on my way to the Mao family home I caught the sons and daughters of those heroes tending their own fields. Land ownership had gone full circle. The first despot holding a whip aloft that the boy Mao knew was his own father, Mao Shunsheng. Back at the turn of the century young Mao was in the paddy, working on his father's thirty-five acres, with water buffalo for ploughing. Mao Shunsheng was an exception in Shaoshan, being upwardly mobile. All the other peasants were poor, forced into paying seasonal taxes in kind – rice, to the landlord of the village. With Liberation, Mao Zedong ended this exploitation, ousting the landlord and implementing the collective. His successor but one, Deng Xiaoping, in turn dispersed the collective and gave peasants land for themselves and with it a personal incentive. Now they ride bicycles or drive 'iron water buffaloes' – versatile two-stroke tractors on which they load up non-staples such as oranges, melons and peanuts. Mao Zedong, commemorated on the 100 *yuan* note, freed them from the yoke of feudalism, but it was Deng Xiaoping who put the cash in their pockets.

In the autumn sunshine Hunan's third crop of rice lay like a spongy quilt of emerald on the flat-bottomed valley floor. The stalks were fully set with grain, leaning over and rustling abrasively in the breeze. It was a landscape changed since Mao's birth by the annual toil of thousands, increasing acreage to improve production and swell the larder of China.

I found the Mao family home tucked into a side valley, sheltered by low wooded hills from which the fruity scent of sweet osmanthus drifted. Approaching the mud-walled building I passed a lotus pond, where rhubarb-like foliage squeaked, frogs croaked, and swarms of flies buzzed. Out of this smelly and muddy pond the beautiful lotus flower bloomed forth. Mao's transformation from peasant boy in heartland China to world leader, military genius, poet and teacher was no less remarkable. Like the lotus too, Mao had always remained attached to his roots, in the mud, the countryside of China. That was his solid foundation.

Miss Cheng Zhenghui, a guide to the Mao Zedong family home, was dressed neatly in a black trouser suit. She wore the name of the 'shrine' on her lapel.

In Mao's bedroom she described the boy's appearance. 'He wore long flowing robes and had the front half of his scalp shaved; the hair at the back was grown very long and plaited according to Qing Dynasty custom.' Pointing out the desk in his room, she explained that he adopted the habit of being a night owl in adolescence, staying up into the early hours studying.

'What influenced him – his teacher's philosophy or books?' I asked Miss Cheng.

In reply, she indicated a pictorial map of the Qing Empire showing caricatures of animals. 'It was these foreign devils,' she tittered apologetically, 'the Black Bear for Russia, the Lion of Britain, the Cockerel for France and the American Eagle. In all, eight imperialist powers infested Chinese territory.' Such a vivid map was surely enough to awaken the nascent patriotism in anyone.

Mao Zedong's mother, Wen Qimei, was a Buddhist and she maintained a small shrine within the household, often making visits to the clan tomb in the village. All the villagers of Shaoshan carried the Mao family name: they were one big family, a clan and often interrelated.

'Young Mao was close to his mother but hated his father who beat him regularly,' said Miss Cheng, 'until one day the boy threatened to jump into the village pond if the beatings continued, thus reducing the workforce by one. From this successful threat, Mao realised that workers were exploited assets who nevertheless had a tool of rebellion: the withdrawal of their labour.' She went on to explain why the pond held such fear for the village peasantry. 'Qing Dynasty China was superstitious – the pond was the realm of evil spirits – Mao saw a young woman drowned there by being strapped to a wooden frame weighted with a boulder.'

'What was her crime?' I asked.

'She refused to recognise her betrothal to a young boy by having close relations with a man she really loved.'

Mao himself almost fell prey to the custom of the arranged marriage when he was fourteen, being paired-off with a girl of twenty. His father hoped to inherit a new family member, child bearer, servant and labourer in one fell swoop, but young Mao rejected her, and the all-important *yuan fang* (the first night together) never took place.

With the evils of feudalism and imperialism exposed, I wondered if Buddhism, coming from his mother whom Mao loved and admired, had taken root in the boy's mind. Miss Cheng referred to the article 'Learn from Mao Zedong' written by Zhou Enlai and delivered posthumously in 1978 to the National Youth Congress. In it, Zhou described Mao as a typical Chinese, not a god, a man who had, like everyone, been shackled by superstitious and religious beliefs – but cast them away. (However, Mao is rumoured to have remained deeply superstitious throughout his life, even consulting diviners as to the outcome of battles. A bizarre illustration of Mao's regard for the words of diviners surrounds the naming of the 8341 Brigade. This group of crack soldiers were responsible for Politburo, and particularly Mao's, personal safety. The significance of this number, provided by an oracle in answer to a question concerning Mao's future on the eve of his entering Beijing in 1949, remained a mystery until Mao's death in 1976.)

I asked Miss Cheng if any village elders had known Mao as a boy. I was being somewhat optimistic: such people, if alive, would be centenarians.

'There are Mao Kaiqing and his wife Tang Ruiren. They were visited by Chairman Mao in 1959, and tried to prove they were related to him.' I thought of those North Americans who try to find their roots in the British aristocracy.

Across the lotus pond from the Mao family home I identified Tang Ruiren by the small red Mao badge on her jacket on which the Chinese character *zhong*, meaning loyalty, was inscribed. She gripped and held my hand, as is the custom upon initial meetings, throughout the lengthy exchange of salutations. Not ten minutes before, Miss Cheng had said that Mao Zedong was an ordinary man, not a god – an opinion in line with Chinese Communist Party (CCP) policy since the late Seventies when the dismantling of the Mao personality cult began. Yet Tang Ruiren kept holding my hand tightly, speaking dreamily of the day the Chairman came to her home. 'No Chairman Mao, no New China – this is where New China was born; the Red Sun rose right here in Shaoshan!'

Tang Ruiren owned the appropriately named *Mao Jia Fandian* (Mao Family Restaurant). On the wall was the equivalent of a 'By Appointment to the Chairman' – a black-and-white photograph immortalising the moment when Tang Ruiren saw the Messiah. The encounter moved her so much that she changed her name. 'I was born Tang Yangchun but became Ruiren in memory of Chairman Mao's leadership of the Long March,' she said. (Ruijin is the place from which the March commenced.)

We looked at the photograph – Mao seated, smiling and smoking. I noticed Tang's family did not put on any airs and graces. One peasant sat barefoot opposite him. I asked Tang Ruiren what Mao said in that hour back in late June 1959.

She replied: 'Chairman Mao cared about our family, our food and home and the production figures for the year. He cared for us peasants.' She leapt up, leaving me to look at the joy on all their faces in the picture, smiling from ear to ear.

Tang Ruiren returned with a bunch of bamboo chopsticks bound together with grass. Dividing the bunch into pairs she placed them higgledy-piggledy on the table. 'Separately like this the chopsticks are weak,' she cried, handing me a pair to snap. I flexed them obligingly but stopped short of filling my hands with splinters. Rebundling them with the grass, she philosophised, 'Chairman Mao had believed from his childhood days that united the peasantry is strong, an indestructible army; so he founded the Revolution upon them.' Handing me the bundle of chopsticks, she chuckled. 'Now try to break those!' Snapping one pair was task enough, a bunch impossible. I handed them back, but she refused them saying, 'They're yours to keep, to represent the friendship between Chairman Mao and the people of the world.'

The warmth of her welcome continued as the staff served a dish of frogs' legs – the frogs' croaking accompanies the trill of cicadas and rustle of rice on this Hunan landscape. Next came a fiery dish of hot and peppery vegetables where chilli, ginger and garlic were used as vegetables themselves rather than mere flavourings. 'Chairman Mao loved hot food like this,' she said.

Before leaving, I asked Tang Ruiren about her favourite Chairman Mao teaching. 'Serve the people!' she replied without hesitation.

At that moment, some potential patrons refused to eat in the restaurant, presumably because of its high prices as a result of its By Appointment to Chairman Mao status. They had been inspecting the walls plastered with Maoist memorabilia whilst eavesdropping on our conversation. One surly man of the group asked the price of a bundle of chopsticks as used in the demonstration of Mao's chopsticks philosophy.

'Three *yuan* (Thirty pence),' replied Tang.

'The Mao Family Restaurant should serve the people, not swindle them,' he moaned sarcastically, drawing mocking chuckles and applause from his entourage. How easy it was to knock a loyalist when loyalty was out of fashion.

Outside the Mao family home a group of forty middle-school students were being photographed to commemorate their visit, and it did not require a vivid imagination to envisage what queues must have existed during the Cultural Revolution. Down in the village, in an attempt to ease the pressure, two identical Mao Zedong Exhibition Halls were built then, side by side. The duplicate hall was now closed – a sign of the times.

Inside the remaining hall maps, models and photographs trace the story of Mao's life – or at least those parts of his life that the Central Committee of the CCP have instructed their historians to permit and promote. The curator here is only secondarily a servant of history; his prime role is that of an organ of an Orwellian-type Ministry of Truth. His guiding brief is straightforward: to rewrite history by the removal of anything that could be construed as an embarrassment to the memory of Mao. Above all, he must allow no doubts over Mao's infallible judgement. It is akin to the task facing the unfortunate divorcee who must rearrange his photograph album, humiliated by his proven lack of insight into his ex-wife's true character and motives. Hence Jiang Qing of Gang of Four infamy is neither seen nor mentioned; yet as Mao's third wife she was closer to him than anyone else from the late Thirties onwards. Lin Biao too, Mao's 'close comrade in arms' – a synonym for heir apparent – who attempted to stage a *coup d'état*, is nowhere to be seen.

Total removal of such bad elements is the major responsibility of a party-servant in the Ministry of Truth, Shaoshan sub-branch. Other desirable skills for the assignment are photographic darkroom techniques. Characters can be blurred beyond recognition or completely eradicated by burning-out. More favourable juxtapositions, such as Deng Xiaoping in Mao Zedong's presence, can be brought into the limelight by sharper focusing or burning-in to increase contrast, thus drawing the viewer's eye towards the personality being promoted. Any ghostly gaps produced by such darkroom deception can be filled by photo-montage. Gao Gang for example was on the podium for the proclamation of New China by Mao in 1949. Given regional responsibility for Manchuria, he was later accused by the Party of turning it into his own kingdom, but in a ghostly way he still ended up smelling of flowers. In the photograph and in the painting of this proclamation, he has been replaced by a pot of chrysanthemums. Looking in the gallery entitled 'Foreign friends in Shaoshan' I realised that there was scope for future work, for here was Mao greeting Nicolae Ceausescu, now exposed as a closet capitalist by the Romanian revolution.

Shaoshan, the first step on my biographical journey, had provided insight into the influences on Mao during his formative years; yet more than anything it was the great flood his later life initiated that had left its tide-mark there. Nowhere was this more striking than at Shaoshan railway station. In a sense its very being was a tide-mark of the flood, and its maintenance in the face of near desolation a testament to the CCP's adherence to Mao Zedong Thought as the guiding doctrine of the much promoted 'Communism with Chinese characteristics'. Mao's portrait looks out across a station concourse devoid of buses, taxis and vendors. There are no advertisements here because there is no market. Instead the billboards exhort Mao Zedong Thought. 'The force leading our cause forward is the CCP,' pronounced one. 'People, and the people alone, are the motive force in the making of world history,' announced another, extracting the opening quotation from 'The Mass Line' of the *Little Red Book*. But had Lord Beeching seen this line it would have been given the chop.

There were no paintings or statues in Shaoshan which gave me a visual impression of the young Mao when he left Shaoshan to be educated at Changsha. Undoubtedly, like most teenagers leaving home, it was in his mind to change the world. In the park opposite the station a statue of Mao 1927-style showed him wearing flowing robes. Working from that, my identikit picture of him featured a long plait and grass sandals, carrying his possessions on a bamboo pole. With that image in mind I returned to the station, passing between an avenue of seemingly contorted brass on red: plaques of Mao's poems in his own freehand that had greeted pilgrims on their revolutionary *haj*. The red had now faded like the fervour, and many of the brass calligraphic strokes had dropped off. Any Chinese, however, will fill in the missing words for you: they learned the quotations and poems off by heart.

Inside the departure hall a clock ticked around to the one train per day for Changsha, but there was no scrum down for tickets and no stampede for seats. It was the quietest station in all China. Once a museum to a mania of half a million pilgrims each month, its most striking exhibit now was emptiness.

3

Ropes to Cut, Mountains to Climb

Worker, peasant and soldier, setting about a landlord.

Music is an international language. I had often trailed the strains of a melody punctuated with paramilitary yells of '*Yi, er, san, si*' (One, two, three, four) to their source and stumbled upon a checker-board formation of gaily dressed primary school pupils exercising in the morning sun. This time, though, my ears were trailing music of a marching tempo on to a college campus, off the streets of Changsha.

Freshers were on military parade, passing out from a period of army training. In single-sex squads they marched, the boys with squaddie haircuts, the girls with hair off-the-shoulder and stuffed into oversize red-starred caps akin to shower caps – not to keep their hair dry but to hide it from their officers. All in green PLA uniforms, they goose-stepped in green plimsolls, eyes right to their instructing officers shaded beneath parasols on the podium, chanting as they passed: 'Serve the People! Heighten Vigilance! Defend the Country! We love the Party! Learn from the PLA!'

The last slogan surely hurt the most. As it echoed around the campus, it must have been June 4th which came to mind, not the date *Ba, yi* (8.1) marked in Chinese numerals on the Red Army flag heading the parade – the date that commemorates the founding of the army after the Nanchang Uprising of August 1927. For they were here playing soldiers only because the students of the Beijing Spring had 'lost their direction'. Nothing, thought the Party hard-liners, that a spell of parroting in the army could not rectify.

> How bright and brave they look, shouldering five-foot rifles
> On the parade ground lit-up by the first gleams of day.
> China's daughters have high aspiring minds;
> They love their battle array, not silks and satins.

Although Chairman Mao wrote this poem, *Militia Women*, on the back of a photograph in 1961, the girls in this Changsha college still held their automatics with purpose, despite any inner reservations.

A postgraduate student pounced on the chance to practise her spoken English. Managing to bypass the stereotyped exchanges on family, education and my travelling route through China, I quizzed her on the training of her comrades.

'Because of last year's event all new students learn from the PLA for one month – but Beijing students go to Shijiazhuang to train for one year,' she said.

That seemed logical and directed to the root of the unrest, I thought. 'Is it just military training for the whole month?'

'Fighting, marching – including a day's Long March – shooting, running and political education,' she replied.

I knew that every Wednesday afternoon was set aside for political study by each unit throughout the country. 'So it's just like a month-long Wednesday afternoon!' I joked.

'Not so free. They study Marxism, Leninism and Mao Zedong Thought.'

'Useful for China today?'

'Maybe not, but it's the only way; they've no choice.'

One notices how uniforms, whether military or police ones, tend to be abused and worn all the time or in dribs and drabs. I suggested they would be used as such by the students.

'Certainly by the boys – but not by the girls. They want more fashionable clothes.'

Nylons and skirts at least, if not silks and satins, I mused.

'But they'll probably keep their uniforms for later on,' she added.

'What, in the case of war or something?'

She laughed. 'No. Because the baggy green suit is comfortable, it's become the traditional clothing for growing a child in!'

*   *   *

Young Mao Zedong arrived in Changsha, when just seventeen years old, to enter a middle school. It was in 1911, a year that would, once the dust settled, figure as prominently in the chronology of history as the unification of China by Qin Shi Huang or the Ming Dynasty's ousting of the Mongols.

Once out of reach of his domineering father, Mao lost no time in airing his political opinions. He wrote a *'Da zi bao'* (big character poster), and plastered it to the school wall. (Such handwritten opinionated placards covered virtually every public place – walls, trees, noticeboards – even sandwiching people during the Cultural Revolution.) On his poster, the activist Mao called for the establishment of a republic under Sun Yat-sen, Kang Youwei and Liang Qichao. Such a suggestion categorised Mao as a potential monster raving loony. It would have been an absurd alliance, because Sun was a republican while Kang and Liang were monarchists.

Chinese political satirists cite this as the first of Mao's many political gaffes, but I would put it down to a generally confused military and political scene. Think of the Western press coverage of the Beijing Spring of 1989: in spite of real-time communications, spy satellites and intelligence, the daily unfolding of events was as clear as mud. Rumours told of the PLA fighting amongst itself, and of Deng Xiaoping fleeing to Wuhan like a feudal warlord in search of loyalists. It was weeks before we heard what happened in China's other sixty cities with their multi-million populations, and then only by hearsay. Likewise, if one realises that in 1911 not only was the Qing court upon its deathbed, but the nation was spaced-out on opium, then it is no wonder that communications, and hence young

Mao Zedong's political judgement was somewhat muddled. Dynastic China then was an empire only in name. The progress of the railroad had been hampered by the Qing resistance to modernisation. Changsha was connected to Wuhan only via the Xiang River and Dongting Lake, a journey of several days. Guangzhou was over a week away. So when the activist Mao pored over the newspapers the news was often stale and inaccurate.

One thing was certain, however: in 1911 China was on the threshold of a revolution. In Wuhan, a section of the Qing army staged a rebellion which sparked off the proverbial fire throughout China. Dubbed the Double Tenth – and in fact best remembered as the Almost Triple Tenth, happening as it did on October 10th 1911 – the Wuhan Uprising had as great an influence on Mao in Changsha as the events in Tiananmen Square had on the students of China in 1989. Indeed the latter event may be re-evaluated in time as the dawn of the democratic era, just as the Double Tenth is regarded as the beginning of the Republican era. Already students refer the fateful day in the commemorative numerical style of '6.4'.

Student Mao became a militia man in the Hunan Army supporting the Nationalist cause of Sun Yat-sen's Three People's Principles – national freedom, democracy and people's welfare. Just twelve weeks after the Wuhan Uprising over two millennia of dynastic rule were ended by Sun's Presidential declaration in Nanjing. China's last Emperor, Pu Yi, was ousted by his own army under Yuan Shikai, who claimed state power. Perhaps it was from this situation that Mao's later quote 'political power grows from the barrel of a gun' had its origins, for Sun, with no military backing, favoured national unity in repelling Japanese aggression, and so stepped down. I had seen Sun's giant portrait facing Mao's in Tiananmen Square on the National Day of the People's Republic (October 1st) – yet, I am told, one is just as likely to witness similar veneration nine days later across the Taiwan Strait in Taibei as the Kuomintang celebrate the Double Tenth as the National Day of the 'Republic of China'.

Mao's initial spell in the army was just six months. He then moved from college to college, always dissatisfied with the curriculum until finally settling down in the Hunan Provincial First Normal School.

I met Tang Xiao, a middle-aged woman responsible for visitors there. Her title was Propagandist, the Mao Zedong Youth Period

Revolutionary Activities Exhibition Hall. In Britain she would have had the less grandiose and more credible title of Information Officer. We sat in her office drinking green tea in the breeze of an electric fan. There were no photographs of Chairman Mao on the walls, only some red-velvet sashes, decorated with gold tassels and characters – awards to the office for being a model unit. Above her desk was something that resembled a Letts Year Planner. Pointing to it, I asked how many teachers were in the school.

'That is a birth-control chart,' she replied. 'It shows the names of all the fertile women in our unit.' (Ironically it was Chairman Mao's policy of rapidly increasing the country's labour force that has made the strict birth-control implementation of one child per family necessary for the present generation.) 'The census for this year has just announced there are 1.15 billion people in China. The birth-rate is too high. Cadres like me are responsible for limiting births in each unit.'

On the wall-chart were the Chinese characters for population, *ren kou*. Pictographically they are quite appropriate to their literal meaning of 'people's mouths', looking as they do like an inverted 'v' for people's legs and a square for the orifice of the mouth. Why then had Chairman Mao not subscribed to this etymological common sense? An extra birth was another labourer, but it was also an extra mouth to feed. At family level people never forget this. 'There are four mouths in my family,' they say – good Chinese common sense. One thing is clear: when the personal organiser reaches China it should include the birth-control planner for the managerial bureaucrats faced with this unenviable but necessary task.

We stepped outside Tang Xiao's office, leaving behind one of China's contemporary problems, and Tang Xiao introduced me to some of the ills and evils which the student Mao was beginning to confront in 1912. 'Coming to Changsha from Shaoshan,' she said, 'Mao had personally felt the four thick ropes binding the peasantry.'

I asked her to unravel the knots of the encumbering metaphor.

'In 1912 the political rope was already fraying, but the ropes of clan control, religious superstitions and the exploitation of women were the same as they had been for hundreds of years.'

I asked Tang Xiao why imperialism was not one of the ropes.

'Imperialism, together with feudalism and the bourgeoisie, were not ropes,' she replied. 'They were three enormous mountains which lay on the Chinese people like a dead weight.'

'Didn't things improve with the fall of the Qing, and the Republic's foundation?' I asked.

'No. Yuan Shikai simply conciliated the three mountains, and reverted to a monarchical system, crowning himself emperor.'

Walking around the corridors, glancing into classrooms, I realised that this was still a working college. Noticeboards were masterpieces of chalk art, painstakingly written and drawn, and never defaced by smudging. Red and white banners hung in the corridors. '*Qing shuo Putonghua*' (Please speak Mandarin) urged one; for here in Hunan the dialect is particularly strong. I asked Tang Xiao to give me an example of Mao's soft southern tones. '*Wo si Funan ren,*' she said, instead of the standard '*Wo shi Hunan ren*'. Once I started travelling in the remote south, language difficulties would undoubtedly loom large.

We entered a large hall, dominated by an enormous painting of Mao lecturing. 'That's Karl Marx on the wall behind Mao – it was a lecture on Marx's 104th birthday,' pronounced Tang Xiao. '"Teacher" was Mao's most loved title, and it was here he learnt teaching skills between 1912 and 1918.' At that moment a class of girls began spacing themselves out to dance under the painting.

'Dancing for Chairman Mao?' I said to Tang Xiao. In the 1960s dancing became an artistic form of veneration. Whole new routines were choreographed to conform with the decision made by a forum on Revolutionary Literature and Art that all performances should serve the people in their revolutionary struggle.

Looking up towards Mao I tried to imagine the dancing in this very hall a score more years before. Music would have stammered out of an accordion and the students would have faced Chairman Mao's portrait as naturally as sunflowers in bloom rotating with the journey of the sun across the sky. As his good soldiers, they then would momentarily turn away, and like those blooms deprived of sunlight lose their smiles to punch downward, stamp aggressively and chant 'Down with imperialism!' Moving into formation, they would mimic the outline of a ship's hull. On deck a student would hold up a large cardboard cut-out of the *Little Red Book*, like a publisher's promotional prop one might expect to see pushing a bestseller in the window of a bookstore. At the prow, like a living figurehead of a galleon the orchestrator would co-ordinate the oarsmen and lead the chorus in the tone, if not to the tune, of 'All Things Bright and Beautiful'.

> Sailing the sea depends upon the Helmsman.
> Like all living things rely on the Sun,
> Just as water makes crops grow,
> Revolution depends on Mao Zedong Thought.

In 1990 things had changed. Plugging in her Panda-brand cassette player, the dance mistress turned it to full volume, for the sound of Richard Clayderman tickling the ivories to fill the hall. The students, lost in dream, danced elegantly in loose blouses and skin-tight breeches. A group of boy students peered in at an open window through which a gentle breeze wafted. For this was the language of beauty and love.

I asked what were Mao's divertissements back in 1918, during his final year.

'The nature of men,' Tang Xiao replied, 'China and the world – he started the *Xin Min Xue Hui* (New People's Study Society).'

I thought perhaps this group was akin to the Young Conservatives or Socialists in proletarian clothing, and the main purpose there was to meet a partner. Apparently not. Mao had no time for trivialities, love or romance with women.

There is a painting that depicts Mao Zedong examining a world map whilst studying in Changsha's library. He probably considered that Hunan, let alone Shaoshan, was relatively insignificant in terms of China's vast land; hence he yearned to see more of his country. Many of his contemporaries were setting off to study overseas. Mao, however, went to Beiping to co-ordinate a work-study scheme. He did not want to go abroad himself. He felt his time could be spent more profitably in China.

Fortunately for the Revolution, those like Deng Xiaoping, who went to France, would return to serve China – unlike many Chinese students today who study abroad with little intention of returning, despite having signed the pledge 'to serve in the Socialist Construction of the Motherland'. Where had their patriotism been lost? It seemed all the more puzzling when I looked across the street at eight-thirty in the morning to see two hundred or more toddlers of a kindergarten regimented despite their tender age. Holding the gold-starred red flag at each corner the chosen four marched up to the flagpole plinth and with military precision raised the flag to the tune of their national anthem, 'The March of the Volunteers'. Back in ranks, instructed by 'aunties', they all looked up to the flag to sing *'Hong Qi Women Ai Ni'* (Red Flag We Love You). It is a ceremony repeated in thousands of kindergartens throughout China, and continued in primary and middle schools.

What then proves to be a stronger love than that of their country? Perhaps it is materialism. It cannot just be lack of freedom under a Communist regime, as even in dynastic China there were 'economic refugees' who left to set up a Chinatown somewhere across the globe. Yet, through nostalgia they take China with them and look back to the country as children do to their mother to ask what China can do for them, and rarely what they can do for China. As a Chinese proverb goes, they are only interested in harvesting ripe peaches but bear none of the toil in nurturing the tree.

In October 1919, Mao's mother died. In no hurry to return to Hunan, Mao remained in Beiping and tapped his connections. Some months of travelling in Shandong Province earlier that year had left him broke and in need of a job. He looked up his former ethics teacher, Yang Changji, who had been given a professorship in Beiping. Professor Yang introduced Mao to Li Dazhao, a Marxist librarian at Beiping Library.

Li Dazhao gave Mao a job as assistant librarian for 8 *yuan* a month. But the salary was not enough to support a wife. For Mao had fallen in love with Yang Kaihui, his professor's daughter. She was a radical Communist and a brilliant graduate of Beiping National University. The exact date of their marriage – circa 1920 – remains a mystery, inviting speculation that the couple merely lived together. Although they spent much more time apart than together over the following decade, Yang Kaihui's devotion to Mao is without dispute. She was executed in 1930 outside the gates of Changsha, refusing to give warlord He Qian information on her husband.

4

The Secret Congress

Cultural Revolution badge, depicting the inaugural venues of the First
Communist Party Congress.

The characters 'Shanghai' mean 'above the sea' – although the city
is in fact some thirty kilometres from the shore! – but to me Shanghai
means only one thing: humanity.

Even the washing here jostles for space, hung on bamboo poles
and propped out of windows. Below this dripping canopy of cleanli-
ness, pedestrians brush shoulders, side step, dodge each other, over-
flow on to the road making cyclists resort to campanological alarms.

Evening falls heavily on the city of Shanghai. Like victims of an
earthquake fearful of falling masonry, the Shanghainese have vacated
their ovens of brick and wood which re-radiate the heat of the day.
Family groups gather on bamboo and cane furniture, wafting their
noodles cool with woven grass fans or chopping up water melons.
Men lounge in vests hitched up to their armpits revealing midriffs,

and so often, so as to rule out insanity yet still defy reason, have only one trouser leg rolled up. Women in gossamer silks sit the way girls in finishing school are taught not to: their oriental prudery melted by forty degrees they hitch up dresses to thigh-tops and pile the gathered pleats crotchways to give their wide-legged postures respectability. Older women, willingly lumbered with the care of yet another generation (How many babes have passed through their arms?) tilt forward, rocking basinettes of head-shaven talcum-dusted toddlers.

Yet to the devout Communist in China, Shanghai means something else again – the planting of the tree, the founding of the CCP. Mao Zedong came here in July 1921: one of my steering badges commemorated that inaugural congress by depicting its venues. Being a palm width across, it was a striking visual aid with which to quiz Shanghainese on the directions to the First Congress meeting house.

The meeting house is in the former French concession of the city. Old tastes linger here: the one time *rues* are renamed *lus*, and the odd café serves coffee, albeit Nescafé, and *beignets* dusted with icing sugar. While I was indulging in this colonial delicacy I was approached by a man as old as the Party itself and asked to exhume my schoolboy French. This task I found to be almost impossible, all memory space designated for languages now being occupied by Chinese. Hence I was soon in the bizarre situation of walking along Xingye Lu speaking in a cocktail of Franco-Mandarin.

'*Shui jiao ni fayu?*'

'*Mes parents. Ils travaillaient dans une grande maison de Shanghai.*'

Surely such a French connection was most unfashionable during the Cultural Revolution when everyone's past was investigated during 'check-ups'. Bearing in mind that if you do not use it you lose it, how then, I asked, did he retain such fluency?

'*Oui, oui! Très dangereux, très difficile – mais je regarde le Petit Livre Rouge.*'

Marx had described a foreign language as a weapon in the struggle of life, but this man had seemingly used a French edition of Mao's Quotations as his weapon to avoid criticism.

Xingye Lu is not so very different from Coronation Street. Above each terrace door is a semicircular piece of ornate stonework, bright red in contrast to the grey bricks of the walls, perhaps the equivalent of Manchester's red-leaded doorsteps. The street is narrow, and, appropriately, French plane trees with scabby trunks have been trained to act as a street-long parasol.

In 1921, twelve men converged here, on the home of one delegate, Li Hanjun. It is futile to mention all the names of the other participants here, for who, except a fanatic, can recall any player in a foreign football team except for the star: that is Mao Zedong. The rooms, formerly classrooms, are now exhibition halls. One photograph in particular caught my eye – a textile mill with machinery embossed with 'Bolton, England'. The caption exposed foreigners' exploitation of child labour, and the children's eyes told of their premature misery in working more hours each day than their age: ten. All China's ills were rampant in Shanghai 1921: foreign infiltration, exploitation, prostitution, drug addiction. Seeing them can only have fired Mao's resolve and dedication to patriotic work.

The meeting was instigated by Li Dazhao, whom Mao had worked with during his brief stint at the library in Beiping. Li acted as the go-between with Moscow, and Marling and Likonsky, new kinds of missionaries, were despatched to China on the Trans-Siberian railway. Unlike the members of the China Inland Mission, who carried Bibles and crosses, they were Comintern agents carrying Lenin's works, the hammer and sickle. In the wake of the Great October Bolshevik Revolution of 1917, they had come to win China – not for God, but for Lenin. Clearly China cried out for salvation, whether that came from the cross, Lenin or some other messiah.

It is indicative of the hostility towards political cliques of the day that the group met in the French concession of the city. After preliminary meetings, a plenary session was risked on July 23rd. A week later though, a spy tipped-off the *gendarmes* who broke up the congress since such gatherings were prohibited under concession laws. The wife of Li Dazhao, a delegate, suggested that the meeting be reconvened in her home town of 'nearby' Jiaxing.

Nearby means different things in different parts of the world. It took me a whole day to reach the Zhejiang silk town. Travelling via the ancient city of Suzhou the bus ran parallel to the Grand Canal – the longest man-made waterway in the world, stretching some 1,800 kilometres from Hangzhou in the south to the outskirts of

Beijing. Originally built to carry tribute rice to Beijing from the fertile Lower Yangzi, more safely than by the pirate-and-storm-infested Yellow Sea route, the Grand Canal is the result of a mass labour project comparable in scale, technology and innovation with at least some phases of the Great Wall construction. Its length is unequalled; its width makes Suez a stream and Manchester a trickle in comparison. Iron and wooden barges, their decks just inches clear of the water, chug along in convoys looking like the segmented bodies of aquatic centipedes.

Arriving in Jiaxing, I was immediately confronted by the *Gong An Ju* (Public Security Bureau). From bitter experience on the Great Wall, I assumed my journey had been futile. The officer, however, was merely mimicking the archetypal British bobby, welcoming me to Jiaxing and offering his assistance, because I was the first foreigner to visit the town that year. His likes are on the TV news almost every night, being congratulated by leaders in Beijing's Great Hall of the People. Their paper awards and velvet sashes brighten every office and shop, yet the often surly take-it-or-leave-it service dispensed make such trophies seem like hypocritical decor. Now, at last I had met a real model worker, and a policeman at that.

With this memorable encounter in mind, I could see why Marling the Dutchman and Likonsky the Russian had not attended the meeting here. Seventy years ago a foreigner's presence would have aroused too much suspicion. Things had not changed much. If you want to know how a black man felt in Britain during Victorian times then come to China and be pointed out as you walk down every street.

Li Dazhao's wife had rented a landlord's pleasure boat on Nan Hu (South Lake), and while she kept watch on shore the meeting went ahead. The wooden boat, housing a mosquito-netted double bed and a small gaming room with cane-backed chairs is still there. It is ornate to say the least, and I suspect was usually used for afternoon delight rather than tea. To avoid suspicion, the delegates spread out mahjong tiles upon the table and concluded the First Congress of the Chinese Communist Party. They called themselves *Gong Chan Dang* (the share property party). Mao was given special responsibility for the provincial Hunan Communist Party.

* * *

Mao – and I – returned to Changsha.

Following the Party's foundation, Mao enjoyed a relatively peaceful five years compared to the next few decades. The CCP's standing was enhanced by a pact with the KMT and the Soviet Party. Only when Sun Yat-sen died in 1925 did the alliance acquire its unholy tint as Chiang Kai-shek came to power.

Mao worked for the alliance, principally in Hunan where he set about establishing trade unions amongst workers and students. His work was carried out from the Provincial Hunan CP office in Changsha, now preserved in a small park. From the street passers-by can see simply an alloy statue of Mao glistening in the sunshine, but once you approach the plinth, your vision is drawn eastward as if to a roaring blaze; but there is no fire, only a huge red-tiled façade depicting Mao. Its position has crude astronomical significance, as does the siting of a pool which reflects, and therefore doubles, its impact – so much so that the song of praise 'Dong Fang Hong' (The East is Red) seems a reality. How vividly I could recall, even hum, the chime-like melody which Beijing's Telephone and Telegraph Office still rings out every quarter of an hour to the capital:

> The East is Red.
> The Sun is Rising.
> China has Chairman Mao.
> Devoted to People's Happiness,
> He's the People's Saviour.

The young head of Mao is appropriately 1925 vintage although the relic itself dates from 1967, the height of the Cultural Revolution. Both real and painted sun's rays reflect from his head, which is flanked by two large hammer and sickles. Beneath are five burning torches which represent Mao's intention, inherited from Lenin, of spreading the warm, nourishing and bright rays of Communism to even the darkest of continents.

It is a quiet place now, almost deserted except for a courting couple with their bicycles parked under a tree, taking advantage of the seclusion, and two children aged eight and ten. Attracting their attention, and surprise, by calling them 'xiao pengyoumen' (little friends) – a title of affection to which all primary schoolchildren answer – I pointed up to the façade to ask them, 'Do you know this man?'

'He's Chairman Mao,' they pronounced. (Nobody seemed to refer to him as simply Mao or Mao Zedong.) 'Our teacher told us about him,' they added.

'Do you know any other leaders?'

'Zhou Enlai, Li Peng and Zhao Ziyang,' they replied innocently. Their teacher had clearly not brought them up to date, for Zhao was purged from the Party following his display of sympathy for the students in Tiananmen. He has not been seen since.

Changsha means 'big sand' – a name describing the sandbanks midstream in the Xiang River, itself a tributary of the mighty Yangzi. The river was surely, I thought, a good place to catch some fresh air in this stifling, humid city, a place that Mao himself loved and wrote about.

En route I called in at the state run Xinhua bookstore. Amongst calendars of oriental beauties peeping seductively from behind painted fans, posters of revolutionaries were on sale: Mao, Zhou, Lenin, Stalin, Marx and Engels. Significantly *The Truth About the Beijing Turmoil* was not at eye level in the display cabinet. Positioning in China means more than meets the eye: this book was at ground level.

Investing in a weighty four-volume set of the *Selected Works of Mao Zedong* and an anthology of his poems, cloth-bound in red silk, I laboured to the river, crossing over to Orange Island on an arching concrete bridge that spanned the muddy waters of the Xiang. There I stopped to watch the thousands of cyclists flowing lazily past, looking like water themselves cascading from the maze of Changsha's streets and turning the bridge into an aqueduct.

Mao's native soil is red. His rivers are red too. On the Xiang's fertile bank I found seventy-year-old Tong Zhaoyun, once a ferryman in the days before the Communists built bridges. Watering his plot of vegetables he recalled a memorable day in 1956 when Chairman Mao crossed to Orange Island by his ferry. Crowds covered the shore chanting 'Long Live Chairman Mao!' They held red flags and banners – a scene easy for me to envisage as I watched kites diving and flapping in the upcurrents overhead. It must have been a prologue to synchronised swimming, for Mao's entourage accompanied him for a swim whilst carrying flags.

This was one of Mao's favourite hometown places, for he had spent most of a decade here since leaving Shaoshan. People even told me he acquired the Changsha accent. He immortalised his affection for both the place and nature in the poem *Changsha*:

Alone I stand in the autumn cold
On the tip of Orange Island,
The Xiang flowing northward;
I see a thousand hills crimsoned through
By their serried woods deep-dyed,
And a hundred barges vying
Over crystal blue waters.
Eagles cleave the air,
Fish glide in the limpid deep;
Under freezing skies a million creatures contend in freedom.
Brooding over this immensity,
I ask, on this boundless land
Who rules over man's destiny?

In his mind Mao already knew: man himself. In China that meant the peasant. The fighting was about to begin.

5

Old War Horse

'Down with landlords!' Propaganda in a Jiangxi village.

I knew of Jinggangshan from one of its many sons. A man in his thirties, bearing the Cultural Revolution given name of 'Jinggang' had related his namesake's history. He told me how Mao Zedong had sought refuge there with his defeated men after the Autumn Harvest Uprising of 1927.

Preceded only a month before by the Nanchang Uprising, the opening salvo of armed opposition to the KMT, Zhou Enlai's men had held Jiangxi's capital briefly before being besieged and eventually split. Unable to link-up with the Mao-led Autumn Harvest Uprising, Mao's army of workers and peasants fell well short of threatening the Hunanese capital of Changsha and were forced to seek refuge in the highlands. Mao, Zhou and Zhu De had all realised that confronting the KMT openly in towns and cities was not their forte. But out of the two uprisings a mountain-top 'Soviet' was born, and amongst its leadership the belief that guerrilla warfare was the best way for the fledgling Communist army to engage the KMT.

I soon realised why Mao went to ground in the Luoxiao Range straddling the Hunan–Jiangxi border. My bus, crowded with peasants carrying everything but their haystacks crawled up the steep dirt road, its lowest gear never feeling quite low enough for the gradient.

For such a small town there was an extraordinarily heavy presence of *Gong An Ju*. This was not the local force in their green jeeps; these men lounging on the bonnets of their blue and white trim Beijing Cherokee jeeps looked like the provincial police. My enquiries as to what might be going on were met with that I-can't-understand-your-Chinese shrug of the shoulders.

With this response I was left to hedge my bets. Keeping my camera concealed I prepared to stand my ground in the expectation of witnessing a gruesome event I had only seen previously outside Tongchuan in Shaanxi Province: that of an exhibit of criminals en route to the execution ground. Lights, I remembered, had flashed, sirens had howled, and banners criticising the condemned whilst praising the law-enforcing *Gong An Ju* for serving and protecting the people were draped around two giant green trucks. Handcuffed, headshaven and chained to the first truck, the criminals were followed by their executioners: a truck load of immaculately dressed trigger-honed men of the armed police – the *Wu Jing*. But the most striking recollection I had of this motorcade was of the sheer excitement its passage induced in the local people. The road became a race track along which excited young people sped in taxis, on motorbikes, even on bicycles – frantic to beat a path to their bloody entertainment.

Against a repeat of this scenario was the date and the place. Jinggangshan is as sacred to Chinese Communists as Nazareth is to Christians. So why might the soil here be stained with criminals' blood? Anyway, it was not the execution season. Culls normally preceded national holidays and were publicised as the fruitful results of crackdowns and clean-up campaigns to rid society of bad elements.

The hours passed, the peasants waited, and I wandered over to the town's memorial to revolutionaries. The maintenance department were busy at work regilding the giant characters of 'The

People's Heroes are Immortal'. I asked them why they were making so special an effort.

'It's a job we do every two years,' they said, but that proved to be a less than open answer to an interested foreign friend.

Later that day in front of the golden characters glistening in the evening sunshine the mystery was revealed. Premier Li Peng, escorted by Jiangxi Province's top Communist Party officials, arrived in town. Plain-clothes security men formed a human chain with their less than human faces. Switching from a cold scowl to a warm smile a chain-smoking official instructed the crowd to give their Premier a warm welcome, whereupon a burst of loud applause was duly delivered to which Li Peng, as is customary, responded.

The year before Li Peng had signed the martial law enforcement order in Beijing that had ultimately led to the use of force in clearing Tiananmen Square. Yet here he was being given an ecstatic reception for his cliched exhortation, 'Comrades, keep alive the spirit of Jinggangshan, and build up the first revolutionary base area!'

I have always been fascinated by photographs of people surrounding Chairman Mao. The genuine delight and broadness of their smiles, so wide and bright, give the pictures a memorable quality – but these peasants of Jinggangshan looked just as delighted at seeing Li Peng.

Li Peng's popularity rating in the rest of China certainly did not reflect his reception in Jinggangshan, though the comment of a young man behind me that, 'It would be easy to kill him,' certainly indicated that not all was forgiven even there. But nobody can doubt the impeccable revolutionary stock from which Li Peng is bred. His father, Li Shuoshun, was one of the earliest CCP members, and fought alongside Zhou Enlai in the Nanchang Uprising of 1927, just a month before Mao led the Autumn Harvest Uprising – and the Nanchang Uprising is recognised as the beginning of the armed struggle against the KMT.

Li Peng was soon to be orphaned, as his father, captured and taken to Hainan Island, died for the Communist cause. Some years later whilst living in Yan'an, Zhou Enlai heard that his close comrade's son was living with a relative in Chengdu. Zhou asked if he could adopt the boy, who was duly brought to Yan'an. But Chinese people find it hard to associate Li Peng with his late foster parent.

They find it even more difficult to identify any of their beloved Premier Zhou Enlai's fine human qualities in their current Premier. He has an impossibly hard act to follow.

Mao Zedong and his Party's literature have always urged leaders, cadres and grassroots members to keep in touch with the masses and never stand aloof from them. Yet I had never met any Chinese, not even Beijingers, who had spoken to their present day leaders. It is said that there is more chance of meeting someone who has talked to Chairman Mao. With this heartening thought, I approached the Jinggangshan *Jing Lao Yuan* (the respect for elders garden).

Here there was, fortunately, one resident – but only one – capable of relating her experiences of life in the first revolutionary base area during the late Twenties. The rest were bedridden, tired or senile. That was precisely the reason why I was here in China on my biographical journey three years early, pre-empting the centenary of Mao's birth. Had I waited for 1993 I would have faced the risk of hearing fewer testimonies of the revolution.

Ma Lao was clearly well over four score years and her name meant 'old horse'. 'Old', however, was a suffixed title of honour normally bestowed on people over seventy: it emphasised the respect accorded to elders in China, a remnant of the Confucian teaching that treats 'old' as a compliment – because of the likely accrued wisdom – and not as an insult. Clad in a dark blue high-collared Mandarin style jacket with toggle fasteners, black cotton padded trousers and a cord skull cap blacker than her hair coiled beneath it, she walked with a jerky lateral movement on the heels of tiny 'ten to two' feet, a hobble enforced by having suffered footbinding in childhood.

This gait, every bit as revealing chronologically as a silver mark on a tankard, dated her childhood to the end of the Qing Dynasty or the dawn of the Republic. The peculiar custom endured by girls to develop dainty and therefore erotic feet lingered on into the Twenties. Qi's mother, born in 1923, had her feet bound as a child but was mischievous enough to unravel the painful bindings, and what is more, to be unperturbed at her own mother's warnings that finding a husband would, as a consequence, be made all the more difficult.

Ma Lao sat beside an interpreter familiar with the local dialect of *Jiangxi hua*, clutching a gnarled walking stick in her frail hands, an old friend that made up for what she lacked in the size of her feet. Its handle was worn smooth and shiny by years of use to a nut-brown varnished finish, much the same colour as the old lady's face.

'My name is Ma Xiaji, meaning summer's beautiful girl, because I was born in the 28th summer of the Guanxu period.' Guanxu is the title of the reign of Emperor Zai Tian who ruled from 1874 to 1908 of the Gregorian calendar (not adopted in China until the PRC's foundation in 1949). We murmured the arithmetic and agreed her year of birth was 1902.

'I was one of many children – in those days the people believed that that brought more happiness and fortune,' she reminisced, 'but I was only one of a few to survive and stay on the farm in our village near Yongxin.'

Her eyes watered but then she beamed a smile to announce proudly that she was almost ninety, whereas in old China life expectancy was around forty. 'I've been lucky with life and health, all along – many children of Yongxin county were sold off because their parents were so poor. For a pittance they were purchased for life to work in the imperialists' factories of Shanghai and Guangzhou, or forced into renting their bodies to the bigwigs and sailors of those cities.' Ma Lao stayed on the farm in Yongxin county planting rice, weaving baskets and making clothes.

'In autumn 1927 there were rebellions in the Jiangxi–Hunan border area – the Communists had broken their alliance with the Kuomintang. Mao Zedong gathered a small Workers' and Peasants' Army together with miners from Anyuan and peasants from Pinxiang county. They ripped up the railway lines, won many skirmishes but fell short of their target in taking Changsha.' It was during their retreat via Sanwan village, en route to the safety of the Jinggang mountain-tops that Ma Lao first saw Mao Zedong and his thousand men. Several weeks later a Communist propaganda team came to Yongxin county.

'They made speeches, danced and wrote big character posters which were pasted to the village walls with glutinous rice – although few peasants could read them.' More effective were the messages communicated by chanting – Join the Army of the proletariat! Overthrow the Kuomintang! Kick out foreign devils! Down with the landlords!

'It was then I decided to join the Party – it was a light of hope.' There was an initiation ceremony, as there still is to this day, at which new members swore allegiance and lifelong devotion to the Party, fist clenched and raised before the Party flag.

'That first winter was a most difficult time – over a thousand people lived in the misty cold valleys and damp basins of the Jinggang mountains. Most were dressed in tattered rags, but there was an abundance of wood for burning and timber for building shelters.' Yet that was barely survival.

From his youth, Mao had been fascinated by two classic works in particular. He took the commonsense tactic of guerrilla warfare advocated in Sun Tzu's sixth-century BC treatise *The Art of War*, and he combined it with the Robin Hood philosophy of robbing the rich to give to the poor, an outlaw style of living made famous in a Song Dynasty classic *The Water Margin*. The basis of survival, and growth of the First Revolutionary Base Area, was thus formulated.

Hit and run success depended on knowing where to hit, and this is where Ma Lao was used. She collected large fleshy mushrooms and 'wood ears', another kind of fungus, which prosper in the damp mountain forests (and still constitute the best dishes available in the town's restaurants to this day). Walking huge distances with a wicker basket strapped to her back, she took her mountain delicacies down the mountain into the KMT-controlled areas, the flatlands where rice but not mushrooms could grow.

'I'd collect mushrooms at dawn, set off at sunrise and return after sunset.' A painful hike with those deformed feet I reckoned, and I asked whether she had any special remedy for footsores. The reply needed no interpretation. She snorted and mimicked the wiping of her nose on the sole of her foot.

Having penetrated the KMT area and entered a village she would sit on the cobbled street with her mushrooms and wood ears spread out on a cloth. Her own ears were alert for gossip on the bamboo telegraph. Like the best of spies she befriended people, yet being dedicated to the Communist cause had no qualms about informing on their idle talk. Then the proletarian army would act. A quick strike with their red-tasselled spears would be followed by a swift withdrawal back into the forest with a haul of KMT muskets and pistols.

Ma Lao paid the price of spying, being imprisoned twice. 'I was released after bribing the guards – that was always the KMT's downfall – they were corruptible, but even when they beat me I wouldn't talk.' She carried no messages nor membership insignia on her person – she could not read or write, and anyway the Party did not – and still does not – issue a membership card.

Spring 1928 brought warmer weather and several thousand survivors of the Nanchang Uprising. These men were now under the command of Zhu De and Chen Yi, men who would be with Mao for the next half century. The army of Jinggangshan, distributed around the five wells which give their names to the mountain range, by now exceeded five thousand.

'The soldiers of the Workers' and Peasants' Army were disciplined by Mao Zedong,' explained Ma Lao. 'They copied his polite and friendly manner to the locals, calling them friend, brother or sister. Mao Zedong was thin in those days, with long hair and tall for a Chinese – much the same height as you,' she speculated, whilst looking at me from head to toe. 'And the soldiers were honest, putting the "Soviet" before themselves by turning in any food or valuables confiscated from landlords for equal redistribution amongst the masses – no matter how much they needed things themselves.'

Soon the Army was officially disciplined by the 'Eight Points of Discipline' and the 'Three Points of Attention' – the Army's Eleven Commandments, drawn up by Mao and announced at the Hunan–Jiangxi Border Area Congress of Maoping in 1928. Ma Lao began to recite them in poetry-like fashion.

'Replace all doors when you leave a home.'

'Don't you mean *close* all doors?' I interrupted.

'No,' she explained. 'Replace is quite correct, because the soldiers often took doors off hinges to make a firm bed.'

The Points of Discipline and Attention respectively were as follows:

1. Replace all doors when leaving a house.
2. Return straw used for sleeping on.
3. Speak politely to the masses and help them when possible.
4. Return everything you borrow.
5. Replace anything you damage.

6. Pay fairly for what you buy.
7. Be honest in all transactions.
8. Establish latrines a safe distance from people's homes.
and
1. Prompt obedience to orders.
2. No confiscations from poor peasants.
3. Prompt delivery of goods confiscated from landlords to the Soviet.

These guidelines established a good code of conduct in the Soviet and its border areas (a no man's land buffer which was the site of frequent battles). Ma Lao recalled how the peasantry began to volunteer to take part in the revolution: the feeling was that if a Soviet had been established on the mountain tops, then why not throughout all China? The population of Jinggangshan swelled with recruits, and in late 1928 Peng Dehuai and Teng Daiyuan arrived at the Soviet from Pingjiang with men of the National Revolutionary Army of Hunan.

Troop supplies that winter became an acute problem, so much so that Mao Zedong and Zhu De led their forces – known collectively as the Red Army to associate it with its Soviet Union counterpart – to southern Jiangxi to an area adjacent to the already established Western Fujian Revolutionary Base Area. This new Soviet became known as the Central Revolutionary Base Area, and later as the Soviet Republic of China (SRC) with its capital centred on Ruijin. Ma Lao stayed behind in Jinggangshan continuing to work for the Party. It would be on her spirit, that of the old war horse, that the success of the revolution would depend.

6

Sandals Made for Marching

Woven grass sandals were standard footwear on the Long March.

'Revolution is not a dinner party,' predicted Mao in 1927, and neither would my retracing of it be from now on. I was in Ruijin, formerly the capital of the Soviet Republic of China (SRC), a prototype PRC occupying an area the size of Wales in southern Jiangxi, preparing to embark on that legendary trek the Chinese themselves call *Chang Zheng* and we translate as the Long March.

The Long March, like the shift of base from Jinggangshan to Ruijin before it, was enforced by deteriorating conditions within the SRC. The Red Army was under siege and had endured four KMT 'encirclement and suppression campaigns', characterised by ground offensives and aerial bombings, since the SRC's establishment in early 1929. Facing a fifth Chiang offensive throughout 1934 the Long March was conceived that autumn.

By all accounts I had a veritable nightmare in store. The statistics were dazzling, the hardships bloodcurdling. A huge army had left the Soviet to struggle across rivers, over mountains and plateaus, and through deserts and jungles for 9,000 kilometres: a distance that dwarfs the Crusades and in numbers that exceeded Alexander the Great's following on his campaigns in Asia Minor. Such is the stuff of the Long March, an epic tale, yet if you were Chinese your father or grandfather might have experienced it and, if he was a born survivor, related its incredible tales at the dinner table.

Could it possibly be an exaggerated Maoist myth, modelled and manipulated by its protagonists as the Chinese Communists' great escape, their coming back from the dead? If scripture writers embellished religious parables functionally to carry their creed then why should not Communists have done the same to muster followers and gain kudos? Certainly, that is what they say across the Taiwan Strait where the very term Long March does not appear in the indexes of their history books. Similarly, in the West we are fed on the belief that although Communism begins with a 'c' and propaganda a 'p' they belong side by side in the dictionary.

I could, just about, seek truth from participants of the Long March, but there again they were, in most cases, top Communists. A new approach was necessary: certainly to listen to what the witnesses had to say, but also to put their testimonies and feelings to field testing. I needed to walk those sections of the Long March route that encompassed the most strategic locations and varying terrains: to take the Long March from under its revered cloak of secrecy in the museum and back on to the paths crossing heartland China and feel it myself underfoot.

For the time being then, conventional travel was over. Now I would be going back to 1934 reliving the life of a Red Army soldier on the Long March. Mao was in his early forties then. I was somewhat younger, but despite being separated by more than a generation if I was to get to know him at all it would be as we walked and faced difficulties together over the next few months.

Nobody, scholar nor adventurer, except Chinese, had ever retraced the route of the Long March on foot – the most logical way of understanding a story characterised by blood, toil, tears and sweat. As the Dead Sea Scrolls were kept out of reach of interpreters, so was the route of the March through China's backcountry kept strictly out of bounds, thus enhancing its legendary aura. To demystify it required a certain amount of audacity, the ability to speak Mandarin and scribble the nationally understood characters if dialects became problematical, and a stout pair of legs. My linguistics and physique I hoped would be sufficient; all I needed now was the inspiration and that came from Mao himself who wrote, 'Revolution cannot be refined, leisurely and gentle, temperate, kind, courteous, restrained and magnanimous. A revolution is an insurrection: an act of violence by which one class overthrows another.' Freedom of access rather than class struggle was my cause so I replaced the last sentence with 'an act of necessary trespass in which one foreigner outwits the Public Security Bureau'. Fancifully I wondered if my dodging them could be viewed as a modern parallel to the conflict of the Long March.

Sometimes my life seemed to have no pattern to it. At heart I was a geographer whatever that should qualify one to do. I love to run, trek and take photographs. History away from the stuffiness of museums interested me, and as a result Hadrian's Wall had led me to the Great Wall. During that time I met my wife to be, Qi. She has since taught me Chinese. Only now do all these qualifications, likes and events have any pattern. But long before all this I may have been destined to retrace the Long March. As a boy I had looked up my birthday, October 16th, in the encyclopaedia's chronology to find that the Red Army's Long March began on that day in 1934. The omen to finish the journey safely was even stronger since the name of the town in Northern Shaanxi where the March ended was the same as my wife's – Wuqi.

Keeping in step with destiny, I prepared to leave the Soviet exactly fifty-six years to the day that Chairman Mao marched out. For under ten pounds I had put together a complete PLA outfit; it was the grandchild of the Red Army's kit. For rain, I had a green cap, dubbed the Mao cap by foreigners when it became part of the national dress during the Cultural Revolution. For shine, I had a straw hat, which I had lined with polythene as the peasants advocate for use during torrential rain. My green cotton trousers were baggy enough to take the essential heavy knitted long johns when winter came. On top I wore a matching shirt and short-sleeved khaki drill jacket. Its buttons were of impressive looking brass, embossed with the numerals *Ba*, *yi* commemorating August 1st, the foundation date of the Chinese army.

The jacket's abundant pockets were akin to departmental offices. There was an intelligence pocket, with extracts from a paperback atlas and an army compass. The maps were unmarked, and my intended areas of trespass were committed to memory instead, as was the entire March route. Another pocket was psychological. How could the *Gong An Ju* scold me if they found a bilingual copy of Chairman Mao's quotations in my breast pocket? They came complete with a photograph of Mao. I hoped in an absurdly ominous way that they might guide me not only in thought but direction too. But the principal item of this department was a snapshot to prey on the Chinese shutter-bug craze. It showed me amongst a group of students with whom I had chatted at a university's English corner – a free talking outdoor get-together to give scholars of the language a chance to practise debating skills. On the reverse was written, 'We welcome Mr William to serve in the socialist construction of our motherland by helping us gain fluency in English, the world language necessary for the realisation of the Four Modernisations.' With a cigarette in hand provided by my department of public relations, that would make diplomatic reading for my green-uniformed friends.

My rucksack was a green PLA one, matching perfectly my trousers and shirt. Frameless and rubberised on the inside, and secured with old-fashioned draw cords and buckles, it sagged like a sack when half empty. Packed full, however, and carefully secured it would likely be relatively buoyant if I were to fall in a river. Water-bottles were further matching accessories: one of plastic and the other of steel. I kept one outside the rucksack for quick drinking and refilling. This gear was so well camouflaged that the Mao cap and bottles especially could be easily misplaced on the grass when I rested.

Inside my rucksack were just a few concessions to fifty-six years of technological progress. The down sleeping-bag was a more compact and efficient relative of the woollen blankets that Mao's orderly, Chen Changfeng, carried for him; but the duck's feathers at least originated from China. Do-it-yourself is not my forte; so to avoid unscrewing doors from hinges I carried a woven straw mat, a locally made forerunner of the insulating foam type favoured by hikers.

Anyway, I did not have a screwdriver, preferring a simple two-bladed penknife to a bulky multi-tooled one.

I had never wanted to join the army, so how can I explain this Action Man mentality? Dressing up as a PLA soldier was not re-enactment taken to fanatical extremes, nor was it any shade of an attempt at disguising myself as Chinese. Even with black hair dye such deception was too tall an order with my big nose, round green eyes, vigorous beard growth, one metre eighty-five height, and size thirteen feet. It was simply and foremost a ploy to minimise fidgeting and fascination. To be a walking window for the West's manufacturers was just too much of a hassle.

For safety's sake I bought a walking stick which would have an infinite number of uses, besides being a pacemaker and sergeant major when my stride became sluggish. Primarily I envisaged it as a dog deterrent, but it could double up as a rat basher. Since coming south I had had good reason to believe the estimate of the Shanghai-based rodent forecasting station that there were over three billion rats in China – three for every Chinese. They came as standard with lodgings, more reliably than the availability of electricity or running water. The presence of snakes too in restaurant cages was worrying; the stick might also have to be a serpent stabber.

If any of these demons should beat the stick then I might need medicines. This department was a combination of West and East. Vaseline is to the walker what oil is to the engine; it can also stop the sweat running into one's eyes and prevent skin cracking with sunburn. In search of a panacea I approached the herbal medicinalist in Ruijin. His open shop front with its musky smell was enough to beckon anyone inside on the pretext of hypochondria, to marvel at the dark wood-panelled drawers and porcelain jars and wonder with awe or scepticism at the benefit of young male donkey urine for dermatitis or burnt human hair paste for boils.

For a World Wildlife Fund member this dispensary was a nightmare, with its potions made from fauna on the verge of extinction. One can appreciate the danger involved in hunting some of these beasts but the supposed virility induced by consumption of, for example, a tiger's foot was somewhat spurious. It is perhaps a subtle indicator, in a culture where sexuality has been traditionally suppressed, of the importance of male prowess. Yet, I could never understand why, when the population is too large and is being limited by the most intrusive contraception and abortion service in the world, the government should allow the widespread advertisement of such potions.

The doctor on duty wore a white cotton chef-like hat and sat at his desk before a pad of paper, pen and ink well. In case he got the wrong idea I told him about my forthcoming long walk in the remote countryside. He checked my pulse, looked at the whites of my eyes and unhesitatingly scribbled his prescription in unintelligible characters – doctors' writing is awful the world over.

For colds and flu he recommended some tablets containing the very active ingredient of extract of snake bile. After that I intimated that my preferences were vegetarian at heart. Responding, he put great faith in *Yunnan Baiyao*. This panacea was a secret formula concocted from Yunnan Province's abundant flora. For internal or external use, the powder was prescribed for almost anything in anybody: from period pain to sore throats, from internal haemorrhage to gunshot wounds and animal bites. It was to be taken dry, with water or with wine. I had immediate faith in this wonderful stuff: it smelt like a walk through Kew Gardens.

*   *   *

Forty years after Liberation, Ruijin is still a poor county where the trial of life is a close contest between squalor and death. Prosperity seems absent here; mere survival is the most you can aspire to – and even that requires constant toil. Every square metre is cultivated, so much so that the losers of the contest in this overpopulated country cannot rest in peace. Around and over their conical graves the struggle goes on – peasants bent over watering by hand with wooden ladles, women washing clothes in the district pond in which water buffaloes wallow, on which ducks float and over which insects swarm.

Vermin and its dangers are everywhere, familiar, long-time neighbours: rabid dogs, malarial mosquitoes, and rats always carrying some disease one resistant step ahead of any poison. The problems compound with time as too many people re-use what little water there is. The contest starts young, with boys and girls shorter than the bamboo poles springing on their shoulders carrying pails of water back home from the well, barefoot wonders, waddling and bouncing in rhythm with the flexing pole. Such are the scenes in Ruijin during October, for them as always the season of survival, and for me, as fifty-six years before, the secret season of departure.

A bright sun beat down, hot but not scorching by heady Chinese standards, slowly toasting the coarse and brittle bladed leaves of the third crop of rice which would soon be gathered in. Around the farms, peasants rustled amongst the noisy foliage of maize plants that dwarfed them by over a metre, twisting off corn cobs which seemed to squeak in complaint.

On the pounded red earth floors fringing every farmstead, whose contours change with each passage of feet, hooves, morning sweeping and rainstorm, the family elders sorted cobs, grains and pods whilst contenting their life's insurance, the children, with some chewable treasure from the fields. The able-bodied and energetic lugged baskets of corn up bamboo ladders on to the roof, to be stored safe from thieves and prying snouts.

The golden cobs added splashes of colour to these ashen grey ribbed structures whose tiles, being aligned and in high relief, resembled a neatly combed mop of hair that overhung its forehead with a generous fringe curling upwards at the edges. From the corners of the roof deities dangled like earrings to deter the approach of evil spirits, but the yelping dogs had a more practical effect. On the doors too, cast open to fling a beam of light into the farm's dark interior, mystical armoured characters snarled a sinister unwelcome. Across the lintel and down the portals black characters on red fortune paper, the colour of chilli pod strings at their sides, suggested that the fabric of daily and spiritual life had changed little in the fifty-six years since others made their preparation for departure.

Amidst this rustic setting I retreated to the quiet corner of a harvested field to imagine the final homecoming and family circumstances of an average boy soldier on the eve of the Long March.

I pictured a boy known to his parents as Lao Wu (old fifth child) rather than his family name, Wang. He had toiled with farm labour all his young life, as routinely as planting follows winter and famine follows flood. Until 1930. He had never had any schooling but his fingerprint on the Red Army's muster role was enough. However, this had not freed him from back-breaking farm work, for the Reds were a self-sufficient army. But Lao Wu had been to the Soviet's front to fight. As a farm lad used to slaughtering pigs and chickens he had no qualms about killing Whites – KMT soldiers. The Army had taught him something new – a little reading and writing – and introduced him to Lenin and Marx. He had left home as Lao Wu and returned as Wang Tongzhi (Comrade Wang). Before he greeted elders with kowtow and clasped hands, now he used a handshake.

The Communists had given his family thirty *mu* of land – about five acres – but their Red Army had creamed off two teenage sons coming to the primes of their working lives. Too poor to own a water buffalo, these boys had done the family's ploughing. In the last year alone the evil spirits had taken others away with endemic dysentery and malaria as well as robbing the family of its rock: their mother who had produced a dozen children over a fertile twenty years but had recently paid the price of being a baby machine. Father's planned dependence on a pension of people was thus halved and it was increasingly difficult to work the land. He badly needed the dowry a new wife might bring but he had little to offer a woman in return.

The boy soldier had come home to collect a few possessions. A hacker with a blade the length of his forearm might fell Whites as well as bamboo. His sister engaged in 'women's work' would recently have made a trip into the hills and returned with a variety of dried roots, flowers and seeds to grind the family's speciality medicine with pestle and mortar. Perhaps it enjoyed a reputation with Wang's Red comrades as it did with villagers as a cure for dysentery. His grandmother, probably in her early fifties, would not only be the family elder but a village one too. Few lived past forty-five. The youngest grandmothers were around thirty years since most girls were married mothers by their mid-teens. She would have spent the last two months as she had every August and September since the century's turn – weaving the summer's straw and wicker. Lao Wu helped himself to a wide brimmed sunhat and a straw mat. Showing grandmotherly concern, a few pairs of straw sandals would have been pressed into the boy's hands from a pile of fifty or more. The boy reluctantly stuffed them into his knapsack because they took up the place of food, and he was so used to going barefoot anyway that the soles of his feet were like leather. But that was on the terracotta earth of Jiangxi. Little did he know how useful those sandals would be – how vital too the skill of weaving them himself, as taught by his grandmother, for he would soon be carrying loads for distances never before experienced across mountains he had never seen nor heard of. They were sandals made for marching.

That October morning in 1934 brought unusual quiet. Of course the peasants worked – they were the sun's shadow. But the bugle call at sunrise for dawn drills went unblown. There was not the usual pushing and shoving – queueing has never been a Chinese discipline – at the field kitchens because the fires were out, the cauldrons empty of rice gruel. There were no familiarity drills with the latest KMT captured arms. No enthusiastic yells of 'sha' (kill) from new recruits stabbing scarecrows with their red-tasselled spears and pitchforks. The army had gone on to night shift. For the next few weeks they would be the moon's shadow.

As darkness fell the air cooled, but the usually peaceful dusk and its soporific hum and trill of night life were drowned by the movement of the nocturnal army. There were the dead weights of mortars, cannons, bullets and shells to be carried. Field kitchens, medicine chests, printing presses, reams of paper and gold bullion. Until now there had been a policy of self-sufficiency, but this was broken to employ porters; mules were also used, but in the main it was the bamboo pole, that efficient Chinese lever, that shifted the Soviet and its chattels. The moon rose as the heaving and repositioning, the binding and cushioning went on for hours until the scouts led the first soldiers, banner bearers with flags furled, off into the night. There were no flaming torches, as they could not risk being spotted by reconnaissance planes. Any leak of intelligence that an exodus was under way would allow a strengthening of the encircling KMT forces.

Scouts with local geographical knowledge had been earmarked for their jobs weeks before but were summoned by their leaders for briefing only at the last minute. Now they led the way like the leaders of an orienteering race. There was no marching in formation, just a snaking mass of soldiers petering into single file as the paths became steeper, narrower and rockier, developing gaps towards dawn as the men became tired. Then the army went to ground, amidst trees, rocks, fields and in peasants' homes.

The fact that this night-time ritual would be repeated for ten days around the full moon of October gives rise to the disagreement on what single day the March began. If one date must be chosen then it should be October 16th, the day when the recognised leaders of the Army evacuated their headquarters. Because Mao Zedong left the Soviet at a different time, on October 18th, and from a different place, Yudu, inference suggests that he was not part of the decision-making process.

Mao's position had been severely eroded by a group backed and influenced by the Soviet Union. This anti-Mao clique, advocating positional rather than guerrilla warfare and favouring activism concentrating on urban instead of rural areas, was a group of some twenty-eight returned students from Moscow headed by Wang Ming and Bo Gu. Although Mao had achieved the status of Chairman of the Soviet Republic the title was honorary and quite powerless, as he was not in control of the Army. He lived at Yudu with his wife of four years, He Zizhen, a good day's march away from the leaders' headquarters in Ruijin. Most of his comrades knew only of 'Mao Zhu': the name given to the united followers of Mao Zedong and Zhu De from the Jinggangshan days. To much of the army and peasantry Mao Zedong had become a non person – or rather a non existent half person.

The decision to evacuate the Soviet is accredited, or rather blamed on, Bo Gu and Li De. The latter was in fact a German named Otto Braun who had travelled to China from Moscow on the Trans-Siberian railway and been smuggled into Jiangxi. This puzzled those who only knew 'foreign devils' as targets of propagandist slogans or as caricatured beasts on a map. Why, they asked secretly, do we chant 'foreign devils go home' when a yellow-haired, blue-eyed, big-nosed giant is leading our Red Army? It is a generality that in China the uneducated believe everything they are told and the educated believe nothing, but with regard to Braun the former remained sceptical – he was an outsider from an imperialist motherland.

It is interesting to note that the chroniclers of Party history, 1990 vintage, accuse Bo Gu and Li De amongst others of being 'scared out of their wits' by the Nationalist encirclement and failing to consult the Politburo on the decision to march the army out. Furthermore they continue to be accused of 'military flightism' which resulted in 'colossal losses'. So the Long March, usually prefixed as 'Mao's', was in fact not of his planning nor direction at all during its initial stages.

A man closer to the leaders than most was Gu Yiping. I visited him in his spacious eight-roomed home – a retirement perk for having been Zhou Enlai's bodyguard – in Red Capital Street, Ruijin. We sat on creaking wicker chairs, beside a table of homegrown tangerines and beneath a large wall map of China. Gu Yiping at seventy-eight knew full well that the anniversary of departure was coming around again and he had no trouble in recalling those autumn days a lifetime ago.

Standing at the map Gu need not have pointed out the extent of the Soviet. Southern Jiangxi had, through continual pointing and prodding, become soiled and worn to a dark spot. Spreading his fingers and surrounding the black spot he mimicked the extermination campaign of the Nationalists with a theatrical stabbing motion as directed by Chiang Kai-shek from Nanchang.

I asked him if the soldiers knew the March was being planned.

'In hindsight there were indicators,' he responded. 'Peasant women had been ordered to increase their output of straw sandals to extra thick standards – but most peasant lads could rustle a pair up in an hour or so whilst resting in a field.'

Helping myself to a handful of peanuts appeared to act as a prompter to Gu. 'Feasting was another clue – suddenly frugality ceased,' he said. 'You know there's a Chinese saying – "Only a foolish man kills an ox" – because it's more valuable as a draught animal than for meat. Well, from early October rations included duck and pork – most soldiers ate the producers of eggs and piglets.'

Gu Yiping had once been an ordinary soldier himself. 'I joined the Communist Youth in Guangchang but one day was told to report to Ceping – nobody knew that was the leader's headquarters because of internal security: the locations changed often in case of enemy bombing.' Gu was one of four bodyguards-cum-orderlies for Zhou Enlai. He summed up the contrast of his move: 'One day I carried a spear, the next a loaded pistol.'

'You must have been a model soldier,' I suggested, but Gu rejected my praise in the usual humble Chinese way.

Although Gu was so close to Zhou Enlai he was given only a

few days' notice of the moonlight march. What he shouldered in responsibility he lacked in things to carry, being hampered only by Zhou's document case, field-glasses, lamp and foodbox. 'I was just twenty-three when I left Ruijin, but that was older than average – recruitment was frantic in 1934: they were taking teenagers – but despite their tender age they never looked back. Joining the Red Army had improved our life, and we wholeheartedly believed that moving the Soviet would do so too.'

Before I left Red Capital Street Gu revealed his most treasured possession which hung above his mosquito-netted bed – a black-and-white photograph taken with Premier Zhou in Zhongnanhai, Beijing, twenty years after the March. It highlighted a characteristic of Zhou Enlai which became his hallmark – the personal touch on which the love of the people, even to this day, is founded.

At the revolutionary cadres veterans' unit in Ruijin I met Xu Youwan. We talked in a large airy recreation room above which ceiling fans rotated at a lazy end of season pace. The windows, although flung open to catch the afternoon breeze, were not great providers of daylight since the building itself was cloaked in foliage on the outside and unintentionally deprived of any percolating light within by essential iron meshed mosquito shutters. It was so dim that Chairman Mao's quotations adorning the walls were indecipherable, even if one knew the recommended three thousand characters that separate one from illiteracy.

We sat down at a long table on which awaited the diversions of the old men who occupy their historic lives drinking tea, reading good news and building great walls with mahjong tiles. Xu recalled seeing Mao Zedong make a speech.

'After breakfast one morning, in August or September of 1932 – I think, you know I'm getting old now – our leader told us we were going to hear Mao Zedong speak. We were garrisoned at Ningdu. It was about ten o'clock when Chairman Mao arrived. All the men rose from their cross-legged sitting position to welcome him. There were more than ten thousand of us. Mao Zedong stood on some boxes with his hands on his hips. Because I am a Hunanese I understood his every word; so I interpreted his dialect to my Jiangxi and Fujian comrades.'

'What did he talk about that morning?' I asked.

'It was a briefing on the current situation and our tasks, and a call to learn from and uphold the traditional bravery of the Red Army. Chairman Mao called Chiang Kai-shek an imperialist's running dog. He asked us what we should do, and we chanted "*sha, sha, sha*" in reply!'

Xu Youwan became an artillery man and his weapon was a mortar captured from the KMT with a range of up to 2,000 metres. 'But that depended on the shell quality,' he added. 'Being short of ammunition forced us to scour old battlefields for shells and cartridges, many of them unexploded – it was dangerous work.'

It was that kind of thrift and frugality which allowed Xu to march out of the Soviet with a full load.

'On October 19th of 1934 I left Yudu on a starry night marching across a pontoon bridge spanning the river. I was carrying a mortar, four shells, one hundred bullets and five *jin* of rice – total weight about eighty *jin* (forty kilograms).' The pontoon bridge was not a permanent structure. 'It was one of several that were hastily constructed each evening. Boats were stored by day on the bushy banks, leashed together at dusk and spanned with long bamboos.' Once on his way Xu would not see his family again until Liberation – fifteen years away.

*   *   *

Before leaving Ruijin I visited Bao Zhong who enlightened me as to the conditions endured by those left behind. In mid-October of 1934 he was summoned, along with seven or eight hundred others, to a meeting at Yanshi Shan. Mao Zedong had been given some dirty work to do: to tell those gathered why the Red Army was leaving. 'We are too weak to resist the present encirclement and extermination campaign,' Mao said, whilst advising those who sat cross-legged in the dust chosen to remain, to 'fight protracted guerrilla warfare against the KMT who will soon occupy the Soviet. We will return in three to five years.'

'Actually it was three times five – fifteen years later, in 1949,' chuckled Bao Zhong. 'Perhaps I misheard.'

Mao must have hated being the puppet mouthpiece of leaders he outright disagreed with. Nevertheless he abided by the first point of attention which he himself had drawn up, and upon his advice an operation equally as clandestine as the March itself began. Secret meetings were held, records destroyed and identities changed. The elderly, women, sick and children were to be left behind: Mao's two children, amongst many others, were given away to peasants via intermediaries to ensure anonymity. Mao may have fallen from power but in Chiang Kai-shek's eyes he still had the most valuable head. The same went for his own kith and kin.

According to Bao Zhong, some 30,000 were left behind under the command of Chen Yi. They were mainly older ones like himself who at thirty-four in 1934 was almost double the average age. Wrongly they were considered to possess less physiological endurance than boys in their late teens or early twenties, but rightly regarded as being mentally more capable of resisting the fate which awaited them – White terror.

Bao Zhong made repeated treks into the Wu Yi mountains south-west of Ruijin laden with bamboos, their chambers filled with millet through drilled holes. Most rice had been requisitioned by the army. These caches were needed sooner than expected – the millet to eat and bamboo to build mountain shelters. Just three weeks after the last marchers had left the Nationalists were drawn into the vacuum of weakness that was once the Soviet Republic of China.

The KMT found that the Red Army was gone before they knew where it had gone to. It took the same time, three weeks, for news of the exodus to reach the outside world. The *New York Times* of November 9th 1934 was the voice of Chiang Kai-shek. It reported that 40,000 of Mao's 'red bandits' were looting their way through Hunan. Staging his own PR in the United States where it mattered, because that government armed him, Chiang was using the press to publicise the evils of Communism. First impressions, true or false, are important because they stick. The Western press would be anti-Mao for the rest of his life.

On November 10th, Ruijin the Red capital changed colour. Land-lords returned to name the worst Communists. Bao Zhong estimated that about 6,000 were executed in the dark winter of 1934–5. Hardly a tree was without a corpse hanging from its branches. The National-ists could not kill everybody, but they made the people's lives a misery. Peasants branded red were thrown into paddies and pools red from Jiangxi's soil. Many suffocated or drowned in the process.

Chiang Kai-shek got his consanguineous consolation: not Mao's children but his young brother, Mao Zetan, whose corpse was exhibited in Ruijin town.

The Communist Party demands lifelong loyalty from its members, and one of Bao Zhong's most successful raids was to punish a traitor who failed to fulfil this requirement. The hamlet of Lan Tian Bao was defended by eight Whites. With the aid of an infiltrator who tampered with the loading mechanisms of their rifles, Bao Zhong's men swooped on the tip-off of a torchlight signal – one long and two short flashes. Apart from killing an ex-Communist they wiped out the Whites and captured their arms.

Ironically that same fate almost befell Bao Zhong over thirty years later during the Cultural Revolution. After Liberation in 1949 Bao recounted his revolutionary life as a guerrilla fighter in a book, *On the Banks of the Min River*. One of his stories told that by spring 1935 food stores of the Communist mountain cells of resistance were depleted. In order to continue any oppositional activity Bao Zhong and his wife changed their strategy. Surrendering, they denounced the Communists as exploiters and deserters and were eventually rehabilitated into village life. Bao Zhong soon became village leader, a position he used to pass food to the remaining guerrillas. Learning from the Ming and Qing eunuchs who had once set fire to pavilions in the Forbidden City when their thieving activities were in danger of being exposed, Bao Zhong too became an arsonist to cover up the fact that the village barn was empty.

Despite his motives and the benefits he brought, Bao Zhong was severely criticised by Red Guards and branded a spy.

7

Foreign Red Army Marches

Farewell as the Reds leave the Soviet.

The mosquitoes had already scrambled on their pestilent dawn patrol, entering the tattered net which was supposed to prevent them from honing in on the scent of sweat. Nevertheless I lay relatively composed in my violated sanctuary apart from frequent semi-automatic slaps of the hand about my head to swat the whining terrors as they flew in search of their bloody breakfasts. The minute I was *compos mentis*, when dreams were disturbed by itching reality, I cursed the moths who ate the net to allow in the mosquitoes to suck the blood; I subscribed to the theory of interdependence. Moments later, however, I was compensated by the realisation that a big day had arrived. It was October 18th, time to seize the day and hour that Mao Zedong had left the Soviet. I sprang out of my cocoon, eager to be punctual for my appointment with history.

Once outside, my path was blocked by an iron general: a padlock the size of a clenched fist. An arc lamp spotlighted the iron railed gate, casting distorted shadows of its two large decorative stars across the concrete, and I momentarily thought of the first group to set out on the Long March: those women, sick and elderly, deemed to be in danger of execution should they have remained in the Soviet, had departed more than a week before Mao to follow a trail of red stars painted on the ground by scouts. Then a dog barked. I gripped my stick tightly, but it was only the gateman's closed circuit television alerting its master. Fortunately he arrived swiftly to let me out and no on-guard offensive was necessary. All I had lost was my night-sight.

Reduced to four senses I trod cautiously through the streets of Ruijin. Every rattle, bark, snort or sweep provoked a question. An answer ensured continuation. A mystery advised stopping, standing and pondering. After twenty minutes or so, the sky, which had appeared like the only type of black hole I can comprehend, became a star-spangled firmament. Until then, cyclists had proved to be potentially as fatal as meteors falling from it, for only the most decrepit machines rattled any warning of their approach. Absurd but true – China is a place where one can be run over by a bicycle. Regaining the fifth sense, I now could just make out the glowing orange tips of cigarettes wedged in riders' mouths, the closest thing to headlights.

The oldest eyes in town belonged to the Tang Pagoda, witnesses to over a thousand years of history. Surely they had never seen so bizarre a spectacle as the week of nights in 1934. Above me flew thousands of bats, their clumsy flight unchanged in a brief fifty-six years, still unable to answer the question posed by Mother Nature, whether to be birds or mice. On this night, however, the date, time and place meant they could only be the spirits of sandal-shod soldiers who had fallen along the route of the Long March but whose souls had gathered for the anniversary. For I had disturbed the peace of this sacred night by treading on the same red earth and by hearing the unchanged murmur of the Min River fade slowly to silence like a nostalgic voice echoing a farewell. Upon this eerie stage, blanketed with invigorating darkness, I could meet Mao Zedong.

He had trodden this undulating, winding and dusty track many times. The beginnings of all life's journeys pass through familiar lands, yet it is only when one leaves a place, uprooting oneself with no predetermined plan to return, that any emotional notice of the place is taken. One sees different things when one thinks it could be for the last time. A long look is given to the serene paddy fields under moonlight, a final look back to say goodbye to the pagoda. Suddenly hills and woods have personalities which are warm and friendly, simply because in the future cold and foe may be encountered. Nostalgia washes away any boastfulness; confidence wanes, for to survive in the mountains beyond it is best to be cautious.

Mao Zedong was not scared by the prospect of a long trek, although even he did not know, nor did anyone else, just how long it might be. As a boy he had played at his Shaoshan home barefoot. I knew that there is no better way to grow a pair of tough feet. I had seen the unblemished feet of my wife Qi after we had hiked along West Highland footpaths for 170 kilometres.

Yet, more than that, Mao had as a youth walked through the Hunan hills of his home counties not quite knowing where his next meal would come from but knowing for sure his brotherly and sisterly peasants would not see one of their own go hungry. When the skies opened, as they often do, Mao had not run frantically for cover as other Chinese tend to, like cats in the rain, but had taken off his shirt. When the hot sun beat down and drove the locals to the shade for a several hour long *xiu xi* (a midday rest), he strode on to build up his strength.

Mao admitted to being what we would call a fitness fanatic. Now the results showed. Mao was head and shoulders above the average Chinese. As his orderly, Chen Changfeng, struggled along lugging an eighty-*jin* load, Mao took one long loping stride for every two of Chen's. A fair man, and by no means a brutal taskmaster like his own father, Mao grabbed for the makeshift bundle bound by grass cutting into his exhausted orderly's shoulders. Chen, a proud lad not wanting to lose face, refused vigorously and a struggle ensued – as always when any 'gentlemanly' gesture is offered in China. In the end Mao had to order his man to shed some of his load.

This sympathetic hand was offered in spite of Mao's own poor health: he was convalescing from malaria. This somewhat undermined my own holistic approach to the disease. I was not taking any tablets, as I assumed that after two years in China I should have developed a fair degree of immunity.

The Chinese believe any illness is a reflection of the state of mind, and Mao's must have been somewhat depressed. His second wife, He Zizhen, was a week ahead on the trail, with the so-called Red Star brigade because she was pregnant. Mao had already lost Yang Kaihui to the KMT – he knew well that leaving his second wife behind, as others had done, would surely put the local peasantry under pressure of execution to expose her.

On the logistics side, Mao disagreed with the decision to leave the Soviet and felt when the time came to break out of the Nationalists' encirclement there would be heavy losses. But more worrying, apparent even on the first night, was the fact that the army was grossly overloaded. Mao believed when the fighting started his men would be immobilised, like greedy men in danger of dying under burden of goods salvaged from a burning house.

Not wanting to add to his men's burdens, Mao kept these doubts to himself. Instead, he inspired them: their cause was a magnificent one; they represented the hopes of a better China for millions of others throughout the land. He strode out, advising, directing, coaxing, even fathering the lads who were less than half his age.

In sub-tropical latitudes dawn comes quickly – the change from pitch darkness to sunrise takes under half an hour. Now, as day dawned, just as the Red Army had rested to avoid being spotted by the Kuomintang planes, I too faced the practical task of not being spotted by the *Gong An Ju*. My comfortable shroud of anonymity was gone and already I was in enemy-controlled areas – closed regions. China was still restricting foreigners' movements as revenge for the unequal treaties their grandfathers had forced upon her, and – in the case of Britain – for the Opium War.

My first security measure was to get off this dirt road which led to Yudu. A couple of dawn-departure buses had already laboured past kicking up terracotta clouds of dust whose orangey colour was intensified by the rising sun. The adjacent paddies, maize, sugar-cane plantations and I were caked in it. Yet even at this early hour my ears caught cries of '*lao wai*' (old foreigner) drifting out of the windows of passing ramshackle buses.

The old road shadowed the new one behind a very comfortable curtain of maize plants. It passed along the boundaries of paddies and the canal laterals and channels that watered them. Often, in the quest for a few extra yards of land – for that means more *jin* and more money – the path itself was overplanted and I found myself treading on raised mud strands the width of footprints between one terrace and the next. Every few hundred metres these paths led to a hamlet of three or four farms, yet the number of heads they gave shelter to would constitute a village in any country outside overcrowded Asia.

Dogs, although abundant, proved to be of no threat, for this was South China with its adage: 'Anything with four legs, except tables, is eaten.' Dogs were understandably timid, running away yelping mildly as if they instinctively knew their place – on the dinner table of the future. That was the fate of ducks and piglets too eventually, but for the time being they acted as efficient vacuum cleaners on the garbage which littered the apron of every farmstead.

Despite the frequent calls and questioning – '*Ni cong nali lai, dao nali qu?*' (Where are you from and going to?) and '*Ni shi yi ge ren ma?*' (Are you by yourself?) – I just smiled, waved and continued. I had to be selfish and stop only when it suited me for my principal needs. But this was made difficult by those friendly souls who thrust tangerines and sticks of sugar cane into my hands. Replying '*Xie xie pengyou*' or '*Xie xie da ge*' (Thanks friend or brother) aligned me for further acts of hospitality.

Learning from Mao, I resisted the temptation of a midday snooze in an orange grove at the invitation of a peasant who lodged there seasonally in his hide on stilts. He was on the look out for thieves helping themselves to his cash crop which sold at the local Yudu town market for one *yuan* per *jin*.

By evening I had trekked almost sixty kilometres, a daily total which dwarfed any of the Red Army's initial marches, since they were handicapped by carrying the Soviet's wherewithal for being a city on the move. I needed a good rest, but I had made a rule not to check into any kind of lodging house, for that would risk being reported to the *Gong An Ju*. Sleeping rough, however, was out of the question: this landscape was too heavily populated. Every farmhouse housed tens of peasants, so the chances of a peaceful evening there augured badly. A small work unit might present more relaxing prospects; so I introduced myself and my requirements to the leader of a small quarry. 'Being alone,' I said, to allay his suspicions, 'I want to take the chance to speak with the workers and peasants and learn about their lifestyle.'

In the ensuing evening hours until eleven o'clock I had to back up that claim, playing host to a ceaseless stream of visitors, answering the same personal questions over and over again until I was almost hoarse. Though dressed up in Chinese attire, I was still a television to be stared at continuously, even though I was a monochrome set – army green – rather than a colourful foreign one. I had felt quite confident that my clothing, having been familiar to the nation for some thirty years, would be uninteresting. Not so. A joke could be had at my expense over what I had paid for it.

Next morning I set off through Yudu town and was soon walking through a more remote area. The red hills became dusty and barren and being unterraced fostered few peasant dwellings on their slopes. Below the undulating road the Yudu He, a tributary of the Gan Jiang, flowed westwards. According to my map, the latter river drained north to the Yangzi via Poyang Lake and eventually spilt out its silt-laden waters near Shanghai, thus giving the Yellow Sea its name. This source river of China's mighty grandmother was neither lively nor full for, although its course was some two hundred metres in width the water channel itself occupied less than half of this span. Nevertheless it was still a considerable body of water despite its sluggish flow, and being the hue of the hills it drained was opaque and hence of unknown depth to the observer on its bank.

Knowing that the Red Army had bothered to construct five pontoon bridges over the Yudu in this valley I deemed it foolhardy to try wading across. Instead I asked two peasants digging out gravel from the dry river bed where I might find a crossing. They directed me upstream. There was no bridge, they said, but the fishermen were willing to subsidise their earnings from fish sales with a fare across the river.

The fishing craft were long slender rafts – *sampans* as an English dictionary would have it. The native word *sam* means 'three' in Cantonese, and thus defines the number of bamboos lashed together to make the craft. A wider, deluxe version is the *wupan* – *wu* meaning five. In spite of their precarious appearance, they are incredibly strong and buoyant, being made of such wonderful chambered material. Not having the fine balance of the punter, I sat down for the crossing.

Safely on the south bank, though with a wet backside, I proceeded to pick my way along a strand-like riverside path at the foot of steep and crumbling red hills. Looking back, I tried to imagine the scene of those exodus nights under moonlight fifty-six years before. According to Xu Youwan, they crossed by pontoon bridge.

Once across the Yudu He, the Red Army swung southwestward towards Anyuan thus avoiding an early confrontation with the KMT based at Ganzhou, a strategic city where they had tasted defeat in 1932 by trying to capture the citadel at the confluence of two wide rivers.

Under the leadership of Bo Gu and Wang Ming, both strongly influenced by Comintern military adviser Otto Braun, the Red Army advanced at catastrophic cost across Hunan, Guangxi and Guizhou. At the crossing of the Xiang River some 30,000 men had been lost alone. It was a funeral march. Perhaps the fate of the Red Army would change after Mao became leader. I had marched out of the Soviet. Now I headed to Kunming, in Yunnan, to follow sections of the Long March under Mao's direction.

8

Victory and Punishment at Jiaopingdu

Zhang brothers ferrying Reds across the Golden Sands River.

I reached Kunming on a Sunday morning, and paused beneath a painted hoarding of a silhouetted naked man and woman. Almost anywhere else but China this video advertisement would be for pornographic films, or yellow films as the Chinese call them because of the exposure of skin. This, however, was promoting the *New Wedding School* video, which gets down to the nitty gritty of overpopulation, stipulating the rules of marriage and child bearing and promoting the advantages, social and financial, of delaying birth. 'Everybody,' the commentator says, 'must sign the Marriage Law Act of 1981 agreeing to practise birth control according to the regulations.'

Already the brother and sisterless generation has dawned, and as the pruning of the family tree continues cousins, brother and sister-in-laws, aunts and uncles are all set to become extinct. The hero mothers advocated by Mao are out; model one-child families are in.

Mao oversaw a doubling of the nation's population during his leadership, and out on the streets the aftermath is endured by every citizen. People emerge from overcrowded flats to cycle to their over-manned jobs along avenues packed with cyclists. Most of them are under thirty-five. The possible consequences of so many young women being in the child-bearing age are horrific.

In all towns and cities the crude life and death figures are displayed arithmetically at intersections. In Kunming there is a population clock. Its digits clocked on at much the same rate as my watch's second hand. I stopped beneath it for one minute and presided in thought over fifty-six new Chinese citizens arriving in this crowded world.

Attempting to ease congestion in cities, work units give their employees different days off. Sunday is thus a work day for many, but this Sunday stroll had a distinctively relaxed feel about it. People played badminton in the still autumn chill, dancing addicts waltzed in overcoats, mainly man with man and woman with woman. Competing with the Strauss and the mainstream atheism, songs of praise drifted from wide open church doors. The curious sound attracted cyclists. A mélange of their bicycles were parked around the gates through which heads peeped. Braver people ventured inside to see a full congregation at mass, kneeling before a tapestry of Christ, his head haloed in the same reverend manner as Chairman Mao's in the late Sixties. The bravest ones wanted to partake in the worship of something foreign – they genuflected, crossed themselves and knelt down. The Chinese are quick copiers.

At the end of the service, an elderly man with adequate English invited me for a stroll. We ended up at, of all places, a coffee house. The proprietor was Vietnamese. He had married a Chinese girl and imported the coffee drinking habit from his homeland, which French colonialists before him had introduced in plantation form to Tonkin – as North Vietnam was once known. The atmosphere of echoing chatter and the thick, strong, sweet coffee were clearly good lubricants for conversation in 'Chinglish'. The café had become a venue for east meeting west. Foreigners came for a fix of caffeine which they had been deprived of during travels in the land of tea, and locals for their part came to practise speaking. I was about to realise that my elderly friend, an emeritus professor whose name I shall change to Li, had an ulterior motive.

'Have you any Bibles?' he whispered. My answer disappointed him. I suggested he could surely buy one in the Xinhua chain of bookstores.

'Only if I show my citizen's card,' he explained, 'and we Chinese never want to be fat pigs, the first to be slaughtered when things go badly for the Party.'

'Then I'll go and buy one for you,' I replied.

That would inevitably be met with a '*meiyou*' (have not any) response, he said.

Li was an odd-man-out at the café. The other Chinese were children of the Cultural Revolution, but Li at over seventy remembered the Long March. He had a tale to tell.

'It was late spring of 1935. The Yunnan warlord Long Yun brought his men into Kunming. The Communists on their Long March were about to take the city – they were only fifteen kilometres away,' he recalled.

'Were the people afraid?'

'Of course. The Nationalists told us the Communists were bandits. People collected their valuables and fled, especially the merchants and foreigners.' The panic lasted for a couple of days. 'People went south and west – the foreigners by train to Hanoi and soldiers and sandbags in requisitioned carts went to the eastern suburbs.'

Only later did the people realise that Lin Biao had succeeded with a masterful feint of military deception. The Reds had no interest in Kunming. The way was open to the Jinsha Jiang, the river of Golden Sands.

*　　　*　　　*

Back in my Kunming hotel room I sat looking at my maps. The dog-eared ones were tattered and stained the colour of Jiangxi's earth by repeated inquisitive snatchings by peasant hands.

One reminded me of marching out on the night. Another of the Xiang Jiang, and artilleryman Xu Youwan's recollection of the battle there: 'it rained bullets and shells.' Losing over 30,000 men had done nothing for the military résumés of Otto Braun, Bo Gu and Wang Ming. Passing through Zunyi, I had bought a postcard. On the reverse was written, 'Between 15–17th January 1935 the CCP Central Committee held an enlarged Politburo meeting during the Long March. The meeting put an end to Wang Ming's leadership and established Comrade Mao Zedong as both the leader of the Party and the Red Army.' It was now Mao's Long March.

Up until Kunming my route had been along a wide front which reflected the zigzagging retreat of the Red Army itself, but from now on my targets were more specific. My new maps, sealed in plastic – and hope – to protect them from southern rains and humidity, focused on the military epics of Mao's career. They were vitally important sites to reach. There could either be outright wins or devastating defeats. No draws.

The first of these targets was the riverside hamlet of Jiaopingdu, as important to me on my route of badges as it had been to the Communists who wanted to cross the Jinsha Jiang there and to the Nationalists who wanted to prevent them. In Chiang's words, 'The fate of the nation depends on keeping the Reds bottled up south of the Yangzi.' I was prepared to risk all to reach Jiaopingdu.

A local bus from Kunming to its terminus at Luquan left me an estimated two days' walk from the river. I set off along the northward road to Sayingpan where, according to my map, it too would end. History suggested that there was, and inaccessibility made it likely that there still would be, only one crossing in that reach of the Golden Sands, at Jiaopingdu. The footpath used by the Red Army would, I hoped, take me there.

Market-bound traffic, mechanical and animal, flowed and flocked against me. Seeing such mouthwatering produce was like browsing through a recipe book. Carts, mules and bicycles carried freshly picked, live or killed ingredients that when combined in that ingenious Chinese way in the generous company of soy sauce, chilli, garlic and ginger, create the splendour of Chinese cuisine. Muleteers drove cartloads of dew-glistening greens and earth-smelling root vegetables. Bicycles had panniers of basketed chickens and piglets pressed into cages, their pink flesh soon to be golden brown. Some ingredients – the ducks, for instance – even made their own way with immaculate road but little common sense. I was not certain how the racoons dangling from poles would be served, but doubtless they would comprise a health-inducing dish.

Improvising as community transport, iron water buffaloes throttled along picking up passengers at the raising of a hand or a yell of 'Comrade!' People piled high in the trailer like a haystack passed me with a chorus of '*lao wai*'. Nothing unusual about that, except that they were foreigners in a sense too, pots calling the kettle black. For we shared high-bridged noses, round eyes and bigger frames than the average Chinese who are Hans. Hans comprise some 94% of the PRC's billion plus, and dress in such a dowdy regimented way that they look as dull as starlings in comparison to these gaily dressed peacocks. For this is Luquan Yizu Zizhixian, an autonomous county of the Yizu where the women's traditional dress features bright embroideries and headdresses laden with silver amulets. They are very photogenic, at a price – these people demand 'picture money'. Refusing on principle – there was no Red Army Point of Discipline concerning it – I feigned not to understand their *Putonghua* dialect, nor their sign language.

The Red Army actually encountered the Yizu further north, a fact that emphasises the growth of minority nationalities. They are exempt from the one child birth control policy imposed on the Hans. Being a minority people they have historically been driven to occupy marginal lands where the Hans do not want to live. In recompense, the Chinese Government allows them to rear an extra pair of hands.

They have always hated the Chinese – Communist or Nationalist – and demanded 'pass money' for permission to cross Yizu territory. In turn the Yizu are given the derogatory nickname of '*Lolos*' – an insult equal to the usage of 'wog' in Britain. As insularity breeds ignorance, the Chinese are generally racist anyway. Although the flags of Third World leaders fly in Tiananmen Square every week to celebrate state visits, and although national news broadcasts pictures of Li Peng, Jiang Zemin and Yang Shangkun shaking hands with coloured leaders, the average Mr Chen is taken aback at the sight of a black man. Hotel staff will deny having any rooms to spare, and restaurants any food to eat. Taxi drivers will refuse a fare. It is Chinese apartheid.

As always, as the shadows lengthened two necessities came to mind. Evening was the cue for dabbing on that essential perfume of the tropics, insect repellent, and looking for shelter. The former, because of Yunnan Province's high altitude – Yunnan means 'south of the clouds' – was thankfully unnecessary, but consequently it made the latter more so. The temperature was plummeting.

I asked a woman drawing water from a well to fill up my canteen. It was my foot in the door tactic. Before she could feel suspicious of me, I followed the third Point of Discipline by helping her, our legs astride of the dark chasm, to heave up the heavy pails. Beside the well a granite pillar was gouged with black painted characters which read '*Chi shui bu wang Mao Zhu Xi*' (Remember this water was given to us by Chairman Mao). It was not that Mao had dug the well in passing but that all things bright and beautiful had come from him during the Cultural Revolution: the crops were given by him; it was he who sent the soft rain in the summer and the sun to swell the grain.

I knew that she would not fill my canteen with cold water. All Chinese are made aware that their endemic diseases are water-borne. Shouldering her bamboo pole she stooped to engage hook with bucket-handle, then tilted see-saw fashion to counterbalance it and lift the other pail.

We walked along a narrow muddy path between fields which I could see, from the angular sods and hoofprints, had recently felt the slice of the plough and plod of the water buffalo, nature's own rotavator and muck-spreader. We came upon a concrete circle before the farm, but here there was none of the usual autumnal separation of grain from chaff going on, for the stillness of evening had withheld the natural power source. All was quiet except for the clumsy rustling of an off-duty ass tethered to a pole chewing away at the mounds of dried maize plants rimming the outdoor mill.

We entered the farm through a door in a rough wall made of mud and straw. The courtyard was bounded on three sides by buildings. Its Thermos flasks, in the style of twenty-pounder shells, decorated with double happiness characters – symbolising marital unity and hence suggesting that they were wedding gifts – were empty. Although that was in one way bad news, for I was very thirsty, the good news was that water needed to be boiled thus giving me time to get my feet under the table.

'Ma, Ma!' shouted the woman, whereupon an old lady of over eighty shuffled out of the cook house. She wore a dark tunic and had a good head of now grey hair neatly stuffed into a woollen snode the colour her own hair had once been. Soon her wrinkled and weathered round face beamed a broad smile like an inflated football. Sure enough, a fire had to be kindled from tinder, maize cob leaves and orange peel which smoked the whole kitchen out. Retreating to the courtyard I eavesdropped on daughter telling mother that the Englishman was walking the Red Army's Long March route to the Golden Sands.

Their living-cum-bedrooms were large and illuminated by natural light through wooden latticed windows. Like archives, the walls and ceilings were completely covered with a mixture of provincial news and telexed press releases from the Xinhua News Agency – a combination of largely good tidings sold under the title of *Yunnan Ribao* (the Yunnan Daily). The grey newsprint was interspersed with colour calendar portraits, again of yesteryear. The parade of models chronicled the tardy import of dated Western fashions to the middle kingdom: knee-length boots, legwarmers, hot pants, and high-heeled bathing beauties. World fashion on Chinese girls acquired new, often suggestive, names. Bikinis became 'three point style swimsuits', and mini skirts 'attract men skirts'.

Mao himself was a strange bedfellow for the models, an enigmatic juxtaposition that encapsulated in one room what is occurring in China as a whole: bourgeois liberalism permitted within a hard-line Communist infrastructure. Was this reality a means to an end, a concession? As we watched television in that peasant home, it struck me that the leaders had rewritten one of Mao's most famous adages. Having given the populace some 150 million TV sets, they have in as many words told the Ministry of Film and Television that the Chinese people are no longer blank sheets of paper, but they do have their eyes glued to television screens on which any message can be broadcast.

*   *   *

Next morning I set off guilty of breaking the golden rule of dealing with the peasants, that of paying for what I had eaten. My hosts had given me pints of hot water to quench my thirst, rice and eggs to nourish me, a basin of water to wash the dust off my face and their cleanest quilt. However, offering ten *yuan* on departure had, in a friendly way, infuriated them.

Courtesy of their hospitality I was now striding out at top marching pace into the remaining fifty-five kilometres to the Golden Sands. The wide valley of vast ploughed tracts was gradually left behind as the road began to climb, became pot-holed and narrower. Soon road and river, once distant vagrants of the valley, were close neighbours. Convenience of fresh clean water invited frequent rinses and a foot bath for refreshment. Then a series of bends led into a small village on a col, its centrepiece being a concrete monolith crested with a red star and the characters of Sayingpan.

The road went no further, but I did not have to look for village folk to point out the footpath to Jiaopingdu. Vague directions which included 'straight on', 'it's five hours away' or 'you'll be there tonight' came in a chorus. Then a small man stood out from the crowd gathered around me.

'*Wo zou lu dao Jiaopingdu.*' (I'm walking to Jiaopingdu.)

I responded, '*Women yiqi qu hao ma?*' (We'll go together, shall we?)

Once we were past the col, a huge vista opened out before us, dominated by a yawning valley that disappeared beyond the horizon, so deep and steep-sided that my mind doubted whether any path could possibly negotiate its treacherous slopes. Yet on the distant mountainsides terraces stood out like patchwork and paths fell away threadlike to hamlets perched below.

Before I knew my companion's name or could contemplate the arduous descent, he was off, leading the way, zigzagging to tackle the plunge, shuffling along with short and quick steps, controlling his slides, yomping under the force of gravity. In the wake of the dust he kicked up I lagged behind, always trying to slow down, stop sliding and stay on my feet. Occasional respite for braking thigh muscles kept in tension came when we followed contours rather than crossed them. Then the reason for the patchwork appearance of cultivation became clear: some terraces were harvested, others not; some were planted while others were bare. Inevitably they were cut where geology provided a tap, nature's inn on the trail where peasants rested, released their load and straightened their backs bent twenty degrees forward for the climb.

I offered my companion a cigarette. His name was Zhang Changyuan and he was walking to Huili, his home town in Sichuan Province across the river. To reach there by bus was circuitous and expensive; he preferred the three-day walk. 'If we want to rest in Jiaopingdu we should go on,' he suggested.

Zhang was typical of the locals persuaded into guiding the Red Army scouts – living proof, then and now, of the ability to walk through China's vast hinterland with cartographic ignorance, for even the leaders had only the vaguest appreciation of the territory ahead. Maps, if available, were sketchy with great voids in the 'here be monsters' vein, warning of some danger the traveller might encounter, if not in reality then in his mind.

The Red Army and I relied on the likes of Zhang. He was better than a signpost and more reliable than a map. To solicit his help required a good cause, a credible reason. The Reds told of how they would oust landlords and distribute land to the people. My request was to find the footpath to Jiaopingdu and seek out one man's recollection of the riverside events in 1935. Optimistically I sought one of the ferrymen who had helped the Red Army cross the river, if any were still alive – a proverbial needle in a haystack. To my delight, Zhang said he knew one of them.

We yomped along just as the Army had, going with the slope because that is easier than going against it, for the Reds now had teeth – in their feet. Once Mao had become absolute leader in Zunyi, the Communists' greatest weapon was their mobility. Since 55,000 of the men who had left Jiangxi lay in a trail of death across Hunan, Guangxi and Guizhou, Mao made survival his priority. To that end, the Reds were now an army living off the land by their wits, rather than a city of refugees on the march. Chattels had been abandoned, sold off or bartered for primary needs. Mao had confidence in the peasants' hospitality. From teenage wanderings he knew China was filled with brothers and sisters, uncles and aunts – icebreaking terms of endearment used to make friends of strangers who would assist in their cause.

Fifty-six years on Zhang was not unlike a Red soldier. A Sichuanese, he was short and his few possessions were bundled in a small brown bag with makeshift rope shoulder straps. He carried no food, drank from the springs and walked in the straw sandals of the day

– thin-soled black plimsolls, slip-ons nicknamed lazy shoes, and like the black bicycle, Thermos flask and enamel basin a Chinese standard, unchanged for decades and found in every home in the land. Despite their flimsiness, Zhang sped downhill on a rough path not a stride in width and the same distance from death. Through dust, streams and mud, and over rockfalls, he had trodden in the path of history every year since he was a lad.

The patchwork wheat plots were now high above us, and with the moderation of the slope's severity orchards of apples and pomegranates in the mid-levels gave way to terraces of south China's staple. As it was now November the rice was already harvested exposing bare sheets of mud to be pecked over by ducks. A stream which watered them broke the silence of a still afternoon but its babble was soon drowned by a roar as its crystal waters were swallowed up by a muddy torrent, coloured brown by a long journey through Qinghai and Sichuan. The Golden Sands River, the name given to the upper reaches of the mighty Yangzi, scoured a V-shaped valley with fearful force, the sound of its turbulent waters amplified by the steep megaphonic slopes.

Precipitous though they appeared, the slopes proved negotiable, and eventually we arrived at Jiaopingdu, a riverside village which may undergo a name change in a year or two to reflect the ferry crossing, 'du', being superseded by a bridge, 'qiao'. A workforce of perhaps two hundred had provided the biggest influx of strangers since 1935. Some of them kindly invited us to share their woven straw shanty accommodation, but appreciating the security mania surrounding key construction projects I politely refused and reminded Zhang that I sought a ferryman.

We were soon hiking again, asking muscles stiffened during our brief talk with the workmen to carry us further, downstream on a path just tens of metres above the river. Its torrent raged by, drowning our footsteps on the gravel dredged from its own bed, swamping our raised voices – even shouts were whispers – chilling us with the cold eddies in its wake. A log ploughed past, a rider on the waves, its ends kicking like the fore and hind legs of a bucking bronco, as deadly as a waterborne missile if it were to hit a wooden boat. Several such boats could be seen, but they were on shore, upturned, masquerading as giant turtles above the wash line of the not too

Golden Sands – that alluring name, the epitaph of many a dreamer who sought fortune from the placers said to yield nuggets and grains of gold.

We came upon a group of perhaps five farms clinging to the slope, so close together that their boundary walls made something of a tortuous alleyway, a thoroughfare a barrow in width which the size of the hamlet never intended nor warranted. Some geese with seemingly extendable necks hissed an unwelcome which Zhang countered with '*oushi*', the Mandarin equivalent of the interjection 'shoo' – perfectly comprehended by the gaggle who beat a flapping retreat. I realised now why dogs had troubled me. I'd been speaking to them in my mother tongue, not theirs.

'*You meiyou ren?*' (Are there any people?) questioned Zhang as he cautiously edged open a creaking door. Following him I stooped beneath its low lintel to see an oblong courtyard full of seated people, bowls to mouth and chopsticks swooping on a spread of dishes.

'*Wo dai lai yi ge waiguo pengyou,*' (I've brought a foreign friend,) announced Zhang to the silent family, mouths filled and chewing. Once they'd swallowed their food and Zhang's words too, an old man and possibly his son got up and dueted '*Nimen xin ku le, zuo, zuo, he shui, chi fan*' (You're tired, sit, drink and eat) against a chorus of '*Huanying nimen.*' (Welcome you.)

'*Zhe shi ta – ta jiao Zhang Chaoman,*' (That's him – his name is Zhang Chaoman,) advised my guide. The old man singled out beamed a warm smile and asked one of the women to ladle more rice into my bowl. I drank some tea to wash down the gritty rice; it tasted like champagne at a banquet.

*   *   *

As dusk fell on our contentment the women cleared the table and amused the children, leaving the menfolk to smoke in the evening's chill. As Zhang Chaoman's dialect was muddy I asked him to write down his story. Due to a lifetime of no schooling he was illiterate, so a young man of seventeen, Pei Yingfa, was sent for; his characters were said to be the best in the hamlet. With candles lighting our faces and blankets wrapping our torsos, Zhang Chaoman began to relate his experience.

China's premier revolutionary shrine, Mao's birthplace at Shaoshan (above), is now on the itinerary of the middle school children of the consumer revolution. Below, a local Shaoshan couple hold a treasured photo of their meeting with Mao during his return visit in 1959.

The hall of Hunan Provincial Normal School in Changsha still houses an oil painting of its most famous old-boy.

Xu Youwan of Ruijin at 83, one of the few surviving veterans of the Red Army who set out on the Long March 57 years ago.

Primary pupils visiting the Soviet Republic of China government headquarters in Ruijin.

Zhang Chaoman, the ferryman at the Golden Sands River.

Above left, grass sandals made for wearing on the longest mass journey in human history. The pontoon bridge over the Yudu He was assembled at dusk and dismantled before dawn, allowing some 80,000 Reds to evacuate their base area without Kuomintang detection. A similar bridge exists today in nearby Ganzhou, above right. Below, the first sight of the Golden Sands River on the Yunnan-Sichuan border.

A similar structure to Luding Bridge, near Maogong, gives a chilling impression of what the Dadu heroes clambered along to seize Luding.

Ding Li and a shepherd on the summit ridge of Jiajin mountain.

A Tibetan chieftain's *yamen* at Zhuokeji (above), occupied by Mao's men after their crossing of Western Sichuan's Great Snowy Mountains. Below, the ornate woodwork survives in the courtyard of the *yamen* where Mao and Zhou Enlai tethered their horses.

When the Red Army crossed the Grasslands they survived on plants and yak-pelt soup. The Tibetans ate any stragglers.

Inside Mao's *yaodong* in Yan'an, the cave-dwelling he occupied at the end of the Long March.

Top, after the turmoil of 1989 all first year students now face a period of military training. Centre, Mao loved by the people of the world, as depicted in a Cultural Revolution poster. Below, from left to right, Wu Xiaoping, Wu Wanchun and Wu Qi in Tiananmen Square to remember 1966, 1949 and 1988 respectively.

Dr Ma Yanlong (above left), the cosmetic mortician, who served Mao and Zhou in death. Above right, Wang Anting has transformed his tiny Chengdu home into a Maoist temple with memorabilia from the deification decade of the Cultural Revolution. Below, Mao's mausoleum in Tiananmen Square is visited by 13,000 people a day.

'The Red Army's Long March reached Jiaopingdu on the 24th or 26th of April, Min Guo year 24.' (The twenty-fourth year of the Republic which originated in 1911, therefore 1935 of the Gregorian calendar.) 'That night about twenty-four scouts of the front group entered Xiaolongcun (Small Dragon) hamlet. They called at Zhang Chaoshou's – my eldest brother's – caravanserai.' (Jiaopingdu was the river crossing on a Yunnan–Sichuan trade route used by muleteers carrying opium, medicinal flora and brick tea north, and yak hides and Tibetan medicinal fauna south. Zhang Chaoshou catered for these merchants.)

'Zhang Chaoshou saw them with fear knowing they weren't traders. The Reds told him not to be alarmed; they were proletarian fighters – the poor people's army and not the Kuomintang. Their aim was to kill the tigers and rescue the poor.' (Tigers were landlords and bad officials.) '"Help us fellow countrymen; find boats for us to cross the river,"' they asked Zhang Chaoshou and his guests.

'Zhang Chaoshou told them he didn't have any boats but he would take them to his brothers for help – that's me Zhang Chaoman and three more brothers Chaolu, Chaofu and Chaojun in Shangpingzi hamlet.' I offered Zhang Chaoman and the small audience cigarettes, then he resumed.

'We told the Reds that all the boats were controlled by the landlord, and they were all moored and hidden on the north bank – everything that floated was there, out of reach. We all searched the banks for several hours and found one semi-scuttled boat, and patched it up by plugging its holes with material from a merchant at the caravanserai. So we were able to sneak across the river and tow other boats, four in all, back to the south bank. Lao Tu Wang (the landlord), called Zhang Lihan, saw us and ran off to save his skin.'

The women now brought out basins of water for washing: first the hands and face then, pouring the water into a different basin, the feet. Zhang Chaoman bathed first but continued with the story.

'General Liu Bocheng – he lost an eye in battle – arrived with more soldiers and he made a speech. My brothers and I ferried two boats full of Reds across the Golden Sands and moored the boats. First we went to the Li Jinju (tax house), and a villager knocked at the door, tricking Master Liu – the tax collector – into thinking they were paying tax for bringing merchandise to the north side of the river.' The Reds could not do this, because their dialect was quite different and sure to arouse suspicion. 'When Master Liu unlocked the door we charged in, a Red pressed a pistol into the back of his neck and ordered him to tell us where his weapons were hidden. Of course he obliged! The Reds confiscated two good rifles with bullets, and tied Master Liu to a chair.'

It was now my turn to bathe. I sat with feet immersed listening to Zhang's continuing thriller. 'Next we led the Reds to the Zhao family's stables where a group of twenty soldiers of the Kuomintang were barracked. We could hear the slam of tiles on the table so knew they were playing mahjong, half stripped off in the humidity of night. One of the locals knocked at their door and said, "We're from the Huili battalion number 60; we set off late," and they opened the door. The Reds rushed in and the Whites jumped through the windows to escape but were machine-gunned down in their underwear. As a bonus to securing the crossing the Reds confiscated more arms and ammunition.

'Returning triumphant to the south bank, General Liu congratulated us for our hard work. We had been working all night, but couldn't rest for more than a week whilst we ferried thousands of Reds across who waited camped on the valley sides. During the crossing General Liu stood on a huge riverside boulder to direct the operation in which not a single man perished. Once they were across, all the boats were cut free to cascade downstream and smash up on the rocky shores.'

The Red Army owed their bloodless victory at Jiaopingdu to Zhang Chaoman and his brothers, but now with the Communists beating a trail north, the Zhang brothers were left to face the consequences from the pursuing Kuomintang, who had been severely delayed in crossing the Golden Sands by the destruction of boats. Threatened with daggers some people were forced into telling the names of collaborators. Zhang recalled the punishment.

'They took all the Zhang brothers into custody to the home of Bao Zhang (a local leader) where they kept us for five days. I was strung up for twelve hours before they cut me down to be taken to Luquan for execution. Luckily though Bao Zhang believed the many villagers who told him we were forced under threat of our lives to help the Reds. So instead we were fined 280 taels and ordered to serve the KMT leaders banquets of mutton and wine for a week – they confiscated all my furniture as well.'

To my surprise Zhang Chaoman had never mentioned Mao Zedong. I asked him why.

'We didn't know that the Communists were coming here – and when they arrived we thought General Liu Bocheng was their leader. Once they marched off into Sichuan we heard nothing about their fate – only after Liberation fifteen years later did we know about Mao Zedong, and only then did we realise we'd played a role in the so-called Long March! Chairman Mao may have been in my boat but I never knew it!'

The seventy-eight-year-old revolutionary would sleep well on that thought, for I had kept him talking until a late hour. We bade each other a good night with much handshaking, and his son led me upstairs by oil lamp. Our footsteps were met with snorts from the swine styed below which also served as a convenience into which we relieved ourselves. Zhang Changyuan the Sichuanese and another old man were already asleep when I tiptoed into my room. From the flame of the oil lamp I could see its thick stone walls into which tiny windows were so deeply inset that the sills were as deep as cupboards. It was an effective design, for as I strained to look out towards the Golden Sands shimmering under starlight just a good stone's throw away, the roar of its waters was softened to a gentle lullaby.

*   *   *

The grunting of pigs made me think that the poor swine were having another shower, but the footsteps came closer and the aureole of light guiding them entered the room. My eyes, slightly open, saw flames dance on the ceiling like a white cloud upon a dark sky, and as I smelt the burning oil lamp held close to my face my eyes squinted in discomfort. '*Wei lian xian sheng, qi chuang, qi chuang!*' (Mr William, get up, get up!) urged Zhang's son shaking me by the shoulder. I had not asked for an early morning call, nor do the Chinese go in for breakfast in bed. I looked at my watch before pulling on my trousers. It was coming up to one o'clock. My heartbeat raced. Only the *Gong An Ju* would disturb an honest traveller in his sleep like this. The thought of punishment combined with the cold forced me to douse the swine again on the way down to the courtyard.

'*Wo shi Luquan Xian Gong An Ju*,' said the policeman, his finger pointing to, then tapping his Tiananmen national symbol cresting his cap. I offered my hand. He took it, but the speed with which he dropped it suggested he was not too pleased. As the interrogation commenced, I ruled out any fiction – the Zhangs too would surely be questioned, if they had not already been. Who, what, why, where and when came first. I said I was a student of Mao Zedong and the Chinese Revolution and had come to Jiaopingdu to hear Zhang Chaoman's story.

'*Ni shi shenme minzu?*' (What minority are you?) asked the officer.

'*Wo shi Yingguo ren.*' (I'm British.)

'*Shi, shi, danshi shenme minzu?*' (Yes, yes, but what minority?) he continued.

This was absurd, reminding me of the cynical Chinese proverb: 'You don't use good iron to make nails, nor do you put a good son in the police.' How could a foreigner have a Chinese minority nationality? Perhaps this policeman's world was so small that he could not appreciate that anyone could not have a minority like Han, Yi, Moslem, Manchurian, Tibetan and so on. Maybe my ability to speak Chinese in some way compounded his confusion. Whatever the explanation for his ignorance he was becoming so angry raising his voice that the pigs were snorting.

I could not make him understand, so I decided to join him – he looked like a Han. '*Wo shi Hanzu gen ni yiyang.*' (I'm the same as you, a Hanzu.) He wrote it down, nodding proudly, self-satisfied with his technique in extracting vital information that the criminal sought to withhold.

Questions on identity and the notes written by Pei Yingfa necessitated a return to my room, fortunately alone. By sense of touch I rewound my camera film in darkness, and concealed it under my quilt. Quickly taking my passport and *Little Red Book* I hurried down to the courtyard lest the policeman be suspicious of the time I had taken. My reading matter may have impressed him, but it failed to fool him and I was soon returning to the room to retrieve the character script of the ferryman's story. Ominously my passport and notes disappeared into the pocket of the policeman's baggy green jacket. I was immobilised; any thoughts of escape vanished.

I was now questioned on the role of Zhang, my Sichuanese guide. What did I pay him, give him? Five minutes later Zhang himself was summoned from slumber for the back-to-back interrogation, looking understandably concerned at being regarded as a possible accessory to my crime of entering an area closed to foreigners. It was gone 2 a.m., everyone was tired and Zhang the ferryman looked very confused. My case was adjourned until eight in the morning.

*   *   *

Although my own fate was uncertain as the Beijing jeep carried me away, to my relief Zhang the Sichuanese had been freed to continue walking home. I set about exhibiting a good attitude, plying the *Gong An Ju* officer and his driver with smokes on the two hour circuitous journey to Jiaoxi.

As the jeep swept into the *Gong An Ju* courtyard the driver cut the engine and freewheeled to a halt, a fuel saving trick he had applied en route regardless of its dangers. A bunch of villagers engulfed us and I caught sight of their previous entertainment: a dishevelled criminal handcuffed and slumped at the foot of a concrete pillar on a bed of soiled newspapers and rags. My hopes of leniency slumped too.

The commotion alerted the *Gong An Ju* office, and a group of officers bisected the encircling mob with the authority of their uniforms. Among them was a plain-clothed young man, who looked like a middle-school English teacher.

'What's the problem?' he said.

A brief explanation punctuated with puzzled and worried looks soon had him retrieving my passport and notes from my arresting officer.

'I'm Zhao Jinghui,' he said, 'a Yizu nationality representative of the National People's Congress in Beijing's Great Hall of the People. It's very worthwhile to study Mao Zedong by walking the Long March. Here are your documents. Now let's go eat lunch – a banquet is prepared.'

9

Chains of Glory

Storming Luding Bridge, from a contemporary etching.

Once across the Golden Sands, Mao Zedong was faced with the problem of where to go. Sichuan, the largest and most populous province in China lay before his Central Red Army: a basin with Chengdu as its plughole and the Yangzi its main drain, a river whose vast dendritic system of tributaries makes the map of Sichuan appear blue-veined, and four of whose branches – the *Si chuan* of the Yalong, Jinsha, Jialing and Min Jiang – aptly give their name to the province.

If Mao's overall strategy is to be understood, it is now necessary to burden the mind with extra historical detail. As I travelled along the Great Wall, and later talked about it, the most devilish question to answer was the most obvious and common one – How long is the Great Wall? – because the Great Wall is not a single fortification but a network of them. Questions on the Long March regarding route and length are similarly complicated, because the term Long

March is used by Chinese historians to describe several shifts on foot from different base areas by different armies.

The Red Army cells around China, nine in all, can be thought of as sheep separated by the killer dog of the KMT but belonging to the same flock, Communism. Mao Zedong was their shepherd, heading the Central Red Army or the First Front Army. Four other armies were also on the move, on their own Long Marches. Their ultimate goal was unity in the same base area – wherever that should be. In particular, Mao was hopeful of joining up with the Fourth Front Army under the leadership of Zhang Guotao, thought to be in Northern Sichuan.

Yet seven months out from Jiangxi seventy per cent of Mao's army was dead – at that rate Mao's men would not see another autumn – they were heading for an eternal winter. To survive, the Red Army had only one chance – to wriggle through the mountains on the basin's northwestern flank. Going any other way but predominantly north was against the grain of the mountains, but which northern line, which valley? Too close to the basin, in the foothills, would afford the Kuomintang's big war machine easy access. Too far west and the passage of men is confined to narrow valleys, barred by impassable swollen rivers in summer and blocked with snow in winter – in addition to the hostility shown to Hans by indigenous minorities eking out a living on those fringes of Middle China. Mao had to penetrate an alien landscape of snow and ice and breathe a rarefied atmosphere, and his southern soldiers would feel as if they had left China – only Sichuan's fiery food laced with volcanic chillies, whole garlics and tangy root ginger would suggest that they were still in their motherland.

Chiang Kai-shek for his part had failed hopelessly to bottle up the Reds south of the Yangzi – the only thing he was correct about was that the fate of the nation would indeed depend upon it. Mao had called him an imperialist's running dog; but the analogy of a cat and mouse game is more appropriate. Chiang was looking like a toothless domestic cat, for when he held the mouse in his paws, even jaws, he still let it squirm free. The Nationalists were about to be taught another lesson, a lesson that would be taught to the Americans in Vietnam thirty years later: the outcome of a guerrilla war does not depend on might and weapons but on the determination of men's minds, their cause and stratagems, and the strength of their legs – the arts of war of which Mao was becoming a master.

After the success of Jiaopingdu the Reds took Huili where they celebrated briefly and Mao formulated his strategy: to head for Xichang. In the Nationalists' camp Chiang must have fancied his chances. He moved to Ya'an, a town on the trail between Chengdu and Tibet – uncomfortably close to the Reds' intended route bearing in mind their recent deceptions and fleet-footedness. His confidence was based upon the sledgehammer–nut principle, and boosted by omens, the season and geography. As the most likely venue for engagement favoured the Dadu River he could recall that sixty-three years before Prince Shi Dakai and his Taiping rebels, the dissidents of the day with Sinofied Christianity, had been pinned down and annihilated by the Qing army on the banks of the very same river. Even if history failed to repeat itself, Chiang could surely trap the Communists between the Yizu – who hated the Han Chinese – and the Dadu, whose waters in May are at full height with melt-water, thus cutting Mao off from his objective – reunion with the Fourth Front Army in Northern Sichuan. Mao would then be doomed to perish in the winter of Western Sichuan.

*   *   *

As I slurped the piping hot *xifan* in Xichang it was Huili I envisaged, the hometown of Zhang the Sichuanese. He had spoken excitedly, and prematurely, of being my guide there, in showing me the walls that the Reds had scaled despite being scalded. For the Nationalists had poured vats of rice porridge over them. Where else in China could food be wasted so, used as a weapon, apart from Sichuan, China's incomparable larder?

Outside peasants crouched like mushrooms beneath their giant brown capes selling succulent and tasty fruits and vegetables, while in the live market fowl and fish of all descriptions awaited torture and slaughter, to be carried home tethered by string to handlebars, for freshly killed produce is the Third World's answer to lack of refrigeration and the sell-by date. At Xichang in particular the importance of the chicken should not be overlooked. A granite memorial reminds one of the role this bird played in Yizu–Red Army relations. Liu Bocheng, the one-eyed Red Army General, is sculptured clashing bowls with the Yizu chief Xiao Yedan, drinking water into which a freshly killed chicken's blood was added. A bond of friendship was thus sealed, and Chiang's expected allies had become Red Army brothers – and local guides.

I encountered my own guide, the Dadu River, at Shimian on a late midwinter's afternoon. Darkness made our meeting all too visually brief but throughout the long night the river never rested despite the well below zero temperatures, murmuring incessantly to all in this riverside town. My ears heard a different sound, voices from the past. Next morning I hardly needed any arousal: the Dadu's rushing waters had shouted all night like the yells of the Reds beckoning me to march with Mao along its banks. Whence those waters came I would now rush, northward to emulate not only the route of the Reds but their work rate too – 120 kilometres in under two days.

Allowing a few hours for social intercourse, that necessary prelude to obtaining primary needs en route, I anticipated that walking from sunrise to sunset would not be enough to cover the distance. I must start before dawn. I donned all the clothing I possessed, and with my canteen improvising as a hot-water-bottle I set off into the freezing night. The normally troublesome bottle of boiled water was too soon chilled and, feeling confident of the purity of rivulets seeping from the rock walls beside the riverside track, I emptied it to save weight.

The cocks' alarmed 'cock-a-doodle-do' for so long in the total darkness that I began to doubt their reliability as indicators of imminent dawn. Carrion crows were more on the mark, holding back their scavenging cries until the first signs of light began to silhouette billowing clouds to the east. Day was breaking over the Da Xue Shan (the Great Snowy Mountains). From the frozen shadows of the Dadu He valley I saw the shafts of newly born sunlight streaking across the sky of my world, like super spotlights beaming down on to a stage, the opposite horizon, to pick out only the stars, the highest peaks, such as Gongga Shan (7,556 m) and its surrounding massif. The rising sun cast its light on this glacial world like a creator's hand moving slowly through the pastels of a paintbox: from watery pink to mauve, from crimson to lilac and from orange to yellow – all lolly-ice hues that graduated from one into another as the artist, nature, mixed her colours on the palette, the mountains themselves, before one's very eyes.

By the time I reached Anshunchang, the sun had climbed high enough to transform the dawn waters of the Dadu, a raucous dark devil cloaked in mist, into a seductive body of glistening jade waves, churning hypnotically along, crested with pearly white dragons. The water level was low; giants' chopsticks, trunks of timber, were left high and dry on shoals amidstream. Scoured white boulders and washed vegetation allowed one to picture the Dadu's springtime width when the basin it drains – the giant marshy sponge of the permafrosted Aba grasslands – releases its seasonally locked moisture.

This was the focus of Mao's plan – the site of the Anshunchang ferry. The Reds' newly won blood brothers, the Yizu, guided the crack 'Triple Ones' (the First Corps of the First Regiment of the First Army) over the mountain trails, hidden under spring greenery to look down like eagles on the puppet troops of the KMT – warlord forces of Liu Wenhui defending the ferry crossing on the far side.

Xu Youwan arrived the next day, May 25th 1935. Volunteers, he said, were requested to cross the river in captured boats, but so many stepped forward that seventeen had to be chosen – being a crack shot was the prime qualification. Boatmen warned against their madness for the Dadu was seven metres above its normal springtime swell. They advised waiting on weather but were persuaded or cajoled into co-operating. It had happened at Jiaopingdu, then at Xichang with the Yizu and now again at Anshunchang – the Red Army's bargaining offer was a promise of 'liberation from serfdom and land ownership'. But when? It was a hell of an IOU to leave.

It is difficult to imagine how the Reds could have dreamt of ever being in a position to deliver on this, bearing in mind they were not only on the verge of China, but extinction too. Similarly it is surprising that peasants actually swallowed such promises even if the Reds' intentions were good. Some may have been persuaded by the glimmer of future hope, an alternative to life under their heinous landlords – but doubtless others collaborated in fear. However, the Reds managed it, though, their vision of that future, let alone any future, was a testament to the irrepressibility of their optimism that the Chinese people's darkness was only temporary.

According to Xu Youwan, the Dadu was 300 metres wide, bank to bank. Fortunately, the accurate range of his machine-gun fire was 400 metres. So it poured both rain and bullets as the boat of seventeen landed on the right bank. Facing heavy machine-gun fire from the opposite bank, the warlord troops fled at the threat of being surrounded by crack shots. Mao soon secured the Anshunchang crossing.

One month after the Zhang brothers had ferried the Reds across the Golden Sands, another mass ferry job now faced the Communists – but the Dadu was treble the width and its broiling waters and whirlpools made the Golden Sands seem a duckpond in comparison. The operation commenced with only three boats, continuing at night under bonfire and torchlight. The torrential rain must have made it like a wet November 5th. Xu Youwan recalled the river banks being like mud slides and many slipped into the raging torrent to be swept away and drowned. Bamboos and ropes were used to abseil down the treacherous slopes on which no footwear gripped. In wet conditions grass sandals lasted only a few hours but some Reds optimistically bound twigs to their soles, crampon-style, in the hope of some traction. For forty-eight hours the ferrying continued, and then the weather worsened. Only 3,000 Reds had crossed – at that rate it would be a fortnight before the entire force was across.

On the third day it was taking three hours or more for a round trip. Mao knew it was a delay he could not afford. He remembered the fate of the Taiping Prince who ordered a three-day rest at the Dadu to celebrate the birth of his son – he ended up being sliced to death. Xu Youwan reckoned the ordinary Reds knew nothing of this tale. 'We couldn't read or write, and the only history we knew was what we made,' he said.

Frustrated, Mao called a meeting with Zhu De, Zhou Enlai, Peng Dehuai and Lin Biao. Zhu De was a Sichuanese who, in his early guerrilla days, had fled across the Dadu by the fixed bridge of Lu. That was a crossing on the Chengdu to Tibet trail just west of Ya'an where Chiang was stationed. It was over 100 kilometres upstream and there were only intermittent paths – distance and difficulties not to deter Mao. He decided to head for Luding bridge – on both sides of the Dadu.

I crossed the Dadu on a well-maintained cable suspension footbridge, the likes of which have made the Anshunchang ferry part of the romantic past, to enrol in spirit with the 'Right group' of 3,000 Reds moving up the east bank. Over half a century behind in their footsteps I had the luxury of striding out on a track blown by explosives and hewn by pickaxe into the steep valley side. The Reds had to hack their way through azaleas, rhododendrons and cypresses – native exotics of Western Sichuan that scented the air heavily on a winter's morn when the sun burnt brightly through, melting the forest's encrusting rime and turning the valley into a trough of heady Culpeppery vapour.

Frost was an overture to *Da Xue* (the Big Snow) of the lunar calendar which prompted peasants to prepare for deepest winter's onslaught by collecting withered leaves for tinder and branches for firewood. Everybody was already walking the winter shuffle – a unique and contemporary Chinese locomotion induced not by foot-binding but limb-binding. Legs will not bend coddled in several pairs of knitted long johns, and children's arms do not swing. It is as if everyone has become wooden-limbed.

Whilst the middle generation laboured, the newest and oldest – they are made for each other and struggle on for each other in China – basked in the last sunny days of the year, storytelling. The grandparents remembered that when they themselves were children many strangers came in the *Hong Jun* (Red Army). Today's children might well recall a lone stranger coming to eat their rice. But it was hardly a sight to match that of the Reds who marched past for more than a day, continuing through the night, their trails revealed by torchlight climbing high on the valley sides across the Dadu and then plunging down to the river's bank to light up its dark waters.

History from witnesses was inspiring, a reminder too that I should politely refuse their further hospitality despite its warmth. Following the Dadu itself was similarly invigorating under the clear blue sky in the face of a fresh breeze, the river itself changing in character around each bend. Sometimes it was wide and white with valley slopes three or four hundred metres apart, and at other times its deep jade waters were funnelled by vertical cliffs to the width of a well thrown stone.

The western horizon of Great Snowies bit into the setting after-noon sun like a knife through butter. For the next two hours I

marched on at full pace under the valley's pre-empted twilight, breaking into a yomp on the flatter sections to ward off the chill. I had
no intention of sleeping out in such conditions. All day I had
observed the settlement pattern of the valley. Farms were generally
dispersed because each family needed a kilometre or so of the poor
stony valley soils to themselves to grow enough food.

Sure enough, peaceful and secure accommodation was not difficult
to find, and the problem of the local dialect, *Sichuan hua*, was solved
by the unexpected availability of an interpreter amongst my hosts:
not a middle-school teacher but a pupil, speaking not English but
Mandarin, the standard tongue which she interpreted into her provincial mother tongue for her parents. Happily, being just twelve
years old, she used a basic vocabulary.

Huddling around the orange embers in the cookhouse on
which a wok of noodles boiled we warmed ourselves, our faces
reflecting the glow of its radiating comfort. With a burnt front
and frozen back I felt like Baked Alaska and, much to the
amusement of my hosts, began to turn around to get evenly done.
The defrosting process was completed by the noodles themselves
which, spiced up to Sichuanese standards, warmed us from the
inside out.

Talk of distance provided the theme of our after dinner conversation and well within my comprehension provided we were talking
in the same units. Like the British and Americans resisting conver-
sion to the otherwise universal kilometre, the Chinese peasantry are
the last bastion of the *li*, a bizarre and uniquely Chinese distance
which is flexible. A flat *li* is half a kilometre; but an uphill one, being
more difficult, is shorter, and a downhill one, being much easier, is
longer! For a unit to be variable seems quite contradictory until one
realises that the *li* is an indication of not only distance but the
effort needed to cover it, a logical and ingenious measure conceived
specifically for travellers on foot. Through ignorance I had initially
ridiculed this unit but with experience I began to trust it in the
knowledge that a *li* was about five minutes' walking irrespective of
terrain.

'*Dao Luding keneng yi bai er shi duo li,*' (Luding is perhaps more
than 120 *li*,) they concluded. Thereafter my marching plans for the
morrow were made. Before bedding down for the night in the loft

I told my hosts I planned to leave before dawn, thanking them for their hospitality.

*   *   *

When the full moon shone it allowed me to march uninhibited by the proximity and intensity of the roaring Dadu; yet, as if powered by failing batteries, the heavenly torch occasionally flickered to darkness, and I to a crawl, as clouds swept like curtains across its face, making the encircling peaks, which resembled ghosts draped in silvery sheets, vanish mysteriously.

I walked for some three hours, over thirty *li*, before the sunrise artshow of painted mountains began. However, frozen and hungry as I was, seeking out deliverance took precedence over its appreciation. The Reds were no exception to the rule that armies march on their stomach. Whenever possible they carried food with them. Being southerners, they preferred cooked rice, but the contents of any landlord's granary always tasted good. Otherwise they were prepared to march on, like a giant caterpillar stripping the countryside bare of edibles on either side of their trail, making purchases or bartering with the local peasantry. The latter often fled in fear, and those who stayed, being subsistence farmers, were reluctant to sell food in short supply, but the proletarian cause won their sympathy and sacrifice. It was an enormous strain on the local economy, enough to induce near famine conditions in its wake – a situation I started to believe still existed until I found a *fandian* (rice house), where I breakfasted on rice, eggs and cabbage.

The 3,000 Reds were not unopposed in their progress towards Luding, being delayed by skirmishes with warlord troops. On the other bank, the 'Left Group', who had not crossed at Anshunchang, advanced more swiftly spearheaded by a vanguard regiment under Yang Chengwu. Today there are bridges spanning the Dadu every ten kilometres or so: some are the traditional iron chain type, others newer cable suspensions, but most are rickety structures of rusted metal and rotten wood. I chose to cross on a concrete bridge to join the bulk of the Reds moving up the east bank for the attack on Luding. I was saving my nerves for crossing 'the Fixed bridge of Lu', named after the engineer who built it in 1701 for the Qing Emperor Kangxi. In late afternoon it lay between me and the town of Luding.

On May 29th 1935 it had lain between the Central Red Army and any chance of survival – sabotaged.

The first fifty metres of wooden planking – flesh on an otherwise deadly skeleton – had been taken up to reveal bare chains, fresh air and the broiling torrent below. It was too strategic a bridge to destroy entirely, being a profitable source of the warlord's tax revenues. After all, thought the Kuomintang, the Red Army would have to be suicidal madmen to attempt a crossing – only superhumans could overcome this unbreachable defence. Yet defying the limits of human courage such men in Yang Chengwu's group came forward. Apart from having the agility of acrobats and the strength of strongmen these soldiers would need determination comparable to the iron chains over which they prepared to crawl.

I stepped on to the handsome structure formed by the suspension of thirteen huge iron chains spanning more than one hundred metres across the gorge, each link wide enough for a clenched fist to be threaded. I immediately felt a sway as if on a boat. When I looked up the towering mountains moved; beneath me the white waves of the Dadu leapt up like dragons snarling through the cage-like planked floor, which to this day is only sparingly covered. I trod gingerly on towards the centre of the bowing span and, with each cautious step away from the securing bridgehead where the giant chains were embedded, the whole structure, and I with it, began to sway freely. At first it swayed predictably from side to side, up and down, but then more chaotically through interference as other pedestrians, locals, strode nonchalantly across pushing bicycles, carrying baskets of market goods or pulling children for whom the crossing was great fun, like a trip to the swings. A nauseous yet thrilling feeling of air and sea-sickness ensued, for this bridge is not terra firma but terror inducing: a stairway in the sky, the closest thing one can experience to walking the high wire.

Amidstream I looked back at the way I had come, across the thirteen chains of glory. By some miraculous method – one must resort to the dramatic scenes of a far fetched *wu shu* (martial arts) movie to imagine it – the Reds clawed their way on to the second half of the bridge that remained intact, to hurl grenades and dash suicidally towards the machine-gun post at the bridgehead. Too late to strip the rest of the bridge bare, the KMT doused it with paraffin, engulfing it with flames. Cold iron, bullets, the raging torrent and now fire faced the Reds, but still they came. Then, at this most critical time, gunfire was heard on the edge of town – the Right Group of the planned pincer movement were engaging KMT positions. Fearful of being surrounded, many Whites fled. Soon Luding Bridge was under the feet of the Communists.

Doors were found in the town with which to floor the bare chains. During the evening and for three days, thousands of Reds including Mao Zedong marched across the bridge into Luding for feasts on rice, chicken and pork.

*   *   *

Being seasonally out of step with the Red Army – I reached Luding earlier because I only retraced highlights of the March, in December as compared with June – meant that my route ahead through the Great Snowies was impassable. As planned, I prepared to return to my Xi'an base until the following summer.

Before leaving Luding I too feasted – on *jiaozi* (dumplings). The *laoban* (patron) quizzed me on my travels, and for once I did not mind relating how I had telescoped the forty-one years of Mao's life thus far retraced into three months of travel to revolutionary places. Rather sharply the *laoban* remarked that since the Chairman died at eighty-three then I was chronologically more or less halfway through his life story, something I had failed to realise myself. 'The best years are ahead of you,' he said.

We all believe that, I mused. The hope of a better future keeps us going. Mao Zedong in Luding must have been no exception. The past had been dark, recent months the darkest of all. The future did not look much different. Although the Central Red Army was across the Dadu and heading for the region where the Fourth Army was thought to be, the chances of the two Armies actually meeting up were as remote as the mountains themselves. The new battle would be with nature. The Reds were on the threshold of one of the wildest regions of China.

How did Mao change the world from here? One thing I had realised on my biographical journey was why the Communists wanted to change China. When I returned to high Western Sichuan to march with Mao next year in the area where the Long March would be won or lost, for me and the Red Army, perhaps I would learn how.

Fascinated by the bridge I returned there, amazed at the relaxed way locals took its dangers in their stride. Children of just eight or nine raced across unaccompanied. Courtesy of the *laoban*, I knew they walked on wood checked every three years and hand-smelted iron chains checked every five.

Unbelievably just as I was considering the danger of the bridge I saw a large object fall off. Was it a basket? No, people do not shriek about a basket. Whatever had fallen had crashed on to rocks forty metres below then plunged into the swirling current; no, not whatever, whoever, for the discoloured blue jade waters spoke of death with wellings of blood to the surface. A body was being chewed in the teeth of those dragon waves, surfacing and sinking as it was embroiled downstream. Some men raced down to the waterline, but in vain. Body and blood were gone. On the bridge above the scene of the accident, an old woman in hysteria had to be manhandled to safety off the bridge.

The wailing, an unforgettable din of hysteric cries and haunting shrieks, lasted ages. Later, the bamboo telegraph reported the woman in shock was the mother of the deceased. She had seen her thirty-year-old daughter trip up and roll off the bridge before her very eyes. It was told that the drowned woman had used the bridge twice a day almost all her life.

I decided not to cross the Dadu again. I turned my back on the terrible river and its bridge of death.

10

Jiajin Mountain

*Men of Mao's Central Red Army catch first sight of their Fourth Red
Army comrades*

With Mao in Luding and Chiang in Ya'an, they were only eighty
kilometres apart as the crow flew. By road it was more like double
that over Er Lang Shan, a 3,437 metre Great Snowy on the well-worn
caravan route leading from Chengdu via Ya'an, Luding and Kangding to Tibet. That road, icebound, was my hair-raising route back to
Xi'an, aboard a ramshackle bus with unchained wheels. The gantries
across the road prompted travellers for alms of consideration for the
toil its builders went through – 'Hail the People's Liberation Army
who forged this modern highway to Tibet.' The local populace indeed
had reason to give thanks for they benefited by processing the
'western treasure' (the literal meaning of Tibet) of timber and min-
erals carried by the Jiefang truck convoy – full to Chengdu's factories.

After marching initially either west or east from Luding on the

Tibet–Chengdu trail there were several options open to Mao's Central Red Army. He could head off on a northwestern elliptical route via Kangding to Aba in Northern Sichuan. Although this was the remotest route from KMT forces, and therefore the safest, it traversed the heart of the Great Snowies; and the fiercely anti-Han Tibetans would be encountered. An alternative was simply to continue north up the banks of the Dadu He towards Ma'erkang. Or Mao could take his army on a northeastern ellipse. The fact that neither of the latter two routes was an established trail as such – that is to say not well trodden by merchants for centuries as the Aba route had been – probably had little influence on Mao's choice. His decision-making principle when it came to route selection, bolstered by his recent off-the-road success up the Dadu, was inspired by an adage written by Lu Xun, a writer much admired by Mao – 'Originally there were no paths in the world; they are only made by the first man walking.'

Lu Xun's words not only rang true for the Red's routing but also their ideology. They were ground-breakers. Mao chose the northeastern ellipse. It was not thought to be a continuous route but it avoided the spine of the Great Snowies, passing instead through the Qionglai Shan on the eastern flank of the range. The main criteria, however, that probably influenced Mao's choice were the chances of the route leading to a rendezvous with the Fourth Front Army led by Zhang Guotao.

If Mao Zedong were alive today one of the questions on the Long March he would be asked is the reason for picking this route and whether or not he had made contact with the Fourth Army. Everyone wants to know if his decision was an outright gamble, a hunch, or an educated guess, inspired by intelligence, based on contact or even the advice of diviners.

The last known contact between the Politburo and Zhang Guotao was immediately after the Zunyi meeting of January 1935 when Mao Zedong became leader of the Red Army and the Party. Zhang was ordered to head south to assist the Central Red Army's crossing of the Golden Sands River. He never took a step south in response to the orders – it was easy for him to blame bad communications.

Between January and June there was no recorded radio contact. Code books had gone astray. It is quite feasible that they were lost in battle but equally possible there were spies in Red ranks. But as Gu Yiping recalled, his 'Har-tel-ee' (Hartley transmitting equipment, made in Great Britain and captured from the KMT) neither travelled nor functioned well in the humid and mountainous terrain of Western Sichuan. That leaves three possibilities.

Firstly, a net of messengers could have been despatched south by Zhang Guotao to give information on the Fourth Front Army's exact location. But how would Mao have judged them as genuine? Written messages would have been out of the question. They were never used by the Communists, following lessons learnt from their earliest guerrilla days. Passwords were equally unlikely, as their use necessitates prior agreement. That leaves only 'tiger tallies' for verification of the source of the message. These small ornaments – usually matching halves or pairs – were used in ancient China to prove the origin of messages between generals. If they did not tally the messenger was exposed. But once again no testament on record suggests that these were used.

The second possibility is the bamboo telegraph – chatter on the trail between one traveller or merchant and another – which could have relayed a hint to Mao's Central Army on the Fourth's location. If this happened the news would be anything between two and four weeks old. But again, why should Mao believe a stranger, say, who claimed to have 'bumped' into them: he might have followed KMT orders to lay a trail of red herrings?

Finally, there is a small chance that a leak of intelligence occurred from the Nationalist Press. It may have been one of the first wartime media gaffes in history. Just as Saddam Hussein of Iraq benefited from tuning into Cable Network News televising the Gulf War of 1991 by satellite, Mao Zedong in 1935 may have been given a sniff of the Fourth's location from the newspapers, distributed to post stations – there was one at Luding. Such a snippet could have influenced Mao's route – but equally could have been ignored as a hoax . . .

*   *   *

For six months, during three of which Xi'an was under the bitter grip of a dreadful North China winter, I too wrestled, not with which route to take – I was following Mao – but with the logistics of crossing the Great Snowy Mountains. Much torment was derived from watching a recording of the epic revolutionary opera 'Dong Fang Hong' (The East is Red), in Beijing's Great Hall of the People. As the colourful title suggests, the opera dramatically repaints the story of Red China, act by act and scene by scene: from its red-speckled origins in the Twenties when the Communists took refuge in their mountain-top Soviets; through the Long March and the eventual whitewash of the Nationalists in the War of Liberation; and into the Fifties when Mao Zedong shone brightly like the Sun over a new Red China. The scene of the Red Army climbing Jiajin Shan, at 4,100 metres the highest mountain on the Long March, resembled a Himalayan nightmare.

I had to make allowances for artistic licence and revolutionary exaggeration, but soldiers and written accounts of the Long March both emphatically guaranteed the Great Snowies as living up to their name, being snow-capped all year round despite the furnace conditions experienced in the Sichuan Basin just a few thousand metres below. The veterans I had met likened the changeable weather of Jiajin Shan to a child's face – smiling and bright one minute, throwing a tantrum with a snowstorm the next. With moistened eyes they told of comrades losing fingers and feet through frostbite, while others lost their lives, sliding down icy slopes to their death.

A montage of these images formed my 'mind map' of Jiajin Shan as I set out in earnest. But this departure was different. The usual uncertainty of starting out for a target several days away – during which time I could never relax for fear of being 'Gonganed' – was compounded by the possibility of Jiajin Shan being a ski slope when I reached it. For I was taking a gamble, or rather an educated guess, on the likely summit conditions in July. I was purposely as ill-equipped to climb snow-clad mountains as the Reds had been in their cotton uniforms and grass sandals. The success of my sorties too depended upon speed, stealth and flexibility – qualities I could not maintain in high summer handicapped with a winter kit.

Since conditions on the whole would be hot I opted for an ultra-lightweight kit. Even my army trousers had only won inclusion because my legs would feel safer inside them as I crossed the culinary divide and entered regions where dogs eat rather than are eaten. My feelings were that any snow would be confined to the summits: that

the 1935 condition of Jiajin, having never before been experienced
by the southern Reds to whom snowy mountains were likely awesome and frightening, may have been somewhat exaggerated. If my
predictions were wrong I took defiant comfort from my first mountaineering experience, climbing Snowdon as a youngster clad in shirt
and tie, tweed jacket, shorts, ankle socks and crocodile leather shoes.

I found a suffocating quilt of dawn mist lying like a bed of wispy-
white feathers over the valley road leading north from Tianquan.
This is where the Red Army forked off the Luding–Ya'an trail to
march due north to Jiajin Shan. A paperback Sichuan atlas, with
the footpaths used by the Long Marchers labelled and annotated,
had given me high hopes of following in the very tracks of the Reds.
To minimise margin for error Qi had translated charactered place
names on the relevant plates and I had practised their pronunciation
with her. They formed a long list of 'stations' to head for en route
to Jiajin, which looked about three days away. It seemed simple.
Experience told me it would not be. The whole area was closed to
foreigners. Having noted that my first turn was at Lao Chang village,
I switched off from routefinding, strode out, forgot about the *Gong
An Ju*, whistled and tossed my stick – my *bang bang* as the Chinese
called it – from hand to hand.

There was no sun. Low grey clouds hung below a wan sky,
unmoving, lifeless, like those on a theatrical stage. Although there
was no distinct sunlight and hence no discernible shade, passing
under tree branches mopped my brow as soothingly as a cool flannel.
As the heat rose, the verdant valley, emerald with rice paddies,
became more humid as the night's rain returned skyward. Puddles
on the dirt road became dried potholes, mud became red dust, the
valley a clammy greenhouse – totally breathless.

My straw hat, rough, dry and itchy without any headband, was
soon damp with sweat. I took it off and wafted it fan-like to cool
my face. My back was even more uncomfortable. Sweat had spread
out like ink on blotting paper to soak the cotton exterior of my
rucksack, whilst the skin it touched, all my back from shoulders to
buttocks, felt waterlogged. All I could do was occasionally thrust my
hands to the small of my back to provide ventilation.

Approaching Lao Chang I began asking villagers about the *xiao
lu* (footpath) to Lingguan. Successful routefinding in China depends

upon questionnaire techniques – the bigger the sample the better. The most reassuring directions came from the two old men who lounged on bamboo chairs, shaded beneath a line-full of drying tobacco leaves, shrivelled and nicotine coloured like their faces. Their hands held the product, homemade cigarettes rubbed and rolled in local newspapers. '*Ta men zou na bian*,' (They went that way,) they chorused hoarsely as if the Reds were just fifty-six minutes rather than years before me.

A muddy path rutted with cartwheels and pocked with hoof prints followed a small river, which functioned as a communal bath, swimming pool and launderette. Noodle limbed boys wore nothing but sun-given brown suits of high summer for their season of amphibia. Like birds of a feather, women, self-sorted by the topics of their gossip and generation flocked together at the water's edge.

Waddling on the bank were the grandmothers clad in dull tunics. Amidstream, perched on boulders were the agile rock-hoppers, young wives and nubiles, their long black hair fanned out like attractive feathers contrasting with fondant blouses, their whispers and titters only mime-like, being drowned by the rustic laughter, yells, more efficient and less social scrubbing and rinsing of the middle-aged mothers on the bank.

The toil of all blossomed forth on the riverside shrubs, but although the colours matched the exotic rhododendrons on which they were stretched out to dry, these clothes would not have won any shows. There were gaudy purple singlets, army-green trousers like my own, fondant-pink blouses, white bodices, corsets and bloomers that triggered visions of my grandmother's washing-line – but also some much scantier numbers. Underwear reforms had reached deepest rural China.

The path began to meander like the river itself, which I crossed by fords and spindly bridges, some no more than wire fences in the horizontal floored with rotten planks. Soon I realised the details that the PLA cartographers, the atlas compilers, had omitted. They were hardly Wainwrights. The exultation and inner coolness of being on the right path had been lost amid plantations of maize.

I emerged at a small village soaked in a sweat of frustration. The first attempt to leave led me to a dead end, a spring. Returning I trespassed through straw-strewn courtyards – playpens, chicken-runs and pigstyes all in one – where toddlers chased their co-tenants, and future dinners, and I was chased by geese. That typified my predicament. I persisted to escape, intruding where big noses have never nosed, around corners where round eyes have never looked, once comically – for me at least – disturbing a woman reading whilst topping up the manure heap.

Further cross-field walking took me through the peasantry's unharvested larder. An old man picking broad beans advised me to ford the river and climb the valley side, but before letting me go he stuffed a kilogram or so of the pods into my rucksack. Once on the path, I munched on this nutritious windfall which I had always found more appetising raw than cooked. I supplemented them with a few garlic bulbs, doggy-bagged from a Ya'an *fandian* – serving not only as gastronomic condiments but general preventative medicine. Water from one of the many gushing rivulets crossing the path, into which I squeezed fresh lemon – like the garlic a natural antiseptic – completed my lunch.

The valley, and the margin for error in following the once elusive path within it, narrowed as I climbed upwards. A cliff fell away to my side and, as a counter to me doing the same, I walked with a considerable tilt. Other walkers of the trail tilted too like hunchbacks under their burdens of bamboo. Newly felled green trunks, twice to thrice the height of their carriers, were leashed together on the backs of these porters. Their toil must be permanently disabling for these young men articulated themselves so that their burden neither dug into the earth nor caught on the overhanging branches to unbalance them. This involved walking, bent double, with hands on knees. Despite the weight of their load – each pole weighed about ten kilograms and they carried at least six each – they wore no padding on their backs and were shod in grass sandals or paper-thin 'lazy shoes'. But lazy they certainly were not: they crawled along like worker ants carrying twigs much bigger than themselves, pouring with sweat, their trousers rolled up to reveal bulging calf muscles.

Scaffolding standard bamboos prospered on the ground floor of this arboretum, a botanist's wonderland. The middle slopes were dominated by exotics like rhododendrons, camellias, azaleas, japonicas and many other rarer shrubs not bagged by globetrotting plant thieves and popularised for the English border. Far from villages,

these primeval woods were the flying grounds for insects of dinosaur-
ian proportions: furry, fleshy moths, like bats, not only in their
nightshift routine but size too; huge dragonflies with stained-glass
window wings, showering iridescence as they flew by, their segmented tails rattling as they stalled from bush to bush as clumsily
as man's own early attempts to copy the flight of birds; and butterflies
the size of the Chinese kites that they inspired, flitting from flower
to flower, seeming not only to pick up nectar but steal a shade of
each bloom, so multicoloured were their wings.

Many streams watered this Garden of Eden. I stopped as Adam
to bathe in one of their crystal pools. Luckily my ablutions were
completed by the time some peasants ambled by, not knowing they
had just missed a white ghost's bathtime. The ten-minute soaking
felt as beneficial as several hours' rest. I marched on invigorated,
and first heard the background roar then sighted the rushing waters
of the Baoxing He with the town of Lingguan stretched along its
eastern bank.

Spruced up for dinner, I darted unseen into a *fandian* on the edge
of town to banquet in relative peace on *ma po doufu* – bean curd in
fiery chilli sauce, egg and tomato soup and rice – whilst quizzing
the *laoban* on the road ahead. Baoxing, he said, was twenty-five
kilometres upstream. I decided on overtime and strode out on my
evening shift.

The dark green woolly mountains channelling the Baoxing River
were crested in low cloud. Soon it began to drizzle, the damp conditions attracting some giant mosquitoes out for the twilight hunt.
The river's roar seemed weak for its width and broil over such a
rocky bed; perhaps it was muffled by the padded valley slopes or
drowned by the heavenly timpani of thunder. Cicadas trilled in
increasing approval, an audience unseen in the canopy planted to
shade the road, which I tried to use not as a parasol but an umbrella.

It was almost dark by the time I had found a prospective place
for rest. Peasant farms, which I had come to regard as humanitarian
temples where I had never been refused food and lodging, were less
approachable after dusk. A foreign devil dropping in out of the
darkness was, I thought, expecting too much from the good Samari-
tans. There were not many work units in this remote valley because
there was little to work – except at the Malou Shan river-monitoring

station where they measured the height of the Baoxing He. That is where I stayed. My hosts hydrated me with copious mugs of jasmine tea, fed me a noodle supper and provided their table-tennis table for a bed.

A quarry explosion echoing through the mountains awoke me at dawn. I left shortly after because cooking from first principles – a sack of flour and firewood – is not fast food. That I sneaked in the form of *you tiao* (deep-fried dough sticks) on the outskirts of Baoxing amidst workshops where quarry marble was sculptured.

Twenty-five years ago, one old artisan told me, it was all revolutionary work. He recalled the quarry's biggest and most sensitive commission coming from Chengdu for a statue of Mao. Quarrymen fulfilled the order of hewing a 12.26 metre overcoated Chairman. It was difficult to find a huge slab of unblemished rock – veined rock would have been regarded as anti-revolutionary. Delivering a statue of precisely the requested height was also vitally important since the figures corresponded to Mao's birthday on December 26th. Once transported to Chengdu it was erected in the city centre on a plinth of 7.1 metres in height which in turn stood on steps of 8.1 metres in flight. The latter figure corresponds to August 1st (PLA Day), the former to July 1st (CCP's foundation day). The whole arrangement was conceived to embody Mao's control of the Party and the PLA.

'All we work on now are Tang beauties, Buddhas and lions,' said the artisan in an apologetic tone, but he added, 'you can still see our statue in Chengdu today – it was too strong to be destroyed after the Cultural Revolution. It's the largest surviving Mao statue in all China.'

To the north of Baoxing a confluence of two rivers formed the Baoxing He. The geographers who arrived there before me called them the Xi He (West River) and the Dong He (East River), but anyone blessed with a modicum of good directional instinct – or, like me, with a map and compass – would describe them as the Xi He and the Bei He (North River) respectively. I thus followed the East River flowing from the North. It was a long slow grind as the road climbed upstream, I estimated, at about twenty metres per kilometre. But it was cool – no more than twenty-five degrees. I thought of Xi'an's forty-degree summer days, days of exhaustion punctuated by struggles between one water melon and the next.

Like the proverbial frog in the well – a metaphor for the Chinese view of the world before their opening to the outside world – I could not see the surrounding Great Snowies from the confines of the gorge. At Minzhi, only a day's hiking from Jiajin Shan, I began to question locals on the likely weather conditions on the mountain.

'*Hen kun nan; you xue*' (Very difficult; there's snow) was the general consensus.

'*Shang shan, xia shan, duo chang shijian?*' (How long to go over the mountain?) I asked.

'*Gao bu qingchu,*' (It's unclear,) they replied.

'*Nimen qu guo meiyou?*' (Have you been there?)

'*Mei qu guo,*' they replied (Not been there). They were frogs in the well.

But the Reds had been here. 'In the 24th year of the Republic the Red Army came here – and now in the 80th year the Foreign Red Army has come!' said Zhao Diquan, a seventy-three-year-old admiring my PLA clothing, and using the old calendar. Minzhi villagers gave them strings of chilli peppers, ginger root and garlic, he added, for making soup to resist the cold. The Reds made new sandals and some locals joined them as scouts to lead them over Jiajin Shan into Xiaojin County. It was a well-trodden trail to the opium markets.

To the north of Huangdianzi, about fifteen kilometres from the foot of the mountain, I stopped at a timber yard. I had only been there twenty minutes before a jeep pulled in. Out jumped three men, one in a police uniform. The workmen here would not have, could not have, reported me – there were no telephone cables; if there had been, I should not have stopped there.

A middle-school English teacher from Baoxing, requisitioned by the *Gong An Ju* as interpreter for the interrogation, said they had been alerted to my trespass by rangers of the Giant Panda Reserve. Foreigners it seemed were much rarer than pandas there.

It took them under two hours to drive me back in their green Beijing jeep the sixty-five kilometres that had taken me eleven hours to hike. In the foyer of the Baoxing Hotel I was told about the county being closed to foreigners. Moreover, climbing Jiajin mountain was too dangerous, 'even for Chinese'.

'Thank you for saving my life,' I said contritely.

Unscathed apart from verbal flak, I retreated to my room. The only Mao badge I carried showed the Great Snowies: my Long March would be incomplete without Jiajin Shan. Defiantly I consulted my *Little Red Book* for a Chairman Mao quote: 'A dull witted Army cannot defeat the enemy.' The Foreign Red Army therefore must use its wits. Sun Tzu's *Art of War* advocated doing the opposite to what the enemy anticipated. They expected me to be on the bus back to Ya'an. I took a truck back to where they picked me up.

*   *   *

The truck driver wanted to take me to the end of the road, but I insisted on alighting only a minimum safety margin of a kilometre beyond my point of arrest. Jumping down from the cab I felt a rush of adrenalin as if I had escaped, climbed the fence, emerged from a tunnel, broken free. Now it was time to run.

Although the metalled road soon ended, the threat of recapture loomed as I trod a dirt track, an axle in width impressed with jeeps' tyres. The *Gong An Ju* still breathed down my neck, and I would not feel safe until I was beyond the range of their vehicles. Soon I could relax as the track climbed more steeply over rocky ground, on the same northward line, along the west bank of the Dong He, now a gushing mountain stream. Ahead lay Jiajin Shan, the tops clearly visible. The sun shone brilliantly, igniting the dew on the pines into a blaze of fragrance.

Despite these mild and seductive conditions I foraged for some twigs before the tree line was left below, for possible use, crampon-style, bound to my soles. As I did so, a young man clad in a dark blue Mao suit came swiftly up the path behind me. He was clearly going somewhere rather than tracking me, as he was laden with a sack of rice knotted at each corner and made into a rucksack with grass wound rope.

'Ni dao nali qu?' he enquired loudly whilst fumbling in his breast pocket. I beat him to my own Golden Monkeys and tossed him one.

'Jiajin Shan, ni ne?' I replied asking the same of him.

He pointed with the cigarette and said, '*Dawei.*' There was only one way there – over Jiajin. We marched off together.

My partner, Ding Li, chatted incessantly. He had crossed Jiajin Shan over thirty times before, twice a year since his early teens, usually with his brothers or sisters – he had eight of them.

'*Meiyou xue?*' (Any snow?) I asked.

He chuckled pointing skywards. '*Meiyou xue, xiatian meiyou!*' (There's no snow in summer!)

Ding Li strode purposefully on, hopping over puddles, across streams, patches of mud, then breaking into rolling strides: he was trying to race me, I sensed, expecting me to lag behind and suggest a more pedestrian pace. The altitude, approaching 4,000 m, combined with the intellectual task of understanding his broad Sichuan dialect did make me breathless, not only with quick walking, but with talking too.

He quizzed me on Britain: what did the peasants grow? Did they own their land, have machines, televisions, telephones? Did every family have a car? Could I drive? Was there any birth control? What methods were used? This really stretched my vocabulary but made the sign language fun. How many children was I planning to have? In replying I resorted to '*Gao bu qingchu,*' (It's unclear,) whilst turning the question back to him.

'I can have one or maybe two,' he said paradoxically. Was he thinking of twins, or breaking the law in becoming a so-called 'birth-rate guerrilla'? He explained that if his first child was a girl he could have another in the hope of getting a boy because he lived in the poor countryside. 'But if I have a boy first,' he added, 'he won't have any brothers or sisters like me.'

'No, but he'll have loads of aunts and uncles,' I remarked. Ding Li roared in approval.

Like the gradient and our attack on it, the chatter went on constantly. What did I like doing in my spare time? Which sports? I made the mistake of answering marathon running, a reply which Ding Li interpreted as throwing down the gauntlet. 'We'll run then shall we?' he said, breaking off into a jog that lasted for a good steep kilometre. Gasping for breath we stopped, called it a draw to sit on a big boulder and praise each other's fitness, then drink from a gurgling spring and pick over the crimson carpet of wild strawberries.

We marched on in silence, but only for a while. As a distinct summit ridge came into sight the hills came alive to the baritone echoes of Ding Li singing 'Chairman Mao Our Dearest One':

The Sun is the brightest.
Chairman Mao the dearest.
The brilliance of your thoughts
always fills our hearts . . .

He held his palms on his own heart and I nodded in approval
and tried to hum an accompaniment to the second verse:

Spring wind is the warmest.
Chairman Mao, our dearest one,
Your revolutionary guidance leads
us on our journey . . .

He bellowed with arm outstretched towards the summit.
'*Hao ting, hao ting,*' (Sounds good,) I interjected.

Your achievements are higher than the sky.
Your kindness deeper than the ocean.
Your Sun in our hearts will never set
but beat as one . . .

Ding Li pointed to the heavenly bodies and his own anatomy at
the appropriate places. Now familiar with the tune I duetted the
title and chorus on our last few strides to the summit:

Taiyang zui hong, Mao Zhu Xi zui qin!
Taiyang zui hong. Mao Zhu Xi zui qin!!

We shook hands repeatedly before looking into a small Buddhist
shrine. It was a rock-built shelter that housed a wooden image amidst
a litter of offerings from travellers: candles, scented tapers, withered
wild flowers, shrivelled oranges, rock hard unleavened bread, corn
cobs and a live hen. Ding Li added some of his rice. The Reds had
been forced to eat such temple offerings, often years old, in the
remote country ahead.

An old shepherd who watched his flock in the corrie below came
up to the shrine to join us. We sat huddled together on the tufty
grass cushions buffeted by the strong chill wind. The shepherd shared

his sheepskin cape, an enormous blanket of shaggy wool. Ding Li contributed some boiled eggs. I provided water and smokes. There was no snow around, not even in patches. Defiantly I looked back south to Baoxing, knowing there were no policemen up here. It had been a moderately strenuous hike. Ding Li and I had walked together for five hours.

Rubbing his forehead and temples, Ding Li warned of the danger in spending too long in the rarefied atmosphere. Whilst I prepared to perform a ceremony, Ding Li, pressed for time, left for Dawei. Before going he gave me typically detailed Chinese directions for finding the way there by myself – '*Zhi zou!*' (Just go ahead!) he repeated waving his arm to the northern horizon. Off he ran, brandishing friendly bravado to the very end, first sliding down a scree like a mountain goat, unperturbed by the occasional tumble, and then, once safely on to the grassland corrie, turning around briefly to yell, '*Zai jian!*' (See you again!) Soon he was a dark speck amidst many others: they were yaks.

I picked up a thin palm-sized rock to use as a makeshift axehead and walked to the highest point of the ridge. Hacking into the tufty carpet, I exposed the thin stony soil and placed my Mao badge into it: a simple tribute to the young soldiers who marched with Mao over this summit.

In Xi'an I had found one of the youngest Long Marchers – Zhong Ling, a retired doctor. He had devoted his life to treating wounds inflicted during battles, from the Long March to the War of Liberation, injuries caused by both Chinese and Japanese inhumanity to Chinese.

Sitting beneath a calendar of China's Ten Marshals in that winter of 1991, Zhong Ling had told me of joining the Red Army in Jiangxi, in 1932, at the age of thirteen. He could write more characters then than most other Reds twice his age, so he was put to work in the graffiti department, or propaganda team, writing slogans on walls. Becoming ill, he was hospitalised, but when he recovered he stayed in the hospital. Doctors found him a useful orderly and nurse: he could read the medicine names – mainly Chinese herbal preparations – and he washed the bandages well. He must have been good: he was assigned to the Central Committee Hospital when the Long March began. Using needles to lance blisters and cleaning them with *hong yao shui* (red medicine water) was his main duty.

Seeing leaders like Bo Gu, Wang Ming, Zhou Enlai and later Mao Zedong was commonplace for this little Red. He was timid, and spoke only when spoken to but, he recalled, the sight of the foreigner Li De did cause fits of giggles amongst most teenage Reds.

It is unclear how many Reds perished on Jiajin Shan. Only adjectives describe the losses. It was probably in the order of several tens. Zhong Ling played down the difficulty, witnessing no fatalities, only temporary snow blindness and bruises. Some accounts blame not only the icy conditions but the thin air. This seems surprising considering the likely condition of the hearts and lungs which had powered the men for the last eight months. Accumulative exhaustion, however, may have contributed to their inability to tolerate the conditions.

The men, he said, advanced in a single column, following the leader, just a stride apart so as not to get lost. A message was passed up and down the line – the directive of the climb. He does not know who issued it, but he repeated it so often that he has never forgotten it: Loosen clothing on the lower slopes; walk at a steady pace; wrap feet and hands with cotton to prevent frostbite; don't stop on top no matter how tired you are. Fifty-six years later that still seemed good advice. Mist engulfing the summit evicted me by way of the treacherous scree on to the corrie meadow. It was comparatively mild there as the clouds of mist swept above. Surprisingly the directions furnished by Ding Li proved to be ample and my descent was untroubled apart from enduring a brief but chilly torrential downpour.

Three hours later I walked down an undulating narrow mule path hugging the side of a creek whose stream, swollen by the recent deluge, rushed to join the Wori He. As that confluence came into sight the patchwork fields of Dawei's peasants across the river looked like a banner of welcome, promising good food. The same view had given the scouts of the Central Red Army a bigger surprise. They saw encampments. Stopping, the scouts peered through their field-glasses. 'Who are they?' asked those behind. 'What can you see?' The answer was tents, field kitchens, and banners – red banners with the star, hammer and sickle! A bugle call, perhaps a famous Red song was amplified by the creek's own trumpet shape and fell on the ears of the Fourth Army to herald the Central's emergence.

I stood on the Wori He bridge, garlanded in red sashes, to envisage the Fourth and Central's mysterious, incredible, against-all-odds meeting – not to ask questions on how it came about, but simply to share belatedly in their delight. The highest mountain on the Long March was towering behind us.

11

Additional Manoeuvres

*Zhou and Mao contemplate the Grasslands whilst lodging in the
yamen at Zhuokeji*

Dawei is a large village now, its main and only street perhaps two
hundred metres long. There are few signs of life. A group of youths
crowd around a snooker table in the shade. Shops hardly flaunt
commerce, their windows boarded up. Doorways are indicated only
by grubby sheets draped to keep out dust and flies, and by rusty,
dusty bicycles parked outside.

There is a post office where you can phone anywhere in China if
you care to wait for half a day. On the counter stands a tray of
wheat-flour glue littered with matchsticks and a few flies. China
produces neither self-adhesive stamps nor envelopes. Dawei is clearly
not a community of letter writers. The postal clerk dozes on a bed
behind the counter, half curtained by her line of washing. In comes
a peasant who buys one envelope for his note. He takes longer to
write the address than I would.

The only shop open is the state-run store where you can buy any of those classic design standards unaffected by innovation, unchanged by diversification for the past forty-three years. There are Mao caps in green or blue for 2 *yuan*, army trousers 15 *yuan*, jackets 18 *yuan*, Thermos flasks 14 *yuan*, lazy shoes 5 *yuan*, enamel mugs 1 to 3 *yuan*, basins 10 *yuan* and black Flying Pigeon or Forever bicycles for 220 *yuan* – not much to me, but the average annual income of these people is only 300 *yuan* (30 pounds sterling). Perhaps that is why so little purchasing seems to be going on, why the assistants are snoozing on the job.

Some women stand gossiping by the drums of vinegar, soy sauce and cooking oil, shocked by the first price increases since the Sixties. The government has just doubled the price of flour and rice and trebled the price of oil, citing increasing waste as indicative of underpricing and oversubsidy. They arouse an assistant. She yawns and walks slothfully over to the drums, pulling on her army-green sleeve protectors to ladle out the oil into a bottle.

Fandians were easy to spot not only by smell but sound: by the chopping of meat and vegetables, the clanking of utensils and the sizzle of ingredients hitting the smoking oil of the wok; and by the *re nao* (warmth and noise) – the atmosphere created by the guests. All *fandians* are warm in summer, and some vibrate with the boisterous shouts of *hua quan* – the finger throwing game. The two players extend any number of fingers on one hand simultaneously from their clenched fists. At the same time they call out a number, a guess as to what the fingers on both hands total – rather like balancing an equation. The loser drinks a mouthful of fiery white alcohol.

Although four and one makes five, the outcome of the Fourth and First Army's meeting was a less simple equation. Only a few divisions of the Fourth, under the command of Li Xiannian were at Dawei. It seems that Zhang Guotao had cleverly strung out his army along an east–west line from Dawei to Maogong, seventy kilometres to the west, in order to increase the odds of meeting Mao. Nevertheless it was still a miraculous result bearing in mind that Mao might have gone either side of this Fourth wall. Zhang had read Mao's mind well.

A big celebration was held, with Mao and his entourage billeted in the lamasery that basks on the south-facing slopes above the village. The great wooden-roofed structure still dominates the hillside, housing a gaudily dressed Buddha and a score more of peripheral deities.

Today, a terrace of wooden peasant homes, leaning considerably to accommodate the slope and looking like dwellings built with playing cards on the verge of collapse, face the high temple wall. The alleyway formed in between was a throng of communal activity that late summer's evening – until I arrived; for the coming of a foreigner with a camera was akin to the intrusion of a gun. When I raised it, it raised no smiles, only people's fists clenching stones. Elders creaked upright, picked up their tiny stools and skulked indoors. Women took hold of their toddlers, and the children followed, scurrying along the alleyway like chicks behind a mother hen. With the alert sounded and alley cleared, suspicious eyes peeped around corners, through latticed windows and the cracks of doors and from beneath the eaves like watchful birds in fear of a prowling cat violating their nests. Clearly unwelcome, I returned to the village pondering this contemporary xenophobia, a reaction I felt sure was characteristic of feudal religious prejudices induced by the proximity of the temple, in which aliens are represented in sculpture as evil spirits.

More broad-minded and sagacious elders, however, were available for consultation on the summer of 1935. They told me that the two armies had arrived within a day of each other. Although all were Red Army men, the Fourth's soldiers looked well nourished and clothed and relatively clean. Mao's men looked like beggars: dishevelled, harrowed and ill.

For me, the onward route to Maogong was to be treacherous. War waged by weather throughout China – there were catastrophic floods in the lower Yangzi basin – had struck the valley. Yesterday's rain had taken out the road alongside the Wori He with rockfalls and landslides in at least two places. Peasants, mobilised from local hill farms, gave assistance to the permanent highway maintenance gangs who try to preserve road links through these unstable mountains. They laboured with crowbars, barrows and wicker baskets, levering boulders and emptying earth into the river below the road. It was a task of enormous proportion often requiring the use of gelignite – a blast and dash method that either cleared the road considerably or further destabilised the slopes.

Negotiating these hazards entailed scrambling detours high above the scars, and frequent crossings of the Wori He. Many peasants, deprived of community transport, walked too. Some refused to leave their wheels behind. Absurdly they carted chunky black bikes up winding mule paths, along terraces of maize and through orchards.

There were several primitive bridges at water level but I encountered one derelict suspension bridge that had once linked these valley sides an extraordinary 150 metres above the river. The bridgehead still bore Cultural Revolution graffiti: 'Long Live Chairman Mao', and 'Learn from Dazhai'. The latter slogan, a quotation of Mao's, urged the whole Chinese peasantry to take heed of the hard-working example set by Dazhai villagers who terraced the hills high above their Shanxi homes. The peasants here had done exactly that: all around, green patches of culture coloured the otherwise barren hills. But with this bridge now dilapidated peasants faced a long hike to reach the corresponding terraces across the valley. Its remains hung in the sky like a memorial to that fanatical period, its cables still sturdy but its wooden floor twisted like a paper streamer spanning a room, with planks waiting to drop out like rotten teeth, one by one, in the next downpour, gale or earth tremor.

More uncrossable bridges – unless one possessed the necessary acrobatics – hung alongside modern concrete structures at Lao Ying. Here is the confluence of the Wori He, my guide for the last day from Dawei, and the Fubian He, my guide for the next few days making north to Mengbi Shan, the last big mountain of the Great Snowies. These small 'Ludings' are left bare-chained and should give travellers a vivid impression, for the next thousand years, of exactly what the heroes of Dadu had faced.

Mao and his chiefs of staff made a short detour from here to Maogong, now called Xiaojin. (The former name and the name change have no connection whatsoever with Mao himself.) Why they went there, when Zhang Guotao and the bulk of the Fourth Front were on the near side of Mengbi Shan, is open to speculation.

Their meeting place was a Catholic church built in 1901 on the banks of the Xiaojin Chuan. It was a grey stone Sacré Coeur lifted right out of a French village but – *sacré bleu* – occupied by

Communists. Today it is the Xiaojin County CCP headquarters, but foreign influence is making a popular comeback. The church itself houses several billiard tables, a game I was told that had found great favour among members of the Communist Youth League.

It is interesting to note that even in those days of embryonic Chinese Communism, the leaders had no qualms about enjoying the best accommodation that could be had. Mao, it seemed, was developing quite a penchant for squatting in temples and now churches. Apart from it being clean, cool and peaceful, he probably derived a kick from this cuckoo habit of nesting in foreign religious enclaves that he regarded as centres for exploiting the Chinese people.

So why did Mao come to Maogong? Undoubtedly the political and strategic campaigning had begun. Although Mao was theoretically the head of the Party and the Red Army, in practice he had a tiny army compared to Zhang's Fourth. The time was nearing when the appointments made in Zunyi would be proved realistic or honorary. Mao was in Maogong with Zhou Enlai and Zhu De, his staunchest supporters, and, I would think from observing how Chinese develop their connections in modern day China, some leaders of the Fourth sent to meet them at Dawei – perhaps Li Xiannian. He would have been 'wooed' for background information on the Fourth's condition and movements in recent months. Zhang Guotao was not regarded as an enemy, but he had developed a reputation for being a black sheep. To manipulate him Mao would certainly begin by applying principles of the *Art of War* adapted to psychologically persuasive means.

My own inside information on the Fourth had also been gleaned in advance. During my winter recess in Xi'an I had met two '*Guo jia yuan lao*' (founders of the country), as Red Army veterans are known, men of Zhang's Fourth Front Army. They were Tan Bing and Luo Shaoqing.

Tan Bing did not know his birthday as such, but he thought he was born in 1919. He was not exactly treasured by his family. His father thought more of smoking opium. Like drug addicts of today who resort to crime to finance their habit, Tan Bing's father sold his daughter for thirty *jin* (fifteen kilograms) of rice. He did not feed his starving family with the staple; he exchanged it for opium.

Tan Bing did not wait to be traded to the landlord. Some propaganda workers came to his village in about 1929 looking for recruits for the Red Army. He was far too young at ten to join, they said, but he tagged along nevertheless and was eventually befriended by the soldiers rather like a camp dog or cat – a welcome and accepted part of the camp, but not strictly in the Red Army. But soon he began to earn his bowl of rice by acting as a runner, carrying messages around the Fourth Army's base area which occupied north-eastern Sichuan, wedged between the Jialing and Chang Jiang (Yangzi) Rivers and encompassing the towns of Tongjiang, Nanjiang, Chenggu and Bazhong. Tan Bing had been adopted by the Red Army.

Luo Shaoqing was twenty-four when his Long March, also of the Fourth Front, began in November 1934. He carried nothing except some cooked rice and a captured KMT rifle, domestically made in Haiyang near Hankou, now part of Wuhan. Its range was a mere 100 metres and he was only issued with three bullets. Tan Bing at sixteen was too young for arms in such short supply. He was primarily a porter, carrying blankets counterbalanced by a bag of steamed rice and fried flour with salt on his bamboo pole. He walked barefoot and unarmed, but, when conditions improved, he wore sandals and carried a pitchfork.

Their route from the Sichuan–Shaanxi base area was across the well-blockaded Jialing Jiang where they made 'fire in the east and attacked in the west' by herding water buffaloes with lanterns on their horns along the river bank in the opposite direction to where Red Army engineers were constructing a pontoon bridge. Proceeding west they occupied several counties at the juncture between the northern Great Snowies and a plateau known simply as '*Caodi*', or Grasslands.

Tan Bing had a terrible journey, developing pneumonia. The sick and wounded were left behind to fend for themselves. If and when they recovered, they faced a struggle in the wake of their Army, across land stripped of anything edible as if locusts had devoured it. Usually destitute, they were reduced to begging or stealing.

Tan Bing reckoned there was no discipline in the Fourth. However, he added, 'We always respected women.' He lived off the land eating *huanglian* (a kind of wild but very bitter spinach) and various tree barks boiled to soup. Then, with a diet lacking salt, he suffered from dropsy and edema, terrible swellings of the hands and feet, symptoms that worsened on the ascent of Mengbi Shan – the second highest peak on the Long March, only seventy metres lower than Jiajin. After experiencing headaches, nose bleeds and snow blindness on the crossing he arrived in Maogong County to be finally reunited with the Red Army, his family.

Mao Zedong was unheard of then to Tan Bing and Luo Shaoqing. To them, Zhang Guotao was the leader – a fact that emphasised the magnitude of the task that faced the supposed leader of the entire Red Army and Party. Mao stood little hope of taking practical control unless he could dominate his Fourth Front comrade.

They had met twelve years before at the third CCP Congress in Guangzhou. Their reunion took place in Lianghekou (two river mouths) – an apt name for the place where a stream met a river. Mao had under 10,000 men; Zhang had almost 100,000. The venue, as one had come to expect, was in a lamasery which now lies derelict behind a timber yard. I sat amidst its rubble, patching a blister that had developed on my one day-sixty kilometre push there.

Here began the fourth distinct struggle that Mao faced on the Long March adding to those against the Kuomintang, the hostile terrain and the '28 Bolsheviks'. There was an outright difference in opinion on where the united forces of the First and Fourth should now go. Zhang wanted to remain largely in the counties he was occupying and extend what had effectively become a base area there further west into Qinghai and north to Gansu. Mao rejected this as a static, impotent and hopeless plan – there was no chance of Red Army growth there. Instead he advocated that the bulk of the united forces should head north, continue with mobile guerrilla warfare and join up with other Red Army fronts under the leadership of Liu Zhidan in northern Shaanxi.

Mao's plan was far more ambitious, dangerous and patriotic. Japan was infesting northern China and Mao was already focusing on this long-term problem. Zhang Guotao was given the consolatory title of Political Commissar of the entire Red Army, while Mao's plan became the 'Decision on the Strategic Principle After the First and Fourth Armies Joining Forces'. In theory Mao had won the day, but the Army was a long way from Shaanxi. It remained to be seen whether the plan could work in practice. To see if it could, the united Army marched north towards Mengbi Shan, staggering their departure so as not to saturate the land.

* * *

North of Lianghekou the road beside the Fubian He rises gradually, winding its way up Dream Pen Mountain. Attractive blocky thick stone-walled homes of the Zangzu (Tibetans) grace the pine-forested hillsides. Each is a miniature fortress with small windows inset high above the ground, yet nevertheless exuding some friendliness with gaily painted wooden eaves, sills and courtyard doors.

Small bridges leading to the Zangzu villages appear, from a distance, to be improvised washing lines drying none too clean, off-white and tattered rags. On close inspection, however, these were found to be prayer flags, generally elongate: narrow white pieces of material printed with Sanskrit lines of Buddhist text. To those ignorant of this ancient language the prayer flags simply look patterned, although one can distinguish that the prayers on each flag are often different. Their purpose on bridges is primarily to deter evil spirits or persons from crossing and entering the village. Prayer flags also indicate burial mounds and cemeteries from afar, being attached to spear-like rods that seem to have been showered into the earth, tilting at many angles, during the ancestral worship and mourning rites.

It is very unlucky to touch the material of the flags, I was told, as preventing the wind flapping a prayer flag is akin to interrupting a worshipper at prayer. Each flutter is a mutter, as it were, rather like the verbal repetition of a mantra or the rotation of a prayer wheel in a temple, all of which are directed to release from the endless cycle of birth and death.

The First Front Reds must have had a similar yearning with regard to scaling mountains one after another, and marching countless *li* all day and sometimes night. Yet for the first time since leaving Jiangxi they had a destination, a promised land in northern Shaanxi. That, coupled with a feeling of safety in numbers brought about by the combined forces and the knowledge that they were climbing the last Great Snowy, was cause for rejoicing. Geographical ignorance amongst the rank and file, as to what lay in the month ahead, was bliss. A hell on earth was beyond the next horizon.

Mengbi Shan was a grassy mountain in July 1991, its lower slopes the domain of shaggy yaks overdressed for the mild conditions, its tops patrolled by the talons of eagles that preyed upon scampering mountain hares. A road has conquered slope, scree and cliff with switchbacks that slowly wind their way upwards, distance no object, like a blunt knife peeling an apple but getting there in the end, denuding the mountain not of its skin but its core, its spirit and masculinity. The mountain fights back, even in summer, with land-slips, but men and women stationed near the summit work with pick and shovel to keep the upper hand, and offer it to travellers in distress. Warm though their hospitality was – and it did get freezing during the night – I regretted sleeping at that altitude. Dehydrated by a marathon before the long ascent through sultry corries, I suf-fered badly during the night with headache and sore throat, symp-toms which forced me to hurry down the far side of the mountain the next morning.

Across the divide walking was downhill and pleasant under tem-perate blue skies. With the valley carpeted in grasses, sedges and wild flowers – many shades of poppies, orchids, violets, foxgloves, daisies and dandelions – the Zangzu people had vacated their winter fortresses to celebrate high summer's flowering. Whole communities were out on the riverside, sitting cross-legged on brightly woven woollen rugs around low tables piled high with the season's harvest and the hamlet's distilling; potatoes in skins, broad beans and peas, whole roasted piglets, fowls, and two fiery drinks: *bai jiu* – white alcohol made from rice – and *qing ke jiu* – barley liquor.

The Zangzu eagerly beckoned me to join them in celebrating their flower festival. Hanzu people, in contrast, will observe you like a rare animal, talk amongst themselves on the presumption that a foreign devil cannot share their tongue, and then once spoken to will exude warmth and benevolence. The Zangzu, however, are spon-taneous with their friendship. To them, a minority, most others are foreigners, including the Hanzu. The language difference is an opportunity rather than a hurdle, circumvented with universally understood gestures: broad rustic smiles, a courteous bow and wel-coming clasped prayerful hands and ceremony; the offering of a communal vessel held in both hands – best described as a teapot – whose spout delivers a shot of warming rice wine into the guest's mouth. (The fact that this fiery liquor can be used to fuel vehicles is one of its greatest selling points.)

The Reds had never been given such a welcome by the Tibetans. On the contrary, they were the most anti-Han tribe encountered on the Long March. But by fleeing their mountain lodges, which were no better than sheep pens, and unpitching their *yurts* (tents) they unintentionally helped the Reds. Fields were left unharvested with grain to thresh and vegetables to unearth. Once at Zhuokeji the Reds could feast on enormous root vegetables mutated to double the size of agricultural show exhibits by the rarefied atmosphere. Examples of this gigantic produce still graced the barrows of local markets: potatoes like melons, onions like footballs, peas like cherries and carrots like truncheons.

Approaching Zhuokeji I began to look out for the stone tower of its *yamen* (a Tibetan fortress), which Tan Bing had not forgotten in fifty-six years. His first request on my return to Xi'an would certainly be for a contemporary photograph of what he considered the most impressive landmark on his Long March. Zhuokeji is now a small village, and the *yamen*, naturally moated by a confluence, is dilapidated. It is still nevertheless a noble structure that dominates the settlement like a Welsh coastal castle does its harbour.

It was here Mao rested his weary men in the knowledge that 'here be dragons' terrain lay ahead. Comrades of the Fourth Front, being largely of Sichuanese stock, knew of the notorious Caodi (Grasslands) at the northern boundary of their province. To cross that plateau – its average altitude 3,500 metres – required seven days' rations, not to mention great strength, determination and luck with the fickle weather. Zhuokeji was the place to prepare for that next horrendous battle.

Legend had it that the entire First Front could have lodged in the *yamen*. I trod cautiously on the creaking wooden stairs and balconies as if on thin ice, with body braced to react to any imminent collapse. These ruins were now used by a Zhuokeji family as a barn, a place for storing silage and drying bundles of leaves, roots, flowers and pods for eventual medicinal use. Dust and cobwebs masked its former opulence, although fine carving was still visible on the balconies, beams and banisters. The rooms themselves were quite black, for the needle-like fissures in their walls were designed for the exit of arrows and barely admitted any light. From the ground floor up were the stables, the larder and servants' quarters, the lamasery, and the chieftain's rooms, once occupied by Mao.

The previous chieftain, titled Tu Si, had run off like his flock. He was regarded with god-like reverence, albeit a god concerned with opulence, comfort and worldly pleasures. Subjects kept his larder well-stocked with staples, vegetables, salted yak, sheep meat and wines. He practised polygamy with three wives and, not surprisingly, fathered many children. Local Zangzu people believed that one of those wives, Ke Yuxia, and some of her children were still alive and living in Ma'erkang County.

I had planned to sleep in the *yamen* with the bats and pigeons but the overwhelming hand of friendship proffered by the Zangzu people changed my mind. Their white *yurts*, pitched for the flower festival, were adorned with black appliqué and looked like huge lanterns of welcome sitting on the valley floor beside the river. There I spent my last night in the Great Snowies, a long and memorable one, feasting, drinking and jigging.

12

The Grasslands

Crossing the Grasslands.

Like the eerie, fast-forward play of a film in which clouds fly across the sky, I had leapt, during the period of a short journey between Ma'erkang and Hongyuan, from summer into bleakest midwinter. Whilst most of China roasted in the high thirties, or at least simmered, Hongyuan, at 3,400 metres, shivered because it was so high.

Hongyuan had not existed in 1935 – otherwise the Red Army might have passed through. Since then little has happened to make settling there any more attractive. Soils, if not stony and thin are waterlogged and, for six months a year, permafrosted. Water supply is poor and the aspect unsheltered. Yet such conventional settlement criteria do not logically accommodate overpopulated China; hence people have been assigned, some might say exiled, here. Those individuals in the vast sea who make waves, like the classes of 1989 from Beijing, are sent here, their *hukou* (citizenship) changed; a life-long shackle, difficult to break, chains them to this outpost of socialist progress, unless they bribe their way back to the sought-after abode of a provincial capital.

For all that, Hongyuan looked a hastily built town. The newly metalled main street was flooded and devoid of traffic except for a few horses that waded along, their footing doubtless a painful contrast to the spongy turf of surrounding grassland. A chill drizzle, reminiscent of the Scottish Highlands at their worst, had all but cleared the town. Some street-side vendors braved the gloom, their eyes glazed like the yak heads they had butchered and lined up along the gutter. Blood from this outdoor abattoir stained the pools. Behind these butchers were none of the usual dirty-grey Soviet-built tenements, the blight of many a Chinese town and city. Instead, newly built tile-faced blocks, characteristic of the open door period, gave a veneer of modernity to Hongyuan. Yet none appeared to be occupied. It was as if their construction mimicked the purpose of scarecrows on medieval castle ramparts, to deceive. Such is the incongruous encroachment of socialist Han China on the edge of the Grasslands.

Similar developments might, I thought, ease my crossing of the Grasslands compared to that of the Red Army. But I could not forget the sight of Long March veterans Tan Bing and Xu Youwan pointing to their waists as they recounted how many Reds boiled their belts to make soup to survive. It seemed a subtle omen that I should be a belt-and-braces man in carrying food and extra clothing. My PLA standard issue '761' food concentrate biscuit was untouched since I had bought it in Xi'an, but its 250 grams was not enough. To it I added two kilograms of peanut brittle. To keep out the chill, I bought longjohns; for the drizzle I bought a plastic cycle cape, big enough to use as a makeshift tent if I were pushed to find shelter. The Reds had used oiled cotton sheets for cover.

*   *   *

There was a horizon. Low dark hills peeped as landfall beyond an ocean of grass, an expanse of knee-high sedge dripping with dew and dotted with fleets of black boats – herds of yak. It looked like Rannoch Moor, but at 200 by 100 kilometres was more like the size of Scotland north of the Great Glen. Celtic comparisons did not end there. On the drier patches the thistle prospered, a giant altitudinally mutated big brother of its mauve Highland sister. The yaks too were merely black haired breeds of shaggy highland cattle but with the special trait of their water buffalo cousins – they were able to plod through the glutinous mud, which had become the Red Army's chief opponent fifty-six years before as it struggled against nature rather than the warlike nature of man.

The Grasslands are an enormous marshland. As one walks it, fluidity can be felt underfoot. Sometimes it has the spring, the rebound in each stride, of a waterbed, yet if you treat it as a bouncy mattress your foot can easily puncture the superficially playful covering. Heartbeats race. Sweat oozes as you heave your leg, from knee to foot, from its adhesive suction. The bog utters a sucking warning in tone like the dishing out of the first spoonful of trifle.

The Fourth Front Army had crossed the Grasslands before; so for once the Central Army was not entering the landscape blind. They had been advised to collect a week's ration, but that amount of food was not available. Nevertheless they were lumbered with more supplies than usual, more than they had carried since Mao took charge in Zunyi and liberated them from Pickfordian duties. Burdens made wrestling with the glutinous sludge all the more difficult, especially if someone had already grazed its skin. Marching in lines or groups was out. The Reds spread out like a force screening the ground for the clue to a crime, prodding the ground before them with poles to test its strength.

My stick immediately came into its own. Some of the distant black objects were not yaks as such, but *yurts* made of yak hair. Within a couple of hundred metres the animal alarm of the Zangzu was triggered by the approach of my 1.85 metre figure. Any hope of these beasts being shackled was soon abandoned as their barks grew louder as they bounded rapidly over the grassland. They were unshackled to protect the camp whilst their masters tended to the yak on horseback. Using my Mandarin 'oushi' was of little use. The master tongue of these dogs was Tibetan.

Camp protection it seemed was a side benefit of their main aim: meat. The instinct for survival flooded my muscles with adrenalin. These dogs were potential maneaters, if they breached my defence of stick and stones. The killer dogs, three in all, seemed to have a leader, a dominant male to spearhead the attack. I held three well proportioned stones as missiles, and waited until the grisly beast was but seven or eight strides away. I feigned throwing thrice, then released – a direct strike on the head sent the demon yelping in retreat, bemused at my simultaneous eruption into dementia, as bewitching and unexpected as the setting off of a firecracker. The bitches barked and snarled as I whirled and brandished my stick, for face – for it would seem that even Chinese dogs are concerned about losing that – the demon came in once more, but only as a show of paper bravado to its mates. I walked on, and the three dogs had to make do with only camp protection. I had won the first dog fight but more, many more, lay ahead. How would I be able to obtain food from these nomads if all had moats of such unwelcoming teeth?

Feeling badly shaken I sat on the edge of the track, a terra firma thread tacking together towns at opposite ends of the Grasslands. I took several tiny ball-bearing-shaped *rendan* – a kind of Chinese sal volatile. As it had been carried by some Red Army medics, I had no more of an advantage there, but I did with the track which they built twenty years later, a defiant symbol of the Communists' fight against wildest nature across the landscape that had troubled them so by its desolation and disease.

The track curved through low smooth hills, those distant islands at my outset, then eased down the other side to streak across another ocean, this one with no visible horizon except tonight or even tomorrow. Here I saw the Grasslands in a different light as the sun shone, dispersing the cotton wool cumulus and, within the hour, speckling the vista with the colour of a billion wild flower blooms, transforming the monotone green grassland into a pointillist pastel masterpiece by Seurat.

Inky blue and mauve poppies, white starflowers, lemon primroses, miniature orange orchids, giant golden buttercups and dandelions amongst scores more unidentifiable blooms painted a pollen feast for bees whose hives had been carried out here by Han immigrants from the towns. For the brief Grasslands summer they actually live that hypothetical Desert Island Discs existence amidst this floral flood. Home is a rubberised tent, the permitted luxury a sack of rice. Apart from that the apiarists are self-sufficient. Grass is their tinder, yak dung their fuel. Drinking water is ingeniously collected from tent run-off, for it pours almost every day. This dispenses with the absolute necessity of boiling water, for at this altitude boiling point is as low as 85°C, a figure which not only explained my more than 'al dente' rice lunch, but also accounted for the illness that broke out within the Red Army as they crossed the Grasslands, drinking boiled, yet unboiled, water.

I had the same water problem, but thankfully had no fight with the Tibetan nomads apart from their dogs. The Zangzu were the only tribal people not to make peace with the Reds, a mistake one might say they have paid for ever since Mao sent the PLA to their Land of Snows in 1950. For the Tibetans had hassled the Reds at their lowest ebb, hounding the sick and exhausted stragglers of a fragmented herd like scavengers and drawing Red blood with their long knives. The Tibetans ruled the Grasslands then; now the Communists rule Tibet itself; but the Zangzu horseman, a warm, friendly descendant of his fierce grandfather is still the master of this plateau.

He is a fine sight mounted on his steed, an animal groomed only by the wild life, its shiny coat and defined muscles splattered with mud from the steeplechase that is animal husbandry on the Grasslands. Up he gallops at speed over turf and through sedge, a blur of streaking chestnut limbs and trailing tail, a sound of thudding hooves and splashing water, at one with his horse, which instinctively knows solid from sludge, checking and swerving accordingly like a veering wind. He swings his arm like a polo player and whoops like a cowboy in rounding up his *mao niu* (yaks).

The rider is saddled on a bright wool blanket and although the handle of his long bladed knife protrudes from under his yak-hair waistcoat he beams a broad smile of welcome and extends a practical hand of invitation to mount up and visit his *yurt*. This was my Trojan horse past the dogs, yet once inside I was effectively marooned and required an escort even to answer nature's call. This greatly amused my Zangzu hosts, but I took the danger of, well, being eunuched, much more seriously.

The wherewithal for life in this, one of the most remote areas of China, depended upon the yak. Zangzu people herded it, sheltered beneath it, slept on it, ate and drank it. It was truly their livelihood, perhaps in the same way the bison had been to the North American

Indian. The *yurt* of my host family of five was low – one had to walk stooped within it – and made from woven yak wool, its jet black and greasy surface looking like sackcloth. The structure was made safe on its exposed aspect by tens of guy ropes, themselves of braided yak hair secured in the turf with yak bones. The interior was illuminated naturally by a large central aperture beneath which a cauldron of yak milk simmered on a yak dung fire. Scores of plate-like pats of yak dung were drying around the fire.

We sat on huge yak pelts away from the smoky central area where the women prepared tea. They put a chunk of fibrous black matter, brick tea, into the milk. Boiled up this provided a tasty nutritious drink that looked like British tea apart from its thickness. Next came *zanba* – the staple of the Grasslands people. The ingredients were kept in small wooden chests. There was yak butter, very pale in colour, wholemeal roasted barley flour which was mixed with a little hot milk, and bones, half roasted but still too hard for my teeth, which gave added calcium. Each person mixes their own *zanba*, a lump of the dough being palmed, made sausage-like and fed into the mouth, taking care not to break off the dough and mould a ball or egg shape – which is considered unlucky or offensive. The Zangzu horseman carries a small leather bag of *zamba* with him. They advised me to do the same tomorrow.

*   *   *

It had been a dreadfully cold night in the *yurt*, the chill driving me completely, head included, under my blanket and yak skin despite its unpleasant tanny stench. Freezing fog dusting the grasses with frost blanketed the dawn grassland, at the same time immobilising the dog's jaw to silence with the efficiency of a dental jab. I reluctantly left this island of warmth and friendship, bidding farewell to my hosts to plod blindly north along the track. The memory of their generosity would stay with me long after the mug full of *zanba* they prepared for me was eaten, long after the whiff of their smoky yak dung fire was aired from my clothes.

The route of the Reds across these grasslands was tortuous, by way of stratagems, logistics and the uncertain way-finding of stragglers. At the tiny village of Mao'ergai to the east of Hongyuan the Red Army leaders held another meeting. The First and Fourth were reorganised into the Right and Left Columns respectively, primarily so as not to saturate the land but also to reduce friction between Mao and Zhang Guotao. Commander Zhu De led the Left Column for Zhang Guotao, their destination Aba on a northeasterly diagonal, while Xu Xiangqian headed the Right Column for Mao, their destination, and mine, being Baxi on the northern boundary of the Grasslands.

Beyond Aba and Baxi the plan was to reunite in Gansu, but the rift between Mao and Zhang on a suitable base area for the Reds was as pronounced as the national divide they were marching across. Streams flowing south fed the Yangzi system, the eventual direction of Zhang's 'splittist' backtrack after Aba. Across the divide Mao was following entirely different waters, the source streams of the Huang He, his goal being settlement in the base area nestled under the big bend of that Yellow River. It was awesome to think that China's two great rivers roared from such small sources, but more incredible perhaps that Mao's exhausted Red Army struggling across these godforsaken grasslands would achieve similar grandeur related to the affairs of man.

Forsaken but not forgotten, like Fylingdales golf balls on the North Yorkshire Moors, a mass of pure white *dagobas* (hand-bell shaped Buddhist shrines) loomed mysteriously in the now thinning fog. All were six to eight metres high and being almost identical resembled the output of a giant potter's oven. Close inspection revealed that they held small portraits of the Bainquen Lama. He was the leader of Tibetan Buddhism according to the Chinese Government – the puppet leader of Tibetan Buddhism installed by the Chinese Government in the eyes of Tibetans in exile. Between the *dagobas*, whose solid stone structures house some kind of holy relic, were hundreds of tattered prayer flags. This was Wu Qie, a temple village in the heart of the Grasslands.

I took refuge from the chill in the main prayer hall, where three worshippers were immersed in prayer, an activity that required more physical than verbal activity. One old man, wrapped in tattered blankets, burdened with a baby strapped to his back, shod in huge and clumsy yak-hide boots with upturned toes, plodded around pushing a beam that rotated a huge prayer wheel the size of a brewer's vat, which occupied the centre of the hall. The mechanics resembled that of a donkey yoked to a millstone grinding flour. The product here was spiritual staple: repetition of prayer and good karma. A by-product was exercise, for this frail man would surely have collapsed without the support of his holy zimmer.

Two other elders shuffled around the perimeter of the hall rotating much smaller brass prayer wheels with the urgency of jugglers trying to keep as many as possible spinning at once. Six or seven were the maximum. They barely batted an eyelid at me, totally hypnotised by their efforts. More worldly dependants of the temple were hypnotised by my very presence in Wu Qie.

Not that the arrival of a pilgrim on foot was unusual. But most were swarthy Tibetans in cloaks of mauve worsted, with leather fur-lined hats their flaps protruding like wings, necklaces of rough agate, jasper, turquoise or coral and big knives with blades the length of one's forearm for safety on the trail. Some were caked in dirt from prostrating themselves every few metres. They were convinced that I was a member of the big family of fifty-six nationalities, but I sensed it was their parochial insularity rather than my Mandarin tongue or PLA uniform that persuaded them.

It seemed that the cycle of the seasons was crammed into a single summer's day on the Grasslands. Throughout the morning freezing fog of deepest winter, depressing the grassland into a dank and lifeless morass, thinned to patchy mist enlivened by birdsong and water's trickles, sounds of spring. Afternoon sunshine filtered through to emerald the fescue whose sap appeared light-sensitive; its softening breeze rustled the verdant quilt of sedge, scattering the seeds of the countless wild flowers it hosted. Alas it was summer for only a brief few hours, swiftly a fading memory like the sunset's deep red as the giant disc rolled off the plateau's western rim into Qinghai, taking its warming rays and leaving words of warning to anyone crossing the great wilderness – begin seeking out shelter, a place to endure the nightly winter.

My hosts that night were Hans, strangers in the wilderness too. Unlike the Zangzu people, the Hans fought the Grasslands rather than lived off them. Fifty-six years after their grandfathers' generation had crossed this trackless void, they were contributing to the nation's modernisation by maintaining the track built in the late Fifties. The Government referred to their 'contribution towards the

New Long March'. The workers called their employment a bad job.

Just as the Reds could only recall the quagmires and illness, the road workers talked not of Grasslands beauty nor serenity but of backwardness. They were allergic to the yak's dairy products, milk and butter, on which the life of Zangzu people is so dependent. Instead they brought rice with them. The boiling point shortfall spelt indigestion at best, eventual dysentery at worst. My hosts therefore prepared supper using a pressure cooker.

The youngest man at the depot was Xue Dong, a recent middle-school graduate who spoke a few words of English. He shared his bed and quilts. We lay there top to tail talking about the life – or lack of it – out in the Grasslands. Each worker was responsible for different one-kilometre sections of the road. Everything was done by hand. When it rained, they did not work and the routine was six days a week, six months a year. On Sundays Xue Dong would cycle along his road to Zoige, my destination on the morrow and post a letter to his family.

After breakfast Xue Dong loaded up his bicycle with long handled shovel, pickaxe and wicker basket, filled both his water-bottle and mine with pressure-cookered water before we marched off together towards Zoige. After five or six kilometres Xue Dong parked his bike and began smoothing pot-holes on the track with fill scratched from the roadside.

I inferred that it was thirty-one kilometres to Zoige from the name of Xue Dong's depot. He wrote his address for me to mail a snapshot to him. It was the least I could do in return for his hospitality. An hour later I could still detect him working on the road, a dark speck upon a fawn strand crossing the pan-flat grassland, sending up dust clouds with his labour.

On the four and a half hour push to Zoige I saw only three vehicles to erode Xue Dong's road. One bus was at a halt, its dilapidation reminiscent of an amateur football team's changing room. It had, not surprisingly, halted for a pit stop. While passengers gave much needed fertility to the grassland – men on the left of the track, women on the other – one observant peasant yelled '*Tongzhimen, nimen kan kan, yi ge lao wai zou lu!*' (Comrades, look, an old foreigner walking!) There seemed only one response to give: 'Comrades, look, loads of Chinese *sa pao niao!*' You won't find that in the glossary.

Zoige, a Tibetan village, has been turned into a Han town in a deeper sense than merely its new name, Ruo'ergai. Once-proud warriors who rode horses now ride bicycles but their spirit rides with them no longer. Spontaneous waves, wild smiles and bravado charges have gone, replaced by forlornness. These tall swarthy figures with big noses, roundish eyes and thick lips keep their distinctive mauve dress, towering over the Hans, comparative matchstick midgets in their regimented green and blue.

Under a special law the *Gong An Ju* allow the Tibetans to carry their daggers, but they are probably used for cutting up water-melon, imported from beyond the Grasslands and too expensive for most. That goes for most of the products. For the Tibetans of town seem lost, jobless with no iron rice bowls, as alien to town life as the Han on the Grasslands. They amuse themselves with outdoor snooker, but what sport is that compared with the Grasslands version of polo – not with a ball and sticks but with a yak. The Tibetans are simply onlookers, window-shopping the treasures of the reforms which fill shelves with exotic products from legendary kingdoms of the east with evocative names like Beijing, Shanghai, Shenzhen, Zhuhai and Guangzhou. The Tibetans are torn between cultures, their Land of Snows, Xizang, rich in western treasures of the natural and spiritual sense, and the materialistic eastern treasures of the Han on the coast.

On the fourth morning I left Zoige early, striding out well despite patched feet in the hope that, according to my map, I might be out of the Grasslands by nightfall. I would always remember their stunning emptiness and beauty though I had witnessed them at a cost. Sleeping at altitude was at best restless, disturbed by dehydration, over-tiredness and the nightmarish recollection of growing encounters with dogs. Although such confrontations were like sport, exhuming my dormant instinct for survival, I felt that sooner or later I would be a loser.

At the edge of yet another ocean of grassland I began to climb laboriously up into some low hills whose gentle slopes nevertheless reminded me of the 3,500-metre altitude by the breathlessness they induced. Over the top I strode out downhill, continuing down, not into another ocean but down, down for kilometres off the edge of the plateau. The Grasslands had finished.

As I sped along a thickly wooded valley, as buoyant as the crystal

stream waters cascading at my side, I could well imagine the morale
of the Reds being similarly lifted. Gone was that piercing silence, as
lifeless as the grave. The stream gushed, the branches rustled and
within the forest birds sang. A spring had come after the winter of
the Grasslands. Every kilometre fell tens of metres and warmed up
by fractions of degrees. The men loosened their yak hides by untying
ropes and belts softened by boiling. They stank with almost two
weeks of grime, worsened by the mud of the bog and the stench of
the yak hides. Soon it was warm enough to bathe in the Baxi He
and wash tattered rags, then drape them on the bushes to dry
streamside, still used for the same purpose by the Zangzu women
of today.

The Zangzu had fled on the approach of the Reds but the pickings
were sparse – a few acres of unripe wheat and a stray yak here and
there. The forest provided more, some wild strawberries, elderberries
and mushrooms. By now experience had taught the Reds to survive
off the land. While the bulk of the Reds foraged for food, ecstatic
at their deliverance from the threat of suffocation in mud they were
largely oblivious to the crisis brewing between the Red Army leaders.

Mao and Zhou were dishevelled too, despite having ridden much
of the Grasslands on horseback. Mao's tall figure was accentuated
by his thinness. (I too had lost weight hiking the Great Snowies and
Grasslands.) Zhou, as usual for him, wore a beard; it was unusual
for a middle-aged Chinese to have facial hair and as such much
envied by contemporaries, being thought a sign of wisdom. What
Mao and Zhou had always suspected of Zhang Guotao came over
the radio waves. Zhang reported that his route north was blocked
by a flood-swollen river, and therefore he proposed to turn about
and abandon the Lianghekou plan. 'Couldn't' was a word that had
become obsolete in the vocabulary of the First Front Reds. It was
seen as an excuse to split, and for a time the leaders, including Mao,
were thought to have feared a putsch instigated by Zhang Guotao.
Still, with Kuomintang forces likely to be heading for the Sichuan–
Gansu border, Mao and the Right Column wasted no time over
trying to bring Zhang to heel and continued north alone. There
was only one route through the towering Minshan mountains that
straddled the provincial divide, a pass called Lazikou.

For me, it was a two and a half days' hike to Lazikou on legs already numbed and feet blistered from crossing the Grasslands, a mere lick as opposed to a taste of feeling the ingrained fatigue which must have plagued the Reds themselves. Pleasant riverside tracks, going with the flow and still cascading off the elevated Grasslands made kilometres fly. Firstly we followed the Baxi He as far as Chouge where the track ended, then negotiated a thirty-kilometre chain of footpaths through a range of mountains straddling the Sichuan–Gansu border, mountains which funnelled the Baxi He into cage-like gorges and restricted its flow to a few wild and broiling metres until it reached a wider valley north of Dala.

I had crossed more than a provincial boundary. Dropping off the Grasslands I had traversed crop and culinary contours too, as the barley that made *zanba* gave way to wheat and fruits. It was also an ethnic boundary. In the morning I had sat in the forest with brightly clad Zangzu women, drinking milky brick tea brewed on a smoky fire, sharing their *zanba* whose ingredients were kept in leather pouches – waistline lunchboxes that dangled from their belts as they foraged for firewood on the valley sides.

Later that day as I, and the Baxi He, joined the Bailong Jiang (White Dragon River), I found myself with the Hans, something the Reds were pleased about, their ethnic kith and kin. They offered me mugs of jasmine tea 'eureked' by the addition of large lumps of iceberg-like *bing tang* (crystal sugar), opaque in jagged fracture not unlike the Dolomitic peaks of the Minshan that scraped the sky towards the northern aspect. The Minshan rose spectacularly and appeared quite impenetrable. On paper they were a different, lower shade than the Great Snowies or even the Grasslands, but perhaps it was because the eye had been blinded by flatness to the horizon during the crossing of those Grasslands that the Minshan appeared so fearsome.

The sun had long dipped behind the Minshan as I branched off the Bailong to climb upwards from where the Lazi He babbled. I was exhausted by over a week's marching, the last two day push to this tiny stream equalling the fleet-footedness of Yang Chengwu's vanguard Reds. A Moslem, recognisable by his white skull-cap, drew alongside me on his bicycle like a seagull shadowing a ship. He was a welcome and amusing diversion to fatigue. Most Chinese outrightly praised the spirit of my Long March; in me they saw a foreigner feeling the hardships of the epic on which their country was founded. This Moslem was different, or stupid. To him, walking was a necessity enforced by a lack of money. He reached into his breast pocket and withdrew some 'big unities', ten *yuan* notes which portray the single-minded philosophy of the PRC – Socialism; the worker, peasant, soldier and intellectual working for mutual, national benefit. '*You meiyou qian?*' (Don't you have any money?) he asked.

Lazikou – the source of the Lazi River – may have only hosted a trickle of a stream, but nature made up for what it lacked in volume and speed by forming precipitous cliffs that seemed to overhang and block out almost all the sky. Here the KMT men were shielded by blockhouses perched to shower shells and bullets down on any foe crazy enough to attack this impregnable, unbelievably narrow gorge, a veritable needle whose eye could only be threaded by a front fifteen paces of a man in width.

For several hours the Reds sacrificed themselves as sitting ducks, until Mao, encamped to the south, called a halt to the attack. The echoes of the raging battle must have been deafening, a far cry from the absolute serenity, a reverend peace, that slept on Lazikou that balmy August evening fifty-six years after. Mao, ever the master tactician, assembled a group of about forty good scramblers. Men took off their belts – how useful they had been to the Reds, having already been boiled to anaemia – and strapped them together as makeshift ropes. Their job was to climb the cliffs, proceed north and bomb the blockhouses from above with grenades.

Hours later the mountaineering Reds had their revenge on the KMT blockhouses sitting below, and the gorge was a cataclysm of hell once more, as the Reds on the ground, poised for the advance, poured through Lazikou. Mao's route to north Shaanxi was now clear.

13

Reaching the Great Wall

Mao in Shanbei, 1936, from a photograph by Edgar Snow.

On the summit several long-distance truck drivers had stopped to smoke and steam, cooling off both their nerves and radiators. It gave me the chance to check out what might have been an hallucination. As I had shortcut the zigzags up the mountain, I had noticed what looked like Mao portraits through windscreens of passing vehicles. It was after all twenty odd years since the Cultural Revolution. Was I mistaken? Indeed not. Postcard-size pictures of Mao, embellished with red tassels, dangled inside the drivers' cabs. Later, on my return to Xi'an – and in many other cities – I would see them adorning almost every vehicle and being hawked to drivers waiting in traffic jams. It might have been 1967, except that the cars were multi-coloured imported models and the portraits were being sold, not issued free.

Though they labelled them 'Our Great Leader Comrade Mao

Zedong 1893–1993', souvenir makers appeared to be satisfying more than the market for centennial souvenirs. Clearly the portrait bearers had joined a cloaked protest – which they could not be criticised for – against the current leadership, suggesting that the Politburo had fallen short of Chairman Mao in serving the people. 'They judged Mao as seventy per cent good, thirty per cent bad,' one taxi driver told me. 'We rank them as thirty to seventy.'

It was the latest instalment of the Mao personality revival initiated in 1989 by Tiananmen's protesting students, who used the late Chairman to fire their bullets of dissatisfaction at Party corruption. Like the ideological squabble between Beijing and Taibei over the posthumous question of which side of the Taiwan Strait Sun Yat-sen would have stood on, Mao too is being torn between two sides – the masses and the government. The latter's ministries have hijacked the revival by funding a clutch of Mao movies and releasing new soft rock arrangements of revolutionary songs – another echo of the Cultural Revolution – in an attempt to fill the ideological vacuum created by Mao's death.

I was on Liupanshan, the last mountain for me and the Reds on the Long March: a none too taxing spur of Gansu's Longshou Range into Ningxia. In the distance I spotted a shimmering reddish-yellow blur. It looked every bit like a fire, except that there was no smoke.

In fact it was a single huge hoarding covered with calligraphy.

An hour later I stood in its shadow. It was the work of the man who started the fire, and had wafted it so effectively. The Long March was soon to end, and in the long term it would be judged beyond the survival of those few still marching with Mao. For there were tens of millions of peasants in the counties of ten provinces already traversed on the March smouldering with discontent at the Nationalists and their system. Mao's calligraphy read:

> The sky is high, the clouds are pale.
> We watch the wild geese vanish southward.
> If we fail to reach the Great Wall we are not men,
> We who have already measured twenty thousand *li*.
> High on the crest of Liupanshan
> Red banners wave freely in the west wind.
> Today we hold the long cord in our hands.

When shall we bind fast the Grey Dragon?

As the Red Army approached northern Shaanxi, long rumoured to be the base of 25th Army comrades, their overall strategy was put before them, just as it was laid before me here in Mao's poem *Liupanshan*. Mao was focusing on the Great Wall as his Army's next target.

Centuries before, emperors from Qin to Ming had built the Great Wall as a defence against Mongol and Xiongnu tribes. Now it was set to be a battle line once more – this time against the *Riben guizi* (the Japanese devils). Mao was already prioritising foreign invasion as China's most urgent problem whilst not overlooking the Grey Dragon, as he poetically dubs Chiang, who had been only temporarily shaken off.

Any preconceived notion as to the fertility of their promised land was soon brought down to dusty earth as the Reds trod the loess of the Huangtu Gaoyuan – the Yellow Earth Plateau. One of my steering badges, with Mao's inspiring words, 'If we fail to reach the Great Wall we are not men', erroneously depicted a stone-cased Wall, the like of which only exists in Hebei. Like everything else in Shanbei, as locals call the north of their province, the Great Wall is ochre, like the loess it is made from, a dried giant worm-cast segmented by centuries, brown like the sky when the wind from Mongolia blows, brown like the waters of the miserably thirsty rivers that seasonally appear in the steep gullies that dissect the tableland.

On a mid-autumn morning, under grey skies that had already dusted the plateau with the first taste of winter, clouds of dust were kicked up by the swollen and disfigured feet of four thousand Reds shuffling along a mule track to Wuqi. It was yet another alien landscape in the panorama these men had entered since leaving their red Jiangxi hills a calendar year before. Like the snow-capped Great Snowies and the nightmarish Grasslands, these loess hills were a new experience. Everything was dry and brown. Many Reds, hardly geographical scholars, thought they were on the edge of a Central Asian desert. There were few people and seemingly no homes. Some soldiers spotted red calligraphic couplets like those traditionally pasted to house portals for the mid-Autumn Festival. But they appeared to be stuck on rock faces. Indeed they were. Soon the Reds themselves would be tunnelling such *yaodongs* into the loess and living as troglodytes like Shaanxi folk, for this was Shanbei, their new home.

There were Mao Zedong, Zhou Enlai, Yang Chengwu, Deng Xiaoping, Yang Shangkun, Lin Biao, Xu Youwan, Zhong Ling, Gu Yiping. There were infantrymen, messengers, radio operators, scouts, bodyguards, nurses, propaganda workers and just thirty women, one of which was He Zizhen, who had lost her and Mao's third child to the Revolution. None of them were ordinary soldiers any more. Dead or alive they were all heroes.

It was October 19th 1935. Exactly one year before the Red Army had done the moonlight flit from Jiangxi. Their campaign might have been called the One Year War, or even the Great Escape. But one late October day, Mao picked up a writing brush, loaded it with ink and scrawled another poem to commemorate the conclusion of the greatest, most remarkable mass journey in human history. I had rehearsed it to help the countless kilometres pass by, but as I approached Wuqi I looked around at the loess hills, up at the Shanbei skies, and recited Mao's words once more:

> The Red Army fears not the trials of the Long March,
> Holding light ten thousand crags and torrents.
> The Five Ridges wind like gentle ripples,
> And the majestic Wumeng roll by, globules of clay
> Warm the steep cliffs lapped by the water of Golden Sand
> Cold the iron chains spanning the Dadu River
> Minshan's thousand *li* of snow joyously crossed
> The three Armies march on, each face glowing.

Hence the odyssey that had ended became known as *Chang Zheng* (the Long March). Legends would now begin and the epic would never be forgotten. The Revolution was set to continue.

By marching with Mao I had shared the hardships experienced by the Red Army. I had a thin harrowed face from too many miles on too few calories. I had a swollen knee, worms in the bowel from the bad water of the Grasslands, numerous boil-like mosquito bites and many blisters of respect for Mao. It had taken my march to really know the Long Marchers. Perhaps those who lived had suffered the most. The search for a new base had been so protracted and terrible that it was like a year-long crucifixion. Now it was time for the resurrection.

On the face of it, with just 4,000 out of 85,000 surviving, the Long March had been a rout. On the face of it though, the crucifixion had been simply death. Mao himself used the 'frog in the well' to expound his theory. To say that the Long March was a defeat was partially true. He conceded that the Red Army had been weakened by its shift in position. But that was not the full picture. It was not comprehensive – as short-sighted as the frog in the well looking skyward and saying, 'the sky is no bigger than the mouth of the well.' For the Long March was a psychological victory, a defiant act of survival.

Its significance, however, would depend on what this survival by the few against all odds was eventually to lead to, whether that be three days, years or decades later. The heroism of the Long Marchers, their optimism, unshaken devotion to the monumental task, their irrepressibility was set to be seized upon as the Party's role model, its founding myth. It was an entirely tangible one too – essential for a Marxist based ideology – supported by historical facts and promoted by participants. It was enacted by peasant soldiers and that made it reachable. The Communists would urge their soldiers, members and followers to uphold, learn from and emulate the spirit of the Long March – extraordinary and superhuman as it was, yet still attainable. Lowliness held no bars; on the contrary, it was a qualifier.

*　　　*　　　*

Before Mao's Communists could do anything for China they needed to survive themselves. Their year-long nomadic life, sustained by bartering, purchasing, confiscating and peasants' hospitality, was over. Now as Red Army settlers their primary task was to make the dusty hills of loess productive. Most would have regarded the task as monumental. It was. Shanbei soil is dusty, lacking humus and friable. The Reds ploughed and terraced it. The climate, on the fringe of the Ordos Desert was semi-arid. They dug wells to tap the ground-water.

Yields were pitifully poor which meant greater areas needed to be pressed into production. The Red Army was dispersed through the whole Shaanxi–Gansu–Ningxia Liberated Area. At the same time they were, as ever, an active fighting force with fronts to defend. Their Soviet was encircled, besieged. It was the start of an ongoing tradition within the Chinese Army – whether the Red Army of Workers and Peasants of 1935 or the People's Liberation Army of 1992 – to be self-sufficient, a fighting force and a productive machine.

Just two months after the end of the Long March Mao delivered a passionate and prophetic speech to the Politburo at their Wayaobao headquarters, a town halfway between Yan'an and the Great Wall. In what would become known as his treatise 'On Tactics Against Japanese Imperialism', Mao put the Long March into perspective and used the greatest episode of Red Army history to fire national spirit to smash Japan's colonialist dream of transforming China into part of their empire:

> Speaking of the Long March one may ask, 'What is its significance?' We answer that the Long March is the first of its kind in the annals of history, that it is a manifesto, a seeding machine. For twelve months we were under daily reconnaissance and bombing from the skies by scores of planes, while on land we were circled and pursued, obstructed and intercepted by a huge force of several hundred thousand men, and we encountered untold difficulties and dangers on the way; yet by using our two legs we swept across a distance of twenty thousand *li* through the length and breadth of eleven provinces. Let us ask, has history ever known a Long March equal to ours? No, never. The Long March is a manifesto. It has proclaimed to the world that the Red Army is an army of heroes, while the imperialists and their running dogs, Chiang Kai-shek and his like, are impotent. It has proclaimed their utter failure to encircle, pursue, obstruct and intercept us. The Long March is also a propaganda force. It has announced to some 200 million people in eleven provinces that the road of the Red Army is their only road to Liberation. Without the Long March how could the broad masses have learned so quickly about the existence of the great truth which the Red Army embodies? The Long March is also a seeding machine. In the eleven provinces it has sown many seeds which will sprout, leaf, blossom and

bear fruit, and will yield a harvest in the future. In a word, the Long March has ended with victory for us and defeat for the enemy. Who brought the Long March to victory? The Communist Party . . .

In the same delivery Mao criticised the general view held within the Party that the traditionally anti-Communist classes, particularly the bourgeoisie, could never become the allies of workers and peasants in a patriotic struggle against the Japanese.

The September 18th incident of 1931, in which the northeastern provinces of Heilongjiang, Jilin, Liaoning, Jehol and parts of Suiyuan (Inner Mongolia), Chahar and Hebei were annexed by the Japanese, had led to nationwide outrage from all strata of Chinese society. Naming the conquered territory Manchukuo and installing Pu Yi, the last emperor of the Qing, as their puppet emperor, the Japanese had further fuelled Chinese indignation, as had Chiang Kai-shek's non-aggressive stance towards the invaders. That autumn he had withdrawn the *Dongbei* – his Northeastern troops under Marshal Zhang Xueliang – to Shanhaiguan, the town where the Great Wall meets the Yellow Sea to the east of Beijing, prioritising the fight with the Reds rather than with the Red Sun.

Chiang was concerned that fighting the Japanese would weaken his forces whilst allowing Communist ones to strengthen. Fighting 'the disease of the heart' rather than 'the disease of the skin' was his strategy. But like this disfiguring analogy, the Japanese began to spread like acne on a teenager, moving south of the Great Wall to dominate Hebei and Chahar Provinces. Under the names of the Chinese and Japanese Generals He and Umezu a new chunk of China was signed, sealed and delivered over to the invaders with no armed resistance.

The disheartened *Dongbei* troops of Zhang Xueliang had now been moved to Xi'an under Chiang's orders, probably to distance them from staging an independent offensive to recover their Manchurian homeland, but also to add weight to the extermination campaign planned against the Reds in their new Shaanxi Base.

Chiang himself had gone to Lintong, outside Xi'an, to direct the killer blow which he forecast would be completed within one month. One wonders what he had in mind. On past performances, despite vastly superior weaponry and overpowering numbers, the KMT Goliath had always been repelled by the poorly armed Reds. Mobile guerrilla warfare was not their forte.

As I long marched, I had pondered why the KMT had failed repeatedly to exterminate the Reds. Even with odds stacked against them, the Reds pulled off military miracles one after another: at Jiaopingdu, Luding and Lazikou. I put it down to ideology. The Reds had one, the Whites did not. The KMT were a patch-and-paste army of warlords' puppet troops and mercenaries. At the height of battle many were reluctant to lay down their lives for no cause. How often they had fled, earning themselves the title 'bean curd troops', giving landslide victories to the Reds.

If anything the Shaanxi Base looked a tougher nut to crack than had the Soviet of Jiangxi. Lack of roads made it defensible by small forces, whose underground homes were hidden from KMT pilots – they would just be bombing mountainsides. Perhaps that is why Chiang abandoned any concern for the locals in deciding to use poisonous gas.

That was the plan. But Chiang had made the unbelievably naive mistake in surrounding himself in the Xi'an area with discontented troops. Zhang Xueliang had lost his father in a Japanese air raid. In April 1936 he had secretly entered the Shaanxi Base to negotiate with Zhou Enlai on the Communists' proposal for a united front against the Japanese. Most of Zhang's troops had had family members murdered, or wives, mothers and daughters forced into brothel service for the Japanese forces. Their lament was summed up in a contemporary song:

> My family is on the North East's Songhua River.
> There are forests and coal mines there,
> Beans and sorghum everywhere.
> My family is on the North East's Songhua River.
> There are my countrymen,
> My ageing Mother and Father.
> September 18th, September 18th!
> At that atrocious time
> I left my hometown and bade farewell
> to my dear Mother and Father

The time was ripe for mutiny.

*   *   *

It was December 1936. Piercing silence pervaded the Shanbei night. Snow encrusted the plateau and the moonlight flickered from dim to darkness as a bitter Ordos wind swept clouds of loess through the high atmosphere.

In Bao'an all was dark. *Kangs* – bed platforms that can be heated from below – were cold because of a fuel shortage. Peasants and Reds slept like sardines, whole families together, three generations side by side, or comrades together top to tail. Quilts and coats were piled high upon them making it difficult to turn over.

Outside one *yaodong*, however, a faint grid shadow wavered on the snow, for its wooden lattice windows were backlit, making the ovoid entrance look like the stained-glass window of a church illuminated for candlemass. The night owl inside was Mao Zedong. Keeping the candle burning like Chairman Mao in his Shanbei *yaodong* would become a synonym for working late into the night amongst future generations.

In the dim light Mao's silhouette seemed bulkier than it had done a year before at the end of the Long March. Deceptive winter padding was responsible for that. It was ten below zero in the *yaodong*. Under ashen grey cotton trousers Mao wore quilted leggings. As is customary in North China he kept his cap donned even indoors. His huge greatcoat, lined with the pelts of several Ningxia curly lambs, was badly soiled.

For Mao, 1936 had been a year of mixed fortunes. An Eastern Expedition to fight the Japanese had been unsuccessful: the Red Army had been forced to turn back across the Yellow River after meeting heavy resistance from the encircling Kuomintang. Zhou Enlai's secret meeting with the *Dongbei* Marshal Zhang Xueliang had promised much, but as yet had failed to deliver. However, the year had ended optimistically with Red strength increased by the arrival of the Fourth and Second Armies. All Long Marches were over. What would 1937 hold in store?

As with his followers, his ideals had left no room for normal family life. His first wife had been killed in Changsha, his brother Mao Zetan beheaded in Ruijin. He Zizhen had borne him three children, but none slept beside her. They were forcibly abandoned, given away to peasants in Jiangxi and Guizhou.

In Xi'an, just 400 kilometres south of Bao'an, was Chiang Kai-shek. The city, my base for the duration of my biographical journey was now the focus of it. Xi'an had been the ancient dynastic capital of the Middle Kingdom for 1,100 years, and ironically it was at one of its ancient sites, the Tang Dynasty resort of Huaqing Springs, that a crucial incident now decided the fate of China in the face of Japanese aggression.

Huaqing Springs at Lintong, thirty kilometres from the city, was built by Tang Emperor Xuan Zong for his favourite concubine Yang Guifei, said to be one of the most beautiful women in Chinese history. The resort suited Chiang's sybaritic tendencies too. Pavilions set amidst pine and cypress, pools and rockeries, had thermal spring water piped to every room. In his warm pavilion, carpeted with thick Tientsin rugs, fine paintings and potted landscapes, the general-issimo strutted in his long silk gown on the eve of unleashing his 'extermination campaign to suppress the Red bandits'. Coming from Zhejiang, and the warlord class, for him silk was not a luxury. He slept on it and beneath it.

On the night of December 12th trains were chugging to Xi'an from weapons factories and ports, laden with ammunitions for the onslaught. The *Xibei* (Northwestern) and *Dongbei* (Northeastern) armies under Yang Hucheng and Zhang Xueliang were poised for the attack.

In the interests of Sino-Japanese friendship, guides to the Five Chamber Pavilion used by Chiang say little to embarrass Japanese tourists visiting Huaqing, yet they would not be far off the mark if they suggested that had the Xi'an Incident not occurred, Huaqing might now have Japanese administrators rather than tourists. But they are less diplomatic about Chiang, stating that after an exhaust-ing night with his concubine he was disturbed by dawn gunfire as Zhang Xueliang's men overpowered his guards. With no time to dress he slipped on a nightgown and, 'scared to death', climbed out of the window and over the back wall. Hours later, white with cold and fear, he was found crouched in a crevasse up Lishan mountain minus his false teeth, by his own men, officers of the *Dongbei* army acting on Zhang Xueliang's orders. Chiang Kai-shek demanded to be shot but a Captain Sun refused saying 'We will not shoot you. We only ask that you lead our country against Japan.'

Chiang was taken to Xi'an by car and for two weeks kept under house arrest for negotiations on co-operating with the Communists patriotically against the Japanese. Zhou Enlai represented the Red Army. The demands of the *Dongbei* and *Xibei* troops were as follows:

1. Reorganise the Nanjing Government and admit all parties to share the joint responsibility of national salvation.
2. End all civil war immediately and adopt the policy of armed resistance against Japan.
3. Release leaders of the patriotic movement in Shanghai.
4. Pardon all political prisoners.
5. Guarantee the people liberty of assembly.
6. Safeguard the people's rights of patriotic organisation and political assembly.
7. Put into effect the will of Dr Sun Yat-sen.
8. Immediately convene a National Salvation conference.

These eight demands were finally conceded by Chiang on December 24th 1936. Mao had received an unexpected 43rd birthday present.

* * *

For most of the next decade the Chinese people were immersed in their monumental struggle against the Japanese aggressors. This bloody and protracted war, in which twenty-one million Chinese soldiers lost their lives, was not only vital to China's survival, but to the world's too. If Japan had not been entrenched in protracted war with China their venom against the Allies would have been far fiercer. The Allies, however, were in no mood to thank the Communists for their contribution. They threw all their support behind Chiang Kai-shek, as the KMT and the Reds resumed their battle for control of China.

The Allies' efforts were in vain.

In September 1949 – four years after Hiroshima, and twenty-two years after the Communists first split from the Nationalists – the bulk of KMT forces had been wiped out or had surrendered to the besieging PLA. Chiang Kai-shek fled to Taiwan to set up his own independent state, leaving Mao at last in full control of mainland China.

14

Standing-Up

The dawn sentry marching out to raise the Chinese flag, Tiananmen Square.

Qi, her father Wu Wanchun and I waited in the waning darkness to see a flag-raising ceremony Wu Wanchun had not seen for forty-two years.

Beijing was slowly coming alive. Squads of soldiers, crack units barracked behind the Great Hall of the People, jogged past, their leader prompting patriotic chants should the men dawn-dream, like myself.

I felt somewhat less energetic at 5.45 a.m. I sat down and thought of flag-raising witnessed on my travels. Dawn-dreaming took me to a Gansu village, two thousand kilometres from Beijing, to see schoolchildren coddled in padded jackets, trousers and headscarves. My flashback was disturbed by sweeping, a sound of daybreak in Chinese cities just as the cockcrow is to the countryside. I picked out the faint glow of white caps, facemasks and shirts in the waning darkness. They approached slowly and machine-like, their occupants' metronomic action like boatmen paddling across water towards me, each sweep of the besom a pull of an oar. I was obliged to move: Tiananmen Square, said to hold a million at a push, was having its every square metre brushed.

By way of his portrait adorning Tiananmen, the Gate of Heavenly Peace, Mao still presides over the flag-raising each dawn. The First Sentry of the Motherland, as the keepers of the flag are called, part of the *Wu Jing*, emerged from the passage beneath his portrait. A few commuting cyclists kerbed their bikes as the sentry crossed Chang'an Avenue to the flagpole where the colour was raised by the press of a button and a recording of 'March of the Volunteers'. Forty-two years ago a quarter of a million cheered. At the crack of dawn today there were a few hundred. One of them, apart from Mao, was present on both occasions – Wu Wanchun.

Tiananmen is now the biggest square in the world – a size to swallow up twenty Trafalgars, ten St Peters or eight Reds – but in 1949, Qi's father pointed out, it was just a fraction, perhaps one tenth, of its present size. In those days, gates of the Forbidden City crossed the avenue, and none of the Stalinesque buildings now bordering the Square existed. The Great Hall of the People and Revolutionary Museum came in 1959, products of the drive to construct ten big buildings to celebrate China's tenth birthday.

On that day in 1949, a young man, studious and bespectacled, Wu Wanchun was far from his hometown of Chaoxian on the Yangzi River in Anhui Province. He had been born twenty-six years before in 1922 – more or less the time it had taken the Chinese Communists to rise to power after their founding congress in 1921 to this solemn autumn day of 1949. He was the eldest of three sons.

It turned out on detailed questioning that there was a daughter in the family too, but in old China, even if a family had three sons and a daughter, the parents would not include female issue in the admitted size of their household. After graduating from school, Wu Wanchun taught mathematics, but in 1946 he left Anhui for Beiping. He had won a scholarship to study physics at Beiping Da Xue (*Beida*) – the city's premier institution.

The student technicians of *Beida* were given an important task to perform. A public address system, made in the United States, was delivered for overhaul. It consisted of nine loudspeakers and the students who pasted and patched it back to good repair called it the nine-headed bird.

On October 1st, he and his fellow students set off from the university just two kilometres away two hours before the ceremony began. In Beiping's shaded avenues chock-a-block with animal carts, rickshaws and bicycles, notices already adorned the red walls of the Forbidden City informing citizens of Beiping they had a new government. It was too late to change the words of his banner to reflect the city's new name, Beijing.

The weather was fine, characteristic of the capital's golden season, October, when the sapping humidity of high summer has thankfully waned but the chill, dust-laden yellow wind from the north has not blasted the trees bare. Just before ten on that hopeful autumn morning, Mao Zedong, dressed in a brown worsted Sun Yat-sen style suit, flanked by men and women he knew well from the Long March and the Yan'an years, walked slowly and purposefully up the steps for his hard won appointment with the world as the leader of China.

At his side were Zhou Enlai, Zhu De, Liu Shaoqi, Dong Biwu, Soong Ching Ling, Li Jishen and Gao Gang. Huge red silk banners floated in the light breeze reminiscent of the same banners of war first waved by charging Reds in the Twenties.

Now as Mao Zedong stood on the balcony of the Gate of Heavenly Peace he was claiming state power over a country crippled by twelve years of bloody war. Mao himself had been fighting since the 1927 Autumn Harvest Uprising. Peasants had spent more time fighting than planting. Industry was crippled. Railways and roads needed repair. The economy was in total ruins.

Mao's quality as a guerrilla leader and masterly military strategist was without doubt. The big question on October 1st 1949 was whether this same man could unite the country and resurrect the economy. He had some, albeit limited, experience. Mao and his Long March comrades had governed the Shaanxi Base from Yan'an for a decade, organising production, promoting thrift and self-sufficiency and issuing currency. Spiralling inflation caused by the Nationalists' war effort was one of the main problems confronting the new Communist government. As the young Wu Wanchun stood in Tiananmen he carried a large bagful of banknotes necessary to buy a simple lunch of rice and vegetables.

The party moved to the centre of the balcony. Zhu De, in his capacity of commander of PLA forces spoke, urging his men to swiftly wipe out the remnant KMT and liberate all China. As Zhu De's message echoed in the Square below, Wu Wanchun's attention was drawn to a nearby loudspeaker delivering it. It was the public address system which his department, he and his classmates, had overhauled! He felt excitement and more than a tinge of pride in helping the crowd hear the address, but at the same time a hint of fear and anxiety should the system malfunction and not amplify the words of Mao who now stood before the microphone.

'The Chinese people have stood up!'

Wu Wanchun was sceptical. Having lived in Anhui, a province which changed colour from White to Red and back again during long years of guerrilla warfare, he thought Mao's proclamation was a little premature and might be short-lived. Although he returned to the dormitories that afternoon through a new city, Beijing, the capital of the People's Republic of China with a new flag and national anthem, the city streets he passed along were still plagued with the usual ills. Beggars were numerous; in the markets girls, boys and even wives could be bought. Pimps gambled over mahjong whilst their girls extorted cash and kind from opium addicted good-for-nothings. But things were set to change.

After so many years of war the country craved for peace which came surprisingly quickly. By the new year of 1950, whilst Chairman Mao was in Moscow in quest of financial and technical assistance from Stalin for the reconstruction of the economy, all mainland China except Tibet was liberated. Speculation in commodities, to the delight of the general populace, was halted. Instead of being paid in worthless wads of banknotes – which were Kuomintang issued anyway – employees received daily necessities: flour, rice and cooking oil. But everything was in short supply. The students of *Beida* were urged to save one *liang* (about fifty grams) of rice a day. The system was the start of the *liang piao* (crop tickets) and *fushiben* (ration book) era, which Deng Xiaoping's economic reforms have more or less abolished. Life improved quickly in the early Fifties and citizens really believed what the CCP had for so long been saying.

This was New China: gone were the selfish, looting and raping Nationalists; in were the selfless, sharing and caring Communists.

Wu Wanchun was assigned to PLA service in Zhangjiakou to the northwest of Beijing. He managed to arrange a job for his schooldays' sweetheart, Bao Cuiru, as a middle-school teacher in the military college there. Then, as now in China, people wanting to marry must be granted permission from their *danwei* (unit or employer). The Army refused to give them permission. It is likely that Bao's parentage was the problem. She was a landlord's daughter although it was told in Chaoxian county that her father paid and treated his peasants well before Liberation. That opinion was probably correct, as her brother, who inherited the family land, was not one of the many landlords rounded-up, tried and executed during the early Fifties.

There seemed only one way to solve the marriage problem. Bao Cuiru became pregnant and although the couple were criticised for doing things in the wrong order, they were issued with a marriage certificate. On December 18th 1951 their baby was born, a girl, the first of three daughters given names all translating as different forms of 'beautiful jade'. But Wu Qiong sounded too much like 'poor' even though the written character was a semi-precious stone. Dismayed at being nicknamed 'poor girl' at school – this, despite the supposed proletarian pride of New China – she changed her name to Wu Xiaoping. This meant 'little ordinary': common but not the contradiction of value and poverty of her birth name. It proved to be a prophetic change. When the Great Proletarian Cultural Revolution came about, Wu Xiaoping found her name fitted well into the mainstream of desired ordinariness. Aged fifteen in 1966 she was at the young edge of the generation that were the blood of the Cultural Revolution, a bizarre decade that bled all Chinese of ten years of life, and Wu Xiaoping of ten years in her prime.

15

Stuck on Mao

Wang Anting in his Museum of the Cultural Revolution.

Recent Chinese history should be within easy reach. Compared with the rare Long March testimonies, a library of tens of millions of witnesses, perhaps hundreds of millions where the Cultural Revolution is concerned, is theoretically available. A library yes, but hardly full of open books. The bad news is that most people are still, even in the era of the emancipated mind and openness of the early Nineties, reluctant to tell stories that everyone knows, but nobody wants to divulge on the record, especially to a foreigner.

Fortunately, I found myself in a privileged position, being an insider with a Chinese wife. So from now on my biographical journey through Mao's life would at the same time be a biography of my wife's family, and in particular an autobiography – by way of the diaries that she kept – of my sister-in-law Wu Xiaoping.

In telling their story, am I endangering them, should another

Cultural Revolution return? I emphatically think not. China is accelerating and deepening her reforms in order to create a Socialist Market Economy, coming to terms with her past, good and bad, over the past forty odd years. That everything Mao did during his life was great and praiseworthy is well past its believe-by date: that went out of the window in December 1978 when Deng Xiaoping delivered his watershed speech, 'Emancipate the Mind, Seek Truth from Facts'. Anyway, there are no state secrets here, only vignettes of the madness that pervaded all facets of daily life during that decade.

As a prelude to reliving Wu Xiaoping's Cultural Revolution, I went to 23, Wufu Jie in Chengdu, Sichuan province, to visit Mr Wang Anting. It was told he had considerably embarrassed certain authorities by 'holding an exhibition with the nation's dirty underwear'. When I arrived at Mr Wang's home I realised that he was stuck on Mao, warts and all. He had collected over 20,000 Mao badges, hundreds of magazines and newspapers, posters and porcelain busts. Here was preserved New China's darkest past.

'I founded my museum to remind people about Mao's good deeds. I wanted to call it the Museum of the Cultural Revolution but the Chengdu authorities wouldn't let me,' complained Wang. 'You shouldn't forget the man who dug the well to give the people water to drink.'

Government propaganda could hardly be accused of neglecting Mao. However, having judged the Cultural Revolution as an outright disaster, official chroniclers censor that entire decade from national museums. But Wang has centred his collection precisely on that period. In a way he is curator of China's most honest museum, a realm of raw and wild history that was Maoism.

Wang's home is twenty metres square – about one and a half times the size of a standard British garage – and it reeked revolution from every nook and cranny. One could almost hear the shouts of Red Guards who once wore the badges. Wang Anting displays his hoard in home-made cases, pinned on to sheets, glued upon walls and suspended from the ceiling, but many more are unseen, stuffed into sacks in the loft or filling water butts in the kitchen. With his last census recording 10,039 different versions, Wang cannot afford to be seen wearing the same badge twice. He even has luminous ones for nighttime wear.

Ranging in diameter from a tiny one centimetre to a plate-like thirty-eight, they come in porcelain and plastic but the majority are of alloy that would normally have been cast into aircraft fuselages and wings – had not Lin Biao hijacked that industry's production to put Mao up in the sky instead, first to deify him, then to knock him back down to earth for a premature appointment with Marx. Mao reportedly became so fed up with the veneration he ordered Lin Biao, 'Give me my aircraft factories back!' Chinese joke that if Lin had not ruined the aviation industry he might just have found an airworthy plane in which to effect escape to Moscow following the failed assassination of Mao he directed in Hangzhou. After leaving Ulaan Baataar for Beijing on the final stage of my Trans-Siberian return to China, I had looked east into the Mongolian wastes towards Ondor Chaan, the point where Lin Biao's plane crashed. In 1971 Xinhua reported tardily that the escape plane had run out of fuel, but rumour and logic suggest Mao had his comrade turned traitor-in-arms shot down.

Wang Anting's pictorials captured the gut reaction to the news that Lin had tried to kill God. Lin Biao's eyes are, more often than not, neatly burnt out by cigarette ends. On the cover of one magazine a carefully routed tear goes right through his eyes. I asked Wang and Ke Wang, his close comrade, to hold different issues of the pictorials standing at the door of the museum-cum-warehouse of the Cultural Revolution. I chose the magazines carefully to encompass the birth and death of the period. The oldest edition, dated July 1967, showed Mao and Lin reviewing Red Guards from the Gate of Heavenly Peace. The later one, dated November 1976, captured the scene in the Square almost a decade later during Mao's funeral rally. But Ke Wang could not bear to hold up a picture of Lin Biao the traitor, saying, 'It was him who killed Chairman Mao!'

Whereas Wang admitted that Chairman Mao made errors, Ke Wang was adamant that the Chairman was faultless despite the official line of his Party. Even more eccentric than Wang Anting, Ke Wang had been to Beijing many times, and without fail on arrival he goes directly to the mausoleum on Tiananmen to pay his respects to Mao's remains.

Because the badges are, for most, unsightly warts on their youth, haunting memories of the so-called wasted decade, many Chinese abhor, and hence discard, them. This poison, I discovered, was Wang Anting's meat as we sat outside in the alleyway snacking on a Sichuanese speciality of pig's ears in chilli. A ghetto-blaster borrowed from a neighbour beat out the chants of the chart-topping cassette 'Red Sun'.

'Long Live Chairman Mao!' shouted Wang above the din, raising a cup of rice wine. Bemused cyclists rang their bells. To complete the bottleneck up rolled a garbage collector, the two straw panniers of his bike stuffed full with cardboard and newspapers. He pulled out a clutch of badges and an eighteen-inch plastic statuette. This is the source of Wang's collection; badges cost four *yuan* per *jin* (forty pence per pound). The rag and badge man asked two *yuan* for the statuette. Wang spotted a crack on Mao's upstretched arm. He eventually got it for two *mao* (two pence) scrap value.

Wang Anting started collecting at the end of the Cultural Revolution. It was the first time in over ten years that selling all those stored newspapers, posters, badges and busts was not regarded as anti-revolutionary. But Mao's tarnished image was to plummet to an all-time low during the 1980–81 trial of the Gang, when his third wife Jiang Qing said, 'Arresting me and bringing me to trial is a defamation of Chairman Mao because I have implemented and defended his proletarian revolutionary line!' She likened her loyalty to that of a dog. 'When he said bark, I barked, and when he said bite, I bit.' When Jiang Qing said that, the Chinese people threw away their Maoist idols and junk en masse. She received a suspended death sentence, later moderated to life imprisonment, being interned in Qin Cheng No 1, Changping County, Beijing, where many pro-democracy activists would be detained after their capture in 1989. It is believed that Jiang Qing thoroughly approved of the Draconian measures used to suppress that movement. Suffering from cancer she was allowed, from the mid-Eighties, to live in the relative comfort of a Beijing home where she is reported to have studied her husband's works until her last day. She committed suicide by hanging in the early hours of May 17th 1991, the day after the twenty-fifth anniversary of the launch of the Cultural Revolution. On the previous day's *Renmin Ribao* (*People's Daily*) she had scrawled a revolutionary slogan. Twenty-five years before it had carried the May 16th Circular, a directive to begin the Cultural Revolution.

While the Gang of Four prepared to spend the remains of their lives imprisoned, Mao's reputation began to lose its face. His statues were destroyed all over China, mostly under the veil of darkness. 'Chengdu's main statue was too big to be detonated,' explained Wang, and fortunately it survived its suspended sentence until the public's opinion on Mao picked up again. 'Now it's cleaned annually by the city authorities,' he said proudly.

With the backlash against Mao subsiding in the mid-Eighties people looked more objectively at his overall career and his immortal contributions to China therein. Moreover, with the centenary of his birth in 1993, Wang Anting said growing numbers were interested in his home-full of cultural relics, increasing in their scarcity and value. Wang's wife does not bring the washing in every evening; she brings in the Maoist relics of her husband's collection encroaching along the alleyway. 'That embroidery is Suzhou silk,' said Wang, pointing to a two-by-one-metre grey and white portrait.

Wang has put all his money into buying exhibits for the museum. His work papers denote his occupation as 'Propagandist of Mao Zedong Thought'. Entrance fees are set at an appropriate 1 *mao*, takings which are surely absorbed by the jasmine tea and peanuts his wife offers to visitors. Unaffected by consumerism sweeping through China's fourteen-year-long open doors, Wang Anting is certainly no average citizen. As other Chinese strive for personal modernisations Wang buys all his clothing from the rag and badge man. His only electricals are his hearing aid and a dim lightbulb above his bed. When he wakes up Mao is everywhere. 'It makes me feel as if I'm with Chairman Mao; that's all the comfort I need.' But Wang did admit to cherishing one dream – to see Chairman Mao in Beijing. The rail fare however, at two months the average wage of a Chinese worker, is prohibitive. A Dutch visitor once donated a sum specifically for Wang to realise that ambition. Instead he sent his comrade, Ke Wang, to the post office to buy stamps and stationery needed for mailing out his society's newsletter. To serve members is a passion that consumes all similarly intended donations, monies which are meticulously accounted for in a mimeographed newsletter.

In view of the role badges had played in sparking the idea of my biographical journey I applied without hesitation to join the Mao Zedong Badge Collecting and Research Institute, happy to support Wang Anting's service to history uncensored. On the filling out of an application form, forwarding two photographs and a subscription of ten *yuan* I would later receive a red plastic membership card bearing a silhouette of the Chairman on the cover. Inside I was referred to as having the political face of 'the masses' and given the title of Foreign Honorary Director to go alongside my Foreign Red Army nickname.

Wang Anting's life could be set to change whether he likes it or not. He proudly recalls his rejection of a US$50,000 offer for the collection to be exported to the United States. In Mao's centenary year the Museum of Revolutionary History on Tiananmen Square 'urged' Wang to donate his collection in return for Beijing citizenship and a pension. Wang remained unbudged. Indeed it would be a great loss for his atmospheric collection to have such an uncertain future where it might never go on exhibition. China is at best pink but, with loyalist Wang still alive, 23 Wufu Street will always be red.

16

Wu Xiaoping's Cultural Revolution

Wu Xiaoping and fellow Red Guards after seeing Chairman Mao in Beijing.

One and a quarter million of them, mainly teenagers but some in their early twenties, had travelled from all over the country. From the middle of the night they waited, huddled together on the pavements. Dawn brought echoing chants of his approach, and a pressure wave of commotion reverberated through the packed streets. He came with the sunrise. They rose to their feet. An anticipated push and shove began as necks were craned. Up on their toes they were pressed together like meat pie. Cheers grew louder and clearer. A vanguard car swept by to announce that he was coming.

Butterflies on a wave of adrenalin set hearts racing. Breathless, they sweated despite the cool chill of dawn. The climax: he passed slowly by, standing up in the rear of a converted jeep. He was a master of public relations, his wave seeming to be an extended handshake, his roving eyes making hypnotic eyeball contact with all. Boys and girls cried uncontrollable tears of joy in his wake, tears that went unwiped, left to roll proudly off bulging red cheeks to spot collars and breasts. Now they were complete. It was only a fleeting moment, a few seconds at five metres, but it was the greatest thrill of their young lives.

It being October 18th 1966 one could be forgiven for thinking that the Beatles were being welcomed to Los Angeles, Paris or Tokyo. But this was Beijing, Chairman Mao's patch. From August to November he received some eleven million youths who flocked to the capital on Mao worshipping trips, officially sanctioned as *Da chuanlian* (exchanges of revolutionary experiences). They were clear enactments of the personality cult being built around Mao under the direction of Lin Biao, who mobilised the military and requisitioned trains to transport and accommodate the young generation on the move. Their fanaticism, although concurrent with the Beatlemania afflicting Western youth, made the latter look tepid. The legacy of it all would also be a hell of a lot less melodious.

Lin Biao had recently replaced Liu Shaoqi as Mao's chosen successor. Liu and Deng Xiaoping were the moderates within the Politburo who had righted the nation with Rightist policies after the disastrous Great Leap Forward of 1958–59. When Liu became Head of State in 1962 he implemented an incentive-based system to kick start the economy, paying out overtime and bonuses to workers and peasants. Mao regarded Liu Shaoqi's bestselling book *How to be a Good Communist* a 'poisonous weed' that advocated bourgeois revisionist policy. Coupled with Mao's growing mistrust of Liu was the jealousy that Jiang Qing, Mao's third wife, had for Liu's fifth wife, the attractive Wang Guangmei. By promoting Lin Biao, Mao hoped to ensure that he controlled the barrel of the gun.

'*Wenhua Da Geming*' (The Cultural Revolution) had begun five months before Wu Xiaoping – or Sister Xiaoping as I call her, for that is the accepted form of address to such a relative in China – saw Chairman Mao in Beijing. Her family by then had 'five mouths' including two sisters, Wu Lin and my future wife Wu Qi. During the Great Leap Forward in 1959 they moved from Zhangjiakou to Xi'an in Shaanxi under a programme relocating universities and key defence industries to the hinterland, based on Mao Zedong's fear of an attack from the United States. The Wu family, used to the emerald lush rice paddy landscape of Anhui's lower Yangzi basin, thought dusty and treeless Xi'an a step backwards rather than any Great Leap Forward.

This economic plan to accelerate the industrial and agricultural production of China called upon the 650 million populace to compensate for decades of decline by intense hard work. The revolutionary that he was, Mao believed that anything could be achieved with hard graft, long hours and dogged determination: the Long March spirit.

The Long March was however a matter of life or death. Vastly improved agricultural and industrial production was not. Although the Great Leap Forward produced some miracles – high valley terracing to boost acreages, long railway tunnels and the Great Hall of the People put up in eight months – the drive turned into an economic and human disaster.

Why then, I asked Sister Xiaoping, did this attempt to make the Chinese economy run fast end up by making it crawl? She recalled the iron and steel production campaign. Mao had pronounced that China's production must overtake the UK's within seven years. Everyone was urged to make that a reality by setting up local furnaces. Those arriving at the smelter with hands full were praised, those empty-handed were criticised. Sister Xiaoping scoured the family flat for bits and pieces and took away all but the wok and chopper, while cycling at night became dangerous, as some people stole man-hole covers to add weight to their contributions!

Blind obedience, coupled with an achieve-it or lie-about-it attitude also afflicted the peasantry who shouldered the responsibility of feeding the nation. The situation was reminiscent of the stupidity that pervaded the court whose king donned the supposedly invisible clothes. Everyone below the all-powerful Mao was fearful of divulging the facts: that in the wake of the frenetic production drive of 1958 the peasantry were exhausted and disillusioned. This, coupled with freak 1959 weather, made production nosedive. Food shortages became widespread. Anhui, the province where the Wu family have their roots, was severely hit. Sister Xiaoping saw her baby sister, Wu Qi, brought back to Xi'an 'as thin as noodles'. Her father's unit however, in Xi'an, was well supplied because its engineers did research for the PLA.

The PRC's honeymoon years of hope, honesty and common sense of post Liberation were long since gone. The Party's omnipresence based on the *danwei* in towns and the *gongshe* (commune) of the countryside was stringently controlling the people in thought and action. The CCP had lifted a big stone, only to drop it on its own foot. Brainwashing and intolerance of individuality backfired, as Party officials from unit level upwards to Zhongnanhai – the Politburo and State Council's residences in central Beijing – kept Chairman Mao satisfied by leading him to believe the Great Leap Forward was successful. Mao, who prided himself on keeping in touch with the broad masses, had distanced himself. It seems that only one man was determined enough to tell Mao frankly that it was all a big cover up, just like the individual who told the naked king that he should cover himself up. That was Peng Dehuai, a man who had been beside Mao since Jinggangshan in 1928 and would eventually die disgraced in the Cultural Revolution. Meanwhile the pragmatists, Liu Shaoqi and Deng Xiaoping began to rebuild the economy.

*   *   *

What made Chairman Mao, a seventy-three-year-old, so appealing to the generation young enough to be his grandchildren? The answer to this question is, I believe, the key to understanding the mechanics of the Cultural Revolution.

It was that he offered them a chance to rebel. Older generations were fed up with conflict; only the teenagers were interested in revolution any more. They were the sole generation in the populace who had not experienced upheaval and cataclysm. And there were plenty of them. The relatively calm post-Liberation years had produced a baby boom. Bored with daily school life which was, and still largely is, an unimaginative production-line system, they were now treated to *Da chuanlian*, put into army clothes and given delusions of grandeur above their traditional status of children. In one fell swoop the millennium-old Confucian respect for elders was shattered. Their *Little Red Books* and armbands were licences to a rebellion that degenerated into carte blanche for brute violence and disorder. One only has to stand outside any middle school, be that in China or Britain, to see the latent and apparent yobbo nature that Mao masterfully recruited to play out his great experiment – an attempt to brainwash the Chinese people and mould a proletarian clone of obedient workers, peasants and soldiers.

Historically, the Red Guards were originated by the Qinghua University middle school in Beijing. At the first of the eight Tiananmen Red Guard rallies, a teenage pig-tailed *Hong wei bing* (Red Guard) pinned an armband on to Chairman Mao as he stood waving to the million in the Square below. Mao suggested to the girl that she changed her name from Binbin, which meant gentle and graceful, to Yaowu (Desire to be warlike). A wave of name-changing, in adults and teenagers alike, swept the nation. Qi's mother changed hers from Bao Cuiru to Bao Yibing, meaning 'one soldier'.

Red Guard units sprang up in schools, streets and units. Sister Xiaoping, then fifteen, tried to join her middle-school Red Guards. Being the top student of her year, an excellent *san hao* (three goods) scholar, became an immediate yoke to bear. Now was the time to be average, preferably below average and never the best at anything. Although her father, Wu Wanchun, was in the army, being a deputy professor he was regarded as merely an intellectual in a soldier's uniform, an undesirable class rank, the 'stinking ninth' of society alongside landlords, rich peasants, counter-revolutionaries, bad elements, rightists, renegades, enemy agents and 'capitalist roaders'. A good background was parentage and grandparentage in either the worker, peasant or soldier class. Sister Xiaoping had both parents as intellectuals and grandparents who were bourgeoisie and landlords. Only having relatives in the Kuomintang was worse than that.

Rejected by her own middle school, she joined an older Red Guard group at her father's university amongst youngsters who were either top students themselves or intellectuals' children. Hence some Red Guard units were 'redder' than others. In the ensuing months they would criticise, fight and wage war on each other.

As for all Red Guards, the chance to go to Beijing for Sister Xiaoping was a golden, or perhaps one should say red, opportunity. Chairman Mao gave them that chance. She left Xi'an with only ten *yuan* wearing her father's uniform. She used his jacket as a coat with a belt on it and rolled up the trousers. His cap fitted well when she stuffed her two long plaits into it. Only a couple of Mao badges had been issued: the glut – almost one for every speech, meeting, conference, directive, revolutionary episode and site – would come in 1967 and 1968. She pinned one badge that exhorted 'Serve the People' on her left breast – by her heart, for she loved Chairman Mao.

Lin Biao had recently published the *Little Red Book*, the ideological Bible that encompassed the very best of Mao Zedong Thought. Originally aimed at soldiers, it was adopted, like the armband, as an essential part of the Red Guard kit. As this was for her a schools-out period, it was the only book that Sister Xiaoping studied from mid-1966 for almost one year. Her mother recalled that Wu Xiaoping was unaffected by the loss of schooling because she had mastered the necessary characters. Her younger sister, Wu Lin, at twelve was much less advanced. The city's walls became her exercise books. 'She learned to write big character posters knowing characters in context like "*Mao Zhu Xi Wan Sui*" (Long Live Chairman Mao), but she did not know how to use the characters individually.'

Da chuanlian to Beijing was a meticulously planned affair. Sister Xiaoping, along with 3,000 other Red Guards, was trucked by the PLA to Xi'an railway station. Almost the whole passenger train capacity was at the disposal of the military for transporting the youths to Beijing.

They were like sardines. When the train stopped for coal or water the Red Guards swarmed off to rinse their faces, relieve themselves and stretch cramped legs. As engineers tapped the wheels, Red Guards went to the engine to make sure Chairman Mao's portrait was spotless. At night they slept on the seats, under them and on the luggage racks padded with quilts, virtually the only belongings apart from red banners and Mao portraits carried by the youths. Similarly cramped conditions can be experienced by train travellers in China today if they ride the cheapest hard seat class.

Once in Beijing Station the Red Guards were met by commissars of the PLA and piled into the back of green Jiefang trucks, to be taken to a college in the suburbs to be barracked and await the big day. Locals had been urged to donate food to the Red Guards. Twenty-three years later they volunteered to feed students occupying Tiananmen.

Without any notice, the Red Guards were woken up at 2 a.m. to be driven half asleep through cold, dark and empty streets to allocated positions. Sister Xiaoping, hungry and tired, ate her two boiled eggs and *mantou* (steamed bread) well before breakfast time. She had no idea where she was in the city until dawn broke. The Tiananmen rostrum along the avenue then came into view, its glazed tile roof a radiant gold in the first rays of daylight.

Mao coming with the sunrise was not by chance. Not committing himself to precise timing and having the Red Guards on station in the city meant that Lin Biao could afford to wait for a good weather forecast and shuttle the youths into position at the last minute. Thus Mao seemed to be in control of everything, even the weather. But one slogan, 'Defend Chairman Mao to the Last', hinted that struggle was in the air, as did the fact that the October 18th rally was the only one of eight when no speeches were delivered. This mild disappointment was overcompensated by Mao, Lin Biao and Jiang Qing being driven around the Square in jeeps, passing within a few metres of the lucky ones. Avenues to the Square were rivers of red flags flowing to Tiananmen itself, an ocean that erupted into a fervent storm of flagwaving and chanting as the motorcade passed.

Before the Cultural Revolution was finished the popularity of Lin Biao and Jiang Qing would plummet, numbering them amongst the most despised people in Chinese history. Jiang Qing was Mao's third wife, a Shanghai actress who arrived in Yan'an in 1937. Twenty years his younger she caught Mao's eye by sitting in the front row at meetings and lectures, always eager to ask questions, soon replacing He Zizhen in the Chairman's *yaodong*. Mao's night-owl habit was soon broken and it was said that the light in his cave burned into the night no longer. Thirty years later Jiang Qing had lost what sex appeal she had; politics now consumed her energies. From 1970 onwards the latent hatred of the 'empress' who hijacked the Cultural Revolution, and as the ring leader of the Gang of Four would later be accused of instigating the majority of its excesses, would grow to fever pitch. Sister Xiaoping, indeed all her family had read the mimeographically reproduced and secretly circulated book, *Hong Du Nu Huang* (Empress of the Red Capital), a damning account of Jiang Qing's life. In a style typical of Chinese humour she was attributed with 'three falses' – hair, tits and arse in order to maintain man appeal, especially to sportsmen, who were summoned to her Zhongnanhai villa to serve her. One of them, Zhuang Zedong the champion table tennis player, would later undergo 're-education' for his association with Jiang Qing in Beijing's Qin Cheng No 1 prison.

Such gossip is the stuff of many Hong Kong based monthlies, and I myself have been offered accounts that fall into the 'confessions' category. There is no shortage of Chinese with far-fetched stories of naked cabarets, swims and drug use in Zhongnanhai, anonymously offering their accounts to cheque-book journalists. Bearing in mind, however, that Mao Zedong and Liu Shaoqi had eight wives between them, it is only to be expected that the womanising side of their lives would be the subject of attention. Nevertheless, I did hear one reliable inside account of how Lin Biao selected a girlfriend for his son. In Liverpool's Chinatown, a postgraduate medical student recalled how she had been ordered to dance in her swimsuit when she was just seventeen at Zhongnanhai. Lin Biao watched the teenage nubiles with the typical concern of a Chinese parent finding a spouse for their offspring. Fortunately for her, she was not chosen.

*　　　*　　　*

Twenty-five years on, as Sister Xiaoping, Qi and I strolled across Tiananmen, the stage was exactly the same; only the decorations were different. Passing thousands of potted chrysanthemums, dahlias and snap-dragons prompted Sister Xiaoping to recall radical Red Guards doing the rounds back home to smash some 'four olds' – ideas, culture, customs and habits. There were not any to be found in the Wu home, so the potted plants went. 'There was little enough green in dusty Xi'an,' Qi's mother recalled when I mentioned this story. 'They also took away all the photographs of my parents; so now I have none.'

At the south of the Square Sister Xiaoping laughed, saying, 'My husband to be, Xiao Zuo, was about here during a Red Guard Rally. He cried, not because of Chairman Mao, but because he was too far away and couldn't see anyone on the rostrum!' We turned around: the Gate of Heavenly Peace was over 700 metres to the north.

Across Qianmen Xidajie there is a white melamine statue of an old man, a soldier according to his title, and a founder of an empire. The United States finally won the ideological war and Colonel

Saunders of Kentucky Fried Chicken has conquered the Beijinger's taste-buds with his biggest, busiest and most profitable outlet in the world. His restaurant with a view across Tiananmen, epitomises the turnaround of China, Beijing and Sister Xiaoping in the last twenty-five years.

Wu Xiaoping is now the administrative office manager of an electronics company built up over the open door decade and owned by a *Renminbi* multi-millionaire. She earns three times the average state wage and she and her inventor husband are a model Deng entrepreneurial, go ahead and hard working family.

Taken back to those fervent days, Sister Xiaoping could chuckle at my questioning, remembering the Cultural Revolution as all one big joke, rather like her forty-year-old Western contemporaries who laugh at their hippie days of joints and flowery shirts. She could do so because her conscience is clear. She did nothing particularly bad as a Red Guard. She did not spit, vilify, kick, beat or smash any of the 'four olds'. 'Generally speaking, the worst students made the best (most violent) Red Guards,' said Sister Xiaoping, 'but I loved Chairman Mao dearly. He gave us Red Guards opportunity to taste revolution, although I and the whole country paid for it.'

'Know revolution by making revolution.' The Red Guards were the blood of the Cultural Revolution – without them it would have been a non-event. Mao saw them as the essential element to exploit in harnessing nascent youthful desire to wreak havoc. He used them in an attempt to wage class struggle and cleanse first the Party, and later the country, of capitalist roaders, revisionists and the bourgeoisie who had returned to prominent positions since Liberation. The Chairman, none too competent with the daily drudgery of managing the country, was bored and frustrated. Like a mad doctor uninterested in the mundane tasks of caring for his general practice, he leaped into genetics experimentation, by conceiving the Cultural Revolution.

Sanctioning the Red Guards, giving them *Da chuanlian* and encouragement to rebel came after Mao's swim in the Yangzi River – his master-stroke to identify with the youth of China. After having gone to ground for five months Mao returned with a splash and swam some twelve kilometres down the Yangzi at Wuhan one hot summer's day in 1966. All China was astounded at the Chairman's virility, which became the perfect living example of what devotion to a pure revolutionary life could achieve.

As swimming mania swept the nation, Mao's Yangzi swim was re-enacted the following year en masse. With television news cameras at the ready, a producer told the several thousand young swimmers – many of them Red Guards – to enter the water. But like dumplings in a crowded pan they had no room to doggy-paddle, let alone swim. As I witnessed a mass Yangzi swim at Wuhan in 1992, one reliable citizen told me he saw 'at least one thousand' swimmers drowned during the fateful 1967 event. It went, of course, unreported at the time. Ignorant of this disaster caused by blind obedience, Sister Xiaoping recorded the influence of Mao's Yangzi swim in one of her diaries:

> Swimming is a sport that fights nature. However, I always swim in a swimming pool. A thousand mile horse can't be trained in a small courtyard and ten thousand year trees cannot be planted in small pots. So you cannot realise your fighting ability in a calm pool. After Chairman Mao's Yangzi swim he called upon us to temper our minds and bodies in wild rivers and open seas. We can be distinguished as good or bad only in those waters.
>
> I am eager to rush into big rivers and seas, and go forward facing the waves, exercising my body and reddening my heart's loyalty to Chairman Mao. Armed with Mao Zedong Thought, the revolutionary weapon, the huge waves are symphonic music on a voyage.

Sister Xiaoping's veneration illustrates the impact of the Yangzi swim. The fact that Mao at seventy-three was rather fat and floated downstream riding on the river's swift current like a cork was beside the point. He appeared superhuman.

If Mao was a god then the Red Guards were his disciples, the most dogmatic of religious police. Their critical eyes intruded into every aspect of life. Sister Xiaoping recalled that before the mid-summer of 1966 she would rush along to the garbage collector to sell old newspapers once a month. She bought ice lollies of mashed red beans for her sisters with the proceeds. But from July 1966 every newspaper carried the Chairman's photographs and directives. It was counter-revolutionary, sacrilegious to dispose of them. That not only meant no ice lollies but a stockpile of newspapers, stored off the floor, in the Wu family home.

Similarly, postage stamps of the day, which were issued thick and fast to wish Chairman Mao a long life – twenty-four came out over a three-month period in 1967 for that purpose – were treated with the reverence of icons. Postal clerks would not accept letters with stamps glued thereon askew or upside down. Hand franking was slow and laborious, taking care not to mark the Chairman's face. Anyone seen immersing used stamps to separate them from envelopes was asking to be in hot water too.

Lin Biao, seemingly in gratitude for being promoted to heir of the PRC, was orchestrating the deification, making Mao a god and strengthening his own position in the process. I also believe it was the initial tortuously conceived step in Lin Biao's overall strategy of seizing power sooner, rather than wait for Mao's natural death, which in view of his swimming prowess he would have considered happening much later. Besides, Lin Biao was not the healthiest of men despite his illustrious military career.

By saturating the Chinese people's minds with Mao he knew that before long they would become bored with the old man and welcome a divorce. Lin Biao put Mao everywhere. Mao badges were paramount in his plan, capitalising on the Chinese mania for collecting. Portraits of the Chairman became the only decoration in most homes and offices, and statues were erected in units throughout the land. People were obliged to study the *Little Red Book* morning, noon and night. Some eccentrics took Mao worship to greater extremes. Sister Xiaoping heard one soldier lecturing Red Guards on how to fix Mao badges directly on to their skin. With his shirt off, he had twenty or more badges on his chest and abdomen, the scars having healed over.

Meanwhile the masses were recipients of Chinese whispers and cloaked directives which they were left to interpret and act upon like sheep. Red Guard activists 'bombarded the headquarters' by invading Zhongnanhai to vandalise the home of Liu Shaoqi, strip him and beat him up in 'sweeping away freaks and demons' and burning as 'poisonous weeds' his book *How to be a Good Communist*.

Liu Shaoqi would be purged from the Party in 1968 and left to die in the squalor of a Kaifeng prison in November 1969. He was reportedly carted off to the crematorium with half his corpse hanging from the back of a jeep.

By this time Mao had already opened the Cultural Revolution to all by instructing Red Guards to seek out revisionists, capitalist roaders and bourgeoisie outside the Party. Street war between Red Guard factions ensued. Sister Xiaoping recalled the most gruesome event of the Cultural Revolution in Xi'an being a display of corpses: Red Guards killed in open fighting on the city's streets. It was September, hot, and the faces of the dead, hacked and disfigured were riddled with maggots and stenching.

The nastiest side of the Cultural Revolution was still to come to the Wu family. With the spotlight of criticism now turned on to non-Party members, Sister Xiaoping's father was ordered to 'the cowsheds' for being an intellectual. 'I'm finished,' he said on hearing the news. Bao Yibing consoled him saying, 'Criticise yourself and work hard.' After regular self-criticisms, during which he was spat upon by Red Guards, he was dressed up between sandwich-boards that advertised his name crossed out and his mistakes – being an intellectual – and put to work outside the Soviet-built university campus.

During the hot summer of 1969 he swept Xi'an's dusty streets and shovelled shit from the street's toilets, serving peasants who came with mule carts to collect the effluent for manuring their fields. 'Most people didn't abuse me,' said Wu Wanchun twenty-three years later.

Qi's mother told her, 'Father has a new job; take him some lunch.' Even the billycan Qi delivered to her father had a slogan etched upon its lid: 'Don't forget Chairman Mao who gave us rice to eat.' The Red Guards overseeing the cowsheds stopped Qi, then only twelve, from giving him eggs with rice and vegetable, saying that a 'stinking ninth' did not deserve eggs to eat. 'I'll certainly never forget Chairman Mao,' said Professor Wu wryly.

17

Return to Feng Xian

'Serve the People' – A decoration from Wu Xiaoping's diary.

Clinging to a slope in the foothills of the Qin Ling, tucked away in the southwest corner of Shaanxi and not far from the borders with Gansu and Sichuan, is a peasant farm. In all but one way it is like the several score of dwellings I have stayed in throughout northern China, and like the hundreds of millions more whose thresholds I have not crossed: a brown mud-walled home to many, its tiled roof overgrown with weeds. Its interior is sparsely furnished and lit. Newspapers reporting recent history cover the walls, and, appropriately since the people are the experimental matter of the policies and upheavals reported thereon, a mosaic of family snapshots overhangs. That still does not make this farm in Feng Xian any different. But a single photograph does. For within the album on the wall is a picture of the Wu family, a black-and-white photo snapped in 1969. This is where Sister Xiaoping stayed in the countryside under a directive of Chairman Mao's that called upon intellectual youth – that covered anyone educated to middle-school level or above – to learn farm labour from poor peasants.

I felt that I had already been to Feng Xian, but I had not. By reading Qi's translation of Sister Xiaoping's diaries which recorded her countryside re-education from October 1968 to May 1973 I could picture the place, even sympathise and identify with her initial love and respect for Chairman Mao in recognition of his monumental achievements. But then as the months, seasons and years of the late Sixties and early Seventies flew by, the golden teenage of a young woman, Sister Xiaoping's writing hinted of boredom, frustration and dissatisfaction at her time being wasted in a place far from home. She lost her religion. Chairman Mao's glistening image was tarnished in my own eyes too as I reached this, the darkest and final episode of his life. It was also the closest personally, since this wild socio-political experiment was inflicted upon my own kith and kin. We went off him together, whilst seeking excuses and scapegoats in octogenarian senility and the Gang of Four.

I read the diaries like a tourist does a guidebook before setting out, but unlike the tourist I did not know whether I would ever reach there: I might remain an armchair traveller. Reaching Feng Xian was going to be difficult. It was not that Sister Xiaoping felt uneasy about returning to her place of Cultural Revolution exile for the first time in almost twenty years. Perhaps it is because she is so down to earth that she was relatively unaffected in psychological terms by the experience. She did it because there was no choice. Mao had wooed millions of youths like her with his encouragement of *Da chuanlian*, the spoonful of sugar to ensure the nasties of the Cultural Revolution be carried out obediently. At best the experience gave her abounding energy, at worst a hardness and devil-may-care attitude to life.

Our problem was purely logistical, or rather racial. Emotions did not enter into the matter. Feng Xian was not open to foreigners: access would not be granted for any reason whatsoever. Sister Xiaoping said there was a special weapons factory in Feng Xian established under Mao's directive to locate armament facilities in the remote heartland of China. Bureaucrats I knew would not listen to reason and logic, especially when it was related to the blackest episode of

Mao's life. It was useless to argue about China's internal affairs, as it was to tell authorities that spy satellites can know all there is to know about Feng Xian. So we worked out our strategy: I was a foreigner, yes; but my sister-in-law was only showing me where she worked as a youth. That just happened to be Feng Xian. She had every personal right to take me along there too.

The first leg of the journey, and a perfectly permissible one, from Xi'an to Baoji, took longer than scheduled. A woman had thrown herself into the path of the train and found in death more attention than she had ever known in life. Hundreds of passengers struggled for window space to catch a glimpse of the decapitated corpse. Sister Xiaoping told me of the high suicide rate induced by the traumas of the Cultural Revolution. She and Qi reckoned that at least ten suicides were committed on their father's university campus. Its Soviet-built tenements proved to be high enough for that purpose. Those in '*Beida*' had not, as Deng Pufang discovered. As the son of the Party's worst capitalist roader, Deng Xiaoping, he was criticised and hassled into seeking escape through death. He now presides over the China Disabled Association from a wheelchair.

After showing our documentation, including the essential marriage certificate, we lodged at a hotel on Red Flag Street. Whilst I read a Chinglish translation of a notice prohibiting foreigners from entering that section of Baoji south of the Wei He bridge – it was said that there were more weapons factories there – Sister Xiaoping and Qi busied themselves in organising our onward transport on the morrow to Feng Xian.

As a Lada taxi collected us promptly at seven next morning my heart rejoiced: it was a Lada with tinted windows. From its back seat I could gaze out from the windows, my big nose unseen. We soon left the south Baoji weapons district behind and wound our way up into the Qin Ling. Before long Qi was interpreting a clutch of Lada jokes for Sister Xiaoping as the driver fidgeted with the engine. Two decades before, her journeys to and from Feng Xian were similarly precarious. Red Guards, whether on *Da chuanlian* or going to the countryside never bought tickets. Sister Xiaoping rode on fresh-air-conditioned carriages of iron ore, coal or timber, keeping her head down in the long cool tunnels that burrow beneath the divide. Feng Xian station was far from her brigade so she usually hitched and rode perched on the front bumper of a Jiefang truck.

Sister Xiaoping told the driver to stop. 'It's up there,' she said confidently, as if returning after days not decades. Though apparently barren, the hillside had on second looks the contours of terracing. The odd farmstead was given away by its shading copse of trees, now leafless in the November sun. Qi gave the driver five *yuan* for lunch and said we would be back in two or three hours.

At the foot of a path a butcher watched over his fatty meat swaying on cleavers in the wind. Without asking him directions Sister Xiaoping strode past, and we followed up a steep, rock-hard mud path within a creek to emerge at a cluster of buildings, one of three lodgings used by her over her five-year period of labour in Feng Xian.

'*Ni renshi wo?!*' (D'you know me?) yelled Sister Xiaoping to a couple in the courtyard. Their dogs clearly did not but the middle-aged woman, sixteen when they said goodbye last, did.

'*Wu Xiaoping!? Ni hui lai le!*' (You've come back!) she cried whilst brandishing a besom at the snarling hounds. The man giggled stupidly as Sister Xiaoping explained that two of the sons here were '*er bai wu*' – a Chinese idiom for having a screw loose. They were issues of incest. I remembered how Qi's mother had voiced concern over her daughter's so-called re-education at the hands of the peasantry. 'How is a young girl expected to learn from them?' she asked, after hearing Sister Xiaoping relate tales of promiscuity and venereal disease amongst her peasant hosts, people who behaved like the animals they kept when it came to mating.

Another branch of the family occupied the adjacent farm. Da Niang (Big Mother) now an eighty-eight-year-old great grandmother was a small toothless woman hobbling on bandy legs, her cheeks bulging with delight on seeing Sister Xiaoping again. We sat on giant bobbins from the local textile factory huddled around a fire burning on the stone floor of the grain store-cum-kitchen.

'*Qingkuang zenmeyang le?*' (What's life like now?) enquired Sister Xiaoping. The old lady, tossing twigs on to the fire, sighed.

'I have old people's illness, can't see much, and the hens aren't laying – it's too cold.' Her eyes looked watery, a tearful contradiction to the permanent impression of smiling suggested by prominent cheekbones.

Catching sight of a coffin upon a bier in the doorway of the room opposite, I whispered to Qi, 'Somebody's just died; that's why she's crying.'

Sister Xiaoping roared with laughter, saying it was the smoke that irritated Da Niang's eyes. 'Twenty years ago there were two coffins there – her old man has taken one and that's empty and waiting for the day she dies.'

Apparently the peasantry liked to prepare early for death here, investing in a good box when finances permitted. Having a big black coffin, painted annually for the inevitable day, was not in the least bit disturbing. Strangely I had never witnessed this custom before in all my travels through rural areas.

Our first visitor, on hearing via the bamboo telegraph that three strangers were not only in town, but in his *lao jia* (old home) was Gai Ling.

'I heard that a "grandfather intellectual" was back,' he joked to Sister Xiaoping using the sarcastic title. Countryfolk dubbed the intellectual youth 'grandfathers' in terms of knowledge held in proportion to their tender years. 'And this is your little sister?' he guessed. 'You gave us a photograph, remember?' Continuing to sort out the relationships he asked, 'Who's the old foreigner?'

'My little sister married internationally: he's British,' explained Sister Xiaoping.

He offered me a cigarette – which I held for friendship – whilst remarking, 'Your sister has opened her door widely.'

Gai Ling was Party secretary, a position that augured well for us. 'It's nothing, no problem,' he assured Sister Xiaoping. 'They're my friends, and we all welcome you and your family back to Feng Xian.'

*   *   *

The barn used by Sister Xiaoping had been burnt down, and with it a season's grain. As we stood amongst the ruins overlooking the town, I recalled what Sister Xiaoping had written about her frustrating days spent within its walls:

26th September 1969
On the 22nd I received two letters and I've written back. I

should receive letters again. It's not been interesting all day. Damn! It's been raining continually for a few days now. If life passes like this, it's not worth living! I can't do any labour work, only stay in this small room, lie on the bed, drink hot water and read novels.

Time has vanished from my pillow. Hours pass slowly out here. I've been in this production brigade now for ten days. In Xi'an ten days goes by without notice. I feel that two months in Xi'an are like ten days here. I wrote to Ma five days ago. I should get a letter from her soon!

'Life hasn't changed much in twenty years,' said Gai Ling. 'Everything the peasants do is still for their stomachs. There's no electricity up in these hill farms. It's much better down in the valley where I live.'

29th September 1969

Today the brigade distributed some crops to us. Can you imagine that now we start to live the life of 'Peasant's Happiness'? Yes, it's a fact. In the coming winter months we'll grind the wheat and corn, collect firewood for cooking – everything we do is for our mouths!

I've not been happy for several days under this grey rainy sky. Time continues to disappear on the bed, in the room and at the cooking stove. In future, when I recall these days won't my face be red, won't I feel ashamed? Yet I can't do anything.

Inside the home little indeed had changed according to Sister Xiaoping's memory. Gone, however, was Chairman Mao's portrait. Gone too were the papercuts of him amongst billowing red flags which Sister Xiaoping had taught the peasants to cut. The Shaanxi art was now manifesting itself more traditionally in the form of deities, deterring evils from coming in the window, and characters of double happiness to wish well for marital unity.

Bored with life in 1969 Sister Xiaoping took solace in looking back to 1966:

1st October 1969

Today is the 20th National Day! On this happy day who can control their excitement? The announcer on the radio recites some slogans for the occasion: Celebrate the Great Victory of Socialist Revolution and Construction during the last twenty years! Long live Chairman Mao! In summarising the achievements of the Great Proletarian Cultural Revolution she says (the announcer) our country has become more prosperous, the Socialist career more developed and the Proletarian Dictatorship more consolidated. Chinese people are able to live life to the full and in high spirits, basking in the sunshine of Mao Zedong Thought.

The chimes of 'The East is Red' herald the start of the live broadcast. Chairman Mao is walking on Tiananmen's balcony! It's so exciting – last year, no, in 1966 during the period of exchanging revolutionary experiences, I saw him in Tiananmen. I was one of the happiest people in the world. I envy those lucky people in Beijing today. I can only listen to the broadcast. In just a few minutes we'll have to do labour work in the fields. How can I be calm? How can one do things as usual? On National Day I normally join the parade in the streets. But today I'm going to pick corn cobs on the high terraces!

Perhaps life is like this, changing all the time. I don't know the future, but whatever my country and comrades ask of me shall be my ideal.

Sister Xiaoping's thoughts and feelings seemed polarised by mood: swept along in the fervour of the Cultural Revolution whilst parroting the propagandist tone of the radio announcer in memorising her heyday in Beijing one minute, then slumping into despondency the next. The appearance of the diaries themselves were contradictory too. Inside the front covers Mao portraits were protected by tracing paper. Every twenty pages the Chairman's teachings were headed by a line drawing of sunflowers blooming in the sunshine of Mao's smile. Sister Xiaoping's stylish characters must have been a source of awe and wonder to her predominantly illiterate hosts, some of whom she taught to read and write. Yet on the covers of the diaries were postcards of goldfish – themselves, poor creatures, the target of destruction from the more radical of Red Guards who regarded the keeping of pets as bourgeois, not to mention superstitious. Water and fish are thought beneficial to *feng shui* (wind and water), the vibes of a dwelling. Such old beliefs were one of the 'four olds' to be eradicated.

Gai Ling suggested that we visited Tujia, the Tu family home across the creek. Sister Xiaoping had fetched water there, carrying it in pails on bamboo poles to the high terraces. Poling water uphill was not easy. Only the thought of a harvest to fill her empty stomach kept her going.

5th October 1969
Today we've done labour work all day – cutting down rice and picking corn cobs. In the evening some strangers, I don't know who they are, play revolutionary opera.* When I go to bed I feel uncomfortable. This morning I was in the paddy with bare feet, perhaps I have a cold. Rolling one's body in mud to refine a red heart isn't so easy.

6th–8th October
The brigade issued 28 *jin* of rice to each person as the autumn harvest. Ma sent me 10 *yuan*, so I must go to Longkou Post Office to collect it. I'll use some money to buy pork and make dumplings.

Traipsing along paths following the contours of terracing, Sister Xiaoping asked Gai Ling about his Party work. He was responsible for implementing the birth control policy amongst some 400 peasants. He told us that since peasants prefer sons for labour work they are allowed a second child if their first issue is a daughter. Sometimes pregnant women visited the countryside to deliver where medical facilities were less advanced and mothers usually gave birth at home, where accidents – especially to unwanted girls – could easily 'happen'. Then they would return to their town or city of citizenship having 'lost' their child, to conceive again – hopefully a boy.

*Probably an opera group touring the countryside playing one of the eight permitted revolutionary operas and ballets which conformed ideologically to serving the masses by conveying propagandist messages.

11th October 1969
After working all day I wash my body in the factory public bath. In the evening we must attend a meeting and give suggestions to Party members. But nobody said anything. In the end everybody was told to have a think at home and return tomorrow. The meeting was held in our room – I don't know why it's always like that. The meeting lasts too long, we sit on cold benches and nobody opens their mouth. Men smoke and women knit. Damn, it's late! Tomorrow we have to get up early and go to work.

Little had indeed changed in twenty years. When we arrived at Tujia, the man of the house, Tusheng (Born from the earth) was smoking. Only the cigarettes had changed. Now he bought them rather than rolled his own. His wife Gen Lian was knitting up a sweater. Sister Xiaoping recognised the wool. It was her wedding gift to the couple in 1970. In China, sweaters are unravelled to be washed to prevent matting, and then knitted up again. Who could argue that this labour-intensive practice was absurd, if a sweater gave twenty-odd years of service? 'The quality is very good!' explained Gen Lian laughing. 'We were so grateful to receive a really useful wedding gift.' Most offerings in those days were Chairman Mao books – which they still had of course, somewhere in their home. 'This is us on our wedding day,' said Gen Lian, pointing to a five-by-three black-and-white, the centrepiece of her family's illustrated history overhanging the *kang*. I scanned the thirty or more surrounding snapshots and found some familiar faces . . .

6th November 1969
Ma, second and little sister are so happy because our family is reunited. The harvest in Feng Xian is gathered in and I'm back in Xi'an. Pa has come back too from '5.7' cadre school.* He brought many apples and peanuts from Meixian. I brought a

*Wu Wanchun was sent to a rural re-education centre, making agricultural tools under a programme of Mao's initiated by the May 7th directive, which called upon intellectuals to learn manual labour from workers and poor peasants.

sack of walnuts. We killed a chicken. I've eaten so much that now I have stomach ache. I've been greedy. What a day to remember!

Recently the preparation for war has become more hectic.* Long bomb shelters are being dug by citizens under Xi'an. Many people are making ready to leave their families. Last night there was a meeting about evacuating older people to the countryside. Imperialists can't bomb the vast countryside, can they? It was ten o'clock when my sisters were sleeping. I was unrolling my quilt. There was knocking and loud voices at the door. We were astonished. It was the police to check up and register us.

In this mood of uncertainty the photo studios are full. Everyone wants a photograph of their loved ones to take away. Perhaps they'll leave Xi'an and say goodbye to their family and friends for the last time. Who knows the future? We waited for over an hour before we had our whole family happy picture taken. But nobody is happy. I'll treasure the photograph and take it back to Feng Xian. I don't know whether the brigade will receive my family. I don't know Ma's plan. There's talk that they will all go to Meixian, Lantian or Tongchuan counties. In every middle school the PLA is recruiting. But they don't want us 'countryside sticks'. I'd really like to join-up but it's only a dream. I know I must return to Feng Xian and work for food production. I'm ready to fight however. Fight! Fight! Sooner or later the war will break out. The earlier it starts the better – we can wipe imperialists off the face of the earth and begin the reconstruction. War is unavoidable so long as imperialists are alive. It's their nature to invade and seek conflict. They're dogs; dogs don't change their habits of eating dirt! Let's fight for freedom, peace and wipe out the invaders!

Upon her return to Feng Xian carrying the photograph which is still on the wall of Tujia, Sister Xiaoping lived the peasant life as normal, unaffected for the time being by the expectations of war that preoccupied city folk. Her writings continue to reflect ups and

---

*An invasion by US forces was predicted by Mao.

downs, sometimes carefree, more often concerned, but they always give a glimpse of the political background to those winter days of 1969.

27th November 1969

The peasants don't have any Sunday. Every day is the same – unless you think of something different to do. After breakfast we took hoes to the field. I told Xiao Zhu that this afternoon we should go into the mountains to collect firewood, otherwise we wouldn't have any left for the cooking stove. 'Why wait?' she said. So we went back, collected a rope and set off.

We walked many *li* up a zigzagging path to find a place with water and trees. The view was beautiful, and far away from the town the firewood was easy to find. Carrying so much firewood back we were 'countryside sticks' at last!

Today I had a look in our work register book. In our brigade one person logs for everybody, not like the Dongfeng brigade where each person records it themselves. So it's easy to make mistakes. On the 25th we worked for half a day, but it wasn't logged. I'm not bothered about the work points themselves. The economic account isn't important. But we must calculate the political account. If we have more work points, that means we've worked hard. If you don't have work points, how can you show that you've received re-education from peasants well? If we work it should be entered in the book!

18th December 1969

Today is my eighteenth birthday. People say it is a golden year on the threshold of a bright future. But I don't feel that way. I wish I was a child forever. My childhood days were so happy. This Great Proletarian Cultural Revolution has changed everyone. I plunged into the Revolution when I was only 14.

This morning I didn't go to work before breakfast. I was told that many people now start work at 2 a.m. Mao Zedong's Thought is that strong it can change people, their thinking and habits. The work rate of the brigade has really increased lately.

In the afternoon we had a meeting about studying Chairman Mao's teachings effectively. Tomorrow morning at 5 a.m. we'll begin militia training, and in the afternoon 'five goods peasants' will be chosen. Positive activists will be identified and everyone should exchange thoughts study methods. What will I talk about? There must be a road when the cart arrives.

19th December 1969
'Get up Comrades!' shouted the brigade leader before five o'clock. It's very cold as I throw back my quilt to go outside in the frost. We do ten minutes' jogging and some exercises using sticks as weapons. The peasants, producers for all their lives, have suddenly become an army! Countryside sticks are now weapons! This isn't so easy. Go slowly Comrades!

In the afternoon I was chosen as a model political activist to represent intellectual youth being re-educated in the countryside.

It appeared that we had overstayed our welcome. Two plain-clothes policemen came up to Tujia to investigate what had been broadcast on Feng Xian's bamboo telegraph.

'Has he taken any photographs?' asked the policeman.

'Only of us,' replied Gai Ling. Coming from the Party Secretary that statement preserved my film from confiscation. Ironically, now, as the late Chairman's 98th Birthday approached, Sister Xiaoping was asked to record the details of our visit on police files. Twenty-three years before, on Chairman Mao's seventy-sixth, she had made a speech to her brigade.

26th December 1969
Today, the reddest reddest sun in our hearts, Chairman Mao celebrates his 76th Birthday. Our tens of thousands of words, tens of thousands of songs can be condensed into one sentence – Long live Chairman Mao!

Chairman Mao, Chairman Mao! You are the helmsman of this era's ship, the saviour of China and the hope of mankind. Your achievement is higher than the Himalayas. A record of your kindness to us couldn't be written out with ink made from the water of three great rivers and five lakes.

You, *Lao Ren Jia* (Respected Elder), taught us that the country-side is a vast land where we can give full play to revolutionary practice. We are willing to roll ourselves in mud, get calluses on our hands and refine a red heart whilst being pupils of poor peasants!

Sister Xiaoping didn't write anything so flowery in the police files, not even a self-criticism for bringing a foreigner to a prohibited area.

After registering my presence we banqueted with Party Secretary Gai Ling. Much of the talk, between nibbles of titbits that included one-hundred-year-old eggs, focused on family life. Gai Ling clearly remembered Sister Xiaoping's philosophy where marriage was concerned. Like most eighteen-year-olds in China, then more than now because now the model couple marries later and starts a family later, Sister Xiaoping had much pressure on her to find the right man.

21st February 1970

Today Mei was married. We've eaten so much food during the wedding that I needn't cook for several days. Traditions and customs of rural areas die hard.

Mei is one year younger than me. Why does she get married so early? Later this year she's bound to have a baby. The countryside is like that – they say 'have a baby early and enjoy life.' I don't want to do that. If I marry here I'll stay in Feng Xian all my life! But who will I marry! In Xi'an it's said that having a student-husband one's afraid of him going to the army; having a soldier-husband one's afraid of him dying on the battlefield; and having a peasant husband one's afraid of him having poor land and the weather. So having a worker husband is the best catch. In Beijing the girls want strong, handsome men with a reliable political outlook and in receipt of food tickets.

As Sister Xiaoping had done before, we returned to Xi'an laden with delicious walnuts picked from the trees dotted on the hillsides between the farms where she once lived. It was during that journey that our taxi driver sought revenge for the jokes cracked at the expense of his Lada. He had lunched on a bottle of *bai jiu* (rice liquor), and drove back to Baoji at a speed that made me think he had poured some in the fuel tank too.

In 1973 after five years of exile Sister Xiaoping left Feng Xian to attend agricultural college at Baoji, but even then intellectual youth continued to be sent to the countryside. The exile programme had developed into as much a method of reducing the chaotic over-crowding in cities and unemployment as a political re-education. With a population topping 800 million in 1969 Mao made a U-turn on population policy. Having formerly dismissed birth control as a Western idea to keep developing countries weak, Mao himself spoke frankly on the thorny subject saying, 'Free contraception is not enough; they must be delivered into the hands of the masses.' In 1974 that finally happened – but there were not enough to go round!

It was the start of a new decade, one of cataclysm and changes of which population policy was but only the first. Another man, Deng Xiaoping, at the end of the decade, would be left to make the biggest U-turn of all, blaming the Chairman and the Gang of Four on behalf of all China for the entire Cultural Revolution.

Eighty-Three, Forty-One

Mao lying in state in the Great Hall of the People.

I remember an event in 1963 which made the whole of Britain stand still. 'Kennedy is dead,' everyone said. Only six and a half at the time, I knew neither death nor J.F.K., yet on September 9th 1976 when Chairman Mao passed away, in China even toddlers of three or four understood. For *'Mao Zhu Xi'* were some of the first words they ever learnt – before even Mama or Baba. With some 900 million sobbing uncontrollably on hearing the news China was plunged into a flood of grief and sorrow. Not only was Comrade Mao Zedong, their leader, dead; God had died. Despite hundreds of billions of cries of *'Mao Zhu Xi Wan Sui!'* (A life of ten thousand years to Chairman Mao!) Mao had fallen short of immortality. He was eighty-three and had led the Party for forty-one years since the Zunyi meeting of 1935. The gap was catastrophic, a chasm that spelt the loss of a religion.

Qi had just celebrated her birthday then. After graduating from middle school she was saved from a countryside re-education because her parents had no other children living with them in Xi'an. Instead Qi had been assigned a postwoman's job dealing with security mail at the Bell Tower Post Office. All employees were told to gather in the yard at 4 p.m. that afternoon. A news release from the Xinhua News Agency echoed over an unusually silent and still city:

Message to the whole Party, whole Army and the people of all nationalities throughout the country. Comrade Mao Zedong, the esteemed and beloved great leader of our Party, our Army and all the nationalities of our country, the great teacher of the international proletariat and the oppressed nations and oppressed people, Chairman of the Central Committee of the Communist Party of China passed away at . . .

The rest of the announcement was inaudible with wailing, crying and fainting.

'For most people they were crocodile tears,' I was told. People were more concerned about their own future and that of the nation without Mao, rather than the death of Mao as a person. The devil they knew was dead, and the four devils they knew were far worse were struggling in the background for the accession.

In search of a bizarre insight into Mao's death, I set out to interview the man who had ensured that Mao's body at least would last for ever – the doctor who had laid him out.

It seemed a tall order to locate Ma Yanlong, one doctor amongst many thousands in Beijing. The news that he worked in 'Beijing Hospital' was the most infuriating of ambiguous leads: there were literally scores of such city hospitals differentiated only by numbers.

We started in the city centre. Amazingly, on Qi's first enquiry we were assured that a Ma Yanlong worked in an annexe of the main hospital. Walking along a near empty backstreet during the lunchtime *xiu xi* (siesta period) to reach there, the trail grew hotter as I spotted a tearful group of people with black cloth armbands pinned to their white shirts.

Entering a complex of antiseptic smelling buildings unchallenged, Qi led me to the appropriate department aided by the labelling on closed doors. There we found a student clad in a white coat. 'Dr Ma is resting. He'll be along soon. Have you come for treatment?'

A jovial man entered the room bowing, clasping his hands prayer-like and repeating a warm welcome. Bare legs with feet shod in sandals protruded from under a soiled white medical coat. Qi introduced me, and Dr Ma nodded appreciatively, giving a thumbs up sign to show his admiration for my journey through Mao's life. He confessed that he had never wanted to answer a foreigner's prying and possibly disrespectful questions on such a solemn subject before, but I was clearly a special case. Presenting me with his namecard he invited us to his home that evening, saying, 'If Mr William has walked over one thousand kilometres of the Long March then he must love and respect Chairman Mao very much.'

Escorting us off the mortuary premises Dr Ma made a detour, 'to show you some history'. We entered a small chilled hall, empty apart from a trolley. 'This is where Premier Zhou Enlai's last viewing was held,' said Dr Ma. The corpse beneath the shroud on the trolley was a corpse ready to be accorded the same last respects, possibly by those mourners outside. We thought between the lines of history. Premier Zhou, who died nine months before Mao, was denied the usual venue for the last viewing that his position deserved by the Gang of Four. His family, friends and staff came to this small mortuary hall instead of the Great Hall.

*   *   *

When Ma Yanlong shows you his photograph album it is full of dead people draped in Communist Party flags. As a cosmetic mortician, he has prepared the remains of almost every top leader, and many lesser known VIPs, since the founding of the People's Republic in 1949. His work on Chairman Mao differed from all others in one respect. He worked on the bodies of Zhou Enlai, Zhu De, Soong Ching Ling, Hu Yaobang and others in preparation for the traditional *gao bie* (the last farewell), the file past of family and comrades. But he prepared Mao for everlasting viewing.

A few days after I met Ma Yanlong, Xinhua released visitor figures for the mausoleum: on September 9th 1991, the fifteenth anniversary of Mao's death, some 13,000 paid their respects; between its opening to the public in 1977 and the fifteenth anniversary sixty-seven million had filed past his sarcophagus. 'Beautiful,' Dr Ma said in English, 'still beautiful after fifteen years,' as he pointed to a photograph of Chairman Mao laid out under the red flag.

It felt disrespectful to flick through Ma Yanlong's photo albums while eating water melon. But Dr Ma seemed very down to earth about his profession and the public's view of it. 'Some people won't even shake hands with me despite the fact that I've handled all the motherland's leaders,' he explained adding, 'they think my job is terrible. It is, of course, neither easy nor pleasant, as there's always the risk of infection.' Dr Ma has fourteen photo albums, his most treasured showing the CCP hierarchy with Chairman Mao and Premier Zhou sharing page one. Premier Zhou, like Mao, looks totally peaceful, a picture of composure. 'Although I've provided services to many powerful people, I've never asked anything from their relatives apart from a few photos of their loved ones to keep as souvenirs in my files and for study.' The most expensive gift he was given is a domestically made Qingdao camera. 'Now I take pictures of the dead myself.'

Dr Ma passed me his 'process album', full of before and after photographs, to illustrate the procedures of his profession. 'In general terms my job is to beautify. The pallid appearance of a deceased person's face usually bears no likeness to that person when alive.' Firstly Dr Ma puts the corpse in an appropriate position, lifting the head and posturing the chin, then spreading the legs to facilitate dressing.

Antiseptic measures come next, followed by the most difficult, and rewarding, process – the cosmetics, 'actually a combination of make-up and plastic surgery'. His workbox contains scalpels, scissors, gauze and cotton wool, ethyl alcohol, razors, clippers, combs, greasepaint, lipstick and brushes. 'I usually request a good picture of the deceased taken ten or twenty years before,' he said, 'but when I worked on Chairman Mao they provided a picture taken in 1972 during his meeting with Nixon.

'The final and most pleasant step is what I've become famous for – the flower and flag formula,' explained Dr Ma.

Ma Yanlong graduated from a one-year army medical school in 1951, doing his first make-up job that year on a General, 'simply by painting his face, draping the flag over his corpse laid out in a pool of flowers,' he said modestly. 'Lighting is important too – a couple of 500-watt spotlights meet on the dead person's breast.' That was initially done to provide light for press photographers and TV news crews, but then he realised the lighting actually made the corpse appear to be breathing.

Initially he disliked the job, but the advanced age of the leadership meant that he became busier. Eventually accepting the role and regarding his service as beneficial to the motherland, he sought improvement via knowledge of plastics, painting, aesthetics and psychology.

Coming from a reasonably well-off family, and brought up as a Catholic – he is now a Buddhist – he was branded a bourgeois reactionary and intellectual as a result of long research hours spent in the mortuary. Ironically it was during his Cultural Revolution exile at a May 7th cadre school that his two most important assignments occurred. The first was in January 1976. 'Premier Zhou was emaciated and unshaven after dying. Zhou's barber shaved him and I did the cosmetics. We cried our hearts out after finishing the work,' said Dr Ma, almost shedding more tears.

On September 9th 1976 Ma Yanlong was working in the fields of a Changping County commune about fifty kilometres north of Beijing. A large black *Hong Qi* (Red Flag car), the state limousine of China suddenly arrived. 'It must be from Zhongnanhai,' thought Dr Ma, daring to think the unthinkable but inevitable. One of the men was crying as he told him of Mao's death. Dr Ma had been listed as a member of the group to prepare the corpse for the state funeral.

Once in Zhongnanhai Dr Ma waited in a large house with other medical specialists. 'I was shaking and sweating like never before,' he recalled. What followed was surely one of the most bizarre sights in the history of the People's Republic. A group of seven morticians headed by Xu Jing, now the director of the Mausoleum, performed their task. 'Despite Chairman Mao having signed a pledge in 1956 to be cremated, in order to set an example to the masses who were consuming too much farm land with burials, we knew from our orders that we were preparing his remains for permanent viewing.'

The work took more than an hour. Besides the group of seven, over thirty medical assistants supported. The entire procedure was watched over by Jiang Qing, Zhang Chunqiao, Yao Wenyuan, and

Wang Hongwen. 'Were they sobbing?' I asked Dr Ma. 'Someone was, but I dared not look around,' he replied. Neither Hua Guofeng, Mao's immediate successor, Deng Xiaoping, his long-term successor nor any Marshals were present. Once the work was completed, the Gang of Four shook each mortician's hand in conveying their thanks. Mao's corpse was transported to the Great Hall of the People where it lay in state for thirty days. Ma Yanlong stayed there for two days, on hand for any final touches.

The funeral rally was held in Tiananmen Square during the afternoon of September 18th. At 3 p.m. over a quarter of a million mourners, mostly clad in white shirts on which black armbands were pinned, faced north towards the Gate of Heavenly Peace, their heads bowed throughout a three minute silence, observed nationwide. China had never been stiller. Ma Yanlong listened to Hua Guofeng's eulogy on the radio in his Changping commune, farming again. Qi attended the rally relayed nationwide on Xi'an's East Street. It was raining heavily but neither umbrellas nor raincoats were permitted. Qi's mother made some alterations to a cycle cape which she wore as underwear beneath the accepted funerary apparel of white and black. Many caught their own death, pneumonia, whilst mourning Mao's.

Perhaps more people cried in Tiananmen than in Xi'an. Mourners at the northern end of the Square could make out the figures of the Gang of Four standing besides Hua Guofeng and that pecking order augured badly for all China. Mao's coffin was not present, being kept out of the late summer afternoon heat in the relative coolness of the Great Hall, further indication that his corpse was being preserved for longer term viewing. Indeed, a calendar year after his death it would go on display six feet above in a mausoleum to be built at the southern end of the Square.

Unlike peasants in the countryside who prepare for their death well in advance by purchasing coffins, the first brick of Chairman Mao's Mausoleum was not laid until after he passed away, for he had specifically instructed that no tombs or memorials be constructed in his memory. Round the clock construction was probably initiated by the Gang but continued under Hua Guofeng – he must bear the responsibility since it is his calligraphy that greeted me when I visited the monolithic memorial hall completed in an astonishing eight months, in May 1977, well in time for the first anniversary of Mao's death.

The etiquette required to see Mao was somewhat more relaxed than the tomb rules in Moscow for visiting Lenin, where notices and guards warned visitors to stand-up straight, not to slouch nor have hands in pockets. Only the removal of headgear and filing past without stopping was obligatory here: tourists with shorts, the miniest of skirts and shod in sandals entered unchallenged.

One is restricted to only the briefest of glimpses: a few metres for a few seconds. Nevertheless, like those Red Guards decades before when they felt complete, my journey also was complete. I had last seen Mao, four years ago on that New Year's Day, as an enigma. Now I knew him better. I had come to pay my respects to his spirit, which had led me, a Foreign Red Army to follow his own. But I had also come to criticise him in asking why, after so much achievement for the Chinese people, he instigated destruction. Mao had, I knew, through his voluminous works, the knack of answering every question one asked of him posthumously, and he now replied, as a revolutionary striving to achieve a perfect Communism, that upheavals were necessary to prevent a reversion to the old ways.

The familiar form of his head and shoulders reminded me he was that above others with regard to influence on China this century, his century, Mao's century. The vibes in this place, the *feng shui* as the Chinese call them, are a vortex: build and destroy, war and peace, up and down, good and bad. It cannot be explained by diviners or doctors with their medical books, only by history books – yet even they are lifeless, sterile pages compared to the faces of the bewitched and curious beside me in the queue. They see the man who wrote the history of decades with millions of lives – if not their lives then certainly those of their parents. Some had doubtless come to respect, remembering the halcyon years of the early Fifties full of hope, belief and unity; others to despise, a silent curse muttered under the breath on behalf of a shattered family. Perhaps the split was the oft mentioned seventy per cent to thirty per cent.

Even that division seemed applicable to the mausoleum itself. The voice of Dr Ma echoed in my mind. 'To many people, the respect and fulfilment they receive at death is what they've striven for all their lives. It's my pleasure to help them realise their last dreams.'

But this was not Mao's dream: not this mausoleum nor this China, forking off the Socialist road, at best a shade of Maoist red outside. Manipulated as a tool by Mao's successors, Dr Ma, the team of morticians, and the hundreds of labourers who built this place, had, far from help Mao achieve his last dream, actually made him endure his worst nightmare.

Chairman Mao lies uncomfortably. It would, as Deng Xiaoping said of the mausoleum in 1980, 'be inappropriate to remove it, though it wasn't appropriate to build it in the first place'. In a word, Mao was dealt a severe dressing-down posthumously. Moreover, in 1983, on the 90th Anniversary of Mao's birth, three memorial rooms were introduced on the second floor of the mausoleum. Mao would have been delighted to have Zhou Enlai and Zhu De as his companions – but surely not Liu Shaoqi whom he despised, purged and left to die in prison? The Chinese manoeuvre of using a third party to attack the first had been used in masterly fashion: Liu Shaoqi, rehabilitated, was there to haunt Mao.

Only Chiang Kai-shek himself could have made the *feng-shui* worse.

A Chronology of Mao's Century 1893–1993

Street vendor selling calendars to commemorate the centenary of Mao's birth.

1 Twilight Years of the Qing Dynasty

1893	Mao Zedong born in Shaoshan village, Hunan province on December 26th.
1900	Mao works on the family farm.
1901–6	Mao attends local primary school from the age of eight to thirteen, studying Confucian Analects and other Chinese classics.
1907–8	Mao works full time on the family farm, labouring by day and keeping the books at night. Mao refuses to enter into an arranged marriage with a twenty-year-old woman.
1909	Mao registers as a boarder in Xiangtan County school where he studies science from a teacher returned from Japan.
1911	The Double Tenth (October 10th) incident in Wuhan

sparks Republican revolution in Central and South China. Sun Yat-sen declared President in Nanjing, Mao goes to Changsha, provincial capital of Hunan, and joins rebel army for six months.

2 The Republic and Warlord Period

1912 The Last Emperor, Pu Yi, forced to abdicate in Beiping. Sun Yat-sen resigns in favour of the militarily powerful Yuan Shikai. Mao, nineteen, enters Hunan Provincial First Normal (Teacher Training) School.

1912–14 Provisional Nationalist constitution and parliament collapses as Yuan Shikai becomes dictator, eventually restoring the monarchy with himself as emperor. Mao influenced by his ethics teacher Yang and travels through Hunan on foot during his vacation.

1916 Yuan Shikai overthrown. China ruled by regional warlords.

1917 Mao founds New People's Study Society. Bolshevik Revolution in Russia. Sun Yat-sen heads provisional Kuomintang government in Guangzhou.

1918 Mao graduates from Hunan Normal School and travels to Beiping to organise overseas work-study group, thereafter working as assistant librarian in Beiping Library.

1920 Mao, twenty-seven, marries Yang Kaihui.

1921 Chinese Communist Party founded by meeting in Shanghai and Jiaxing. Mao is made CCP secretary of Hunan province.

3 Kuomintang–Communist United Front (1923–7)

1923 Third Congress of CCP in Guangzhou supports idea of KMT–CCP united front against militarists ruling North China.

1924 First KMT Congress in Guangzhou, attended by Mao, formally approves admission of Communists.

1925 Mao returns to Hunan to organise peasant support for a Northern Expedition against warlords. Sun Yat-sen dies. Chiang Kai-shek becomes commander of United Front.

1926   Northern Expedition launched from Guangzhou under leadership of Chiang Kai-shek. Mao undertakes Peasant Movement investigation.

4 Kuomintang–Communist Civil War (1927–37)

1927   Mao publishes a report calling for confiscation of land-lords' land. Chiang Kai-shek initiates anti-Communist coup. Mao leads Autumn Harvest Uprising in Hunan but, defeated, flees to highland stronghold of Jinggangshan.

1928   Chiang Kai-shek achieves patchy control of China with his Kuomintang Government. Zhu De joins forces with Mao at Jinggangshan to form first Red Army and establish a mountain-top Soviet.

1929   The Mao–Zhu army moves to Ruijin, Jiangxi province, adjacent to western Fujian Revolutionary base area to establish the Soviet Republic of China.

1930   Yang Kaihui, Mao's first wife who bore him two sons, Mao Anying and Mao Anqing, is executed in Changsha. Mao Zedong already 'living with' He Zizhen, sixteen years his junior.

1931   Wang Ming elected CCP General Secretary.

1932–4   Chiang Kai-shek launches encirclement and extermination campaigns against Soviet Republic of China.

1934   In mid-October the Long March begins. The Central Red Army moves east in search of a new base. Mao Zedong leaves two children behind. Mao's young brother, Mao Zetan, is executed in Ruijin.

1935   In mid-January, at a meeting on the Long March in Zunyi, Guizhou Province, Mao is elected leader of CCP and Red Army. Mao's third child by He Zizhen is given away to peasants as Long March continues through Guizhou.

In July at Dawei, Sichuan, the Central Red Army, led by Mao, joins forces with the Fourth Red Army, led by Zhang Guotao.

In October Central Red Army forces reach Wuqi in Northern Shaanxi, thus ending their year-long Long March.

1936 Chiang Kai-shek is arrested by Zhang Xueliang in Xi'an, forcing Chiang to form a united front with the Communists against the invading Japanese. The Communists make Yan'an their capital. He Zizhen bears Mao a daughter, Li Min.

5 The Kuomintang–Communist United Front against Japan (1937–45)

1937 War of Resistance against Japan begins. The Red Army renames itself Eighth Route Army and New Fourth Army and is put under Generalissimo Chiang Kai-shek's command. Mao remains in Yan'an to head autonomous regional regime.

1937 Mao's second wife, He Zizhen leaves Yan'an, first for Xi'an and later Moscow, suffering from nervous breakdown caused by Mao's infatuation with Jiang Qing whom he soon marries. In Moscow He Zizhen gives birth to her fifth child by Mao, a daughter who dies in infancy.

1938 Mao enters prolific writing period. The KMT and millions of peasants retreat to heartland China. Communists continue guerrilla warfare behind Japanese lines.

1939 China's struggle against Japanese merges with Second World War. Friction grows between KMT and Communists, the former besieging Yan'an.

1940–1 Chiang Kai-shek attacks Communist forces and United Front breaks down. Jiang Qing bears Mao a daughter, Li Na.

1945 Mao meets Chiang Kai-shek in Chongqing to negotiate on coalition government as the Japanese invaders stare defeat in the face. Atomic bomb dropped on Hiroshima.

6 The War of Liberation (1945–9)

1945 The War of Liberation breaks out. The US continues to support the KMT.

1948 Communists win Manchuria.

1949 Chiang Kai-shek flees to Taiwan as Communist forces under Mao's leadership are victorious nationwide.

7 The People's Republic of China

1949   On October 1st, Mao proclaims the foundation of New China in Beijing's Tiananmen Square. Mao travels to Moscow to solicit Soviet aid from Stalin for China's reconstruction.

1950   Mao sends 'Chinese volunteers' to the Korean War, in which his son, Mao Anying, is eventually killed.

1958   China's Second Five Year Plan becomes Mao's Great Leap Forward which subsides into an agricultural and industrial disaster.

1960   Soviet aid and expertise is withdrawn from China.

1966   In May Mao launches his Great Proletarian Cultural Revolution. In July at the age of seventy-three, he swims in the Yangzi River. Red Guards are established. As disciples of Maoism they travel the country on *Da chuanlian* – exchanges of revolutionary experiences. Mass rallies, presided over by Mao, are held in Tiananmen Square.

1967   Chaos of Cultural Revolution intensifies as inter-factional Red Guard battles take place. 'Revisionists' and 'Capitalist Roaders' – most notably President Liu Shaoqi, Vice-Premier Deng Xiaoping and General Peng Dehuai – are purged.

1969   Instruction of Mao Zedong calls on intellectual youth to go into the countryside for re-education from peasants.

1971   In September, Lin Biao, Mao's chosen successor, stages an unsuccessful assassination attempt on the Chairman's life in Hangzhou. Foiled, Lin Biao and family die escaping to Soviet Union by plane.

1972   Mao welcomes US President Richard Nixon to Beijing.

1973   Deng Xiaoping is reinstated as Vice-Premier by Mao. Jiang Qing and her followers launch 'Criticise Confucius and Lin Biao Campaign' aimed primarily at Premier Zhou Enlai.

1974   Mao coins the term 'Gang of Four' to describe the clique led by his wife Jiang Qing. Mao suffers from Parkinson's disease and Premier Zhou Enlai suffers from cancer. Mao welcomes Edward Heath to Beijing.

1976   In January Premier Zhou Enlai dies. In July Zhu De dies. On September 9th, at the age of eighty-three and after forty-one years leadership of the CCP, Chairman Mao

Zedong dies. On September 18th funeral rally for Mao held in Tiananmen Square. The Gang of Four seize power but Hua Guofeng instigates arrest of the clique on October 6th, thus ending decade-long Cultural Revolution. On October 8th a decision is made by Hua Guofeng to build a memorial hall for Mao.

1977   On the first anniversary of the death of Mao the Memorial Hall of Chairman Mao Zedong, containing his embalmed corpse, is opened to the public in Tiananmen Square.

1980   Historical role of Mao reaffirmed, whilst CCP pledges to uphold and develop Mao Zedong Thought as its guiding ideology. In November the trial of the Gang of Four commences.

1981   In January, Mao Zedong's widow, Jiang Qing, is accused of instigating the most heinous crimes of the Cultural Revolution and given a two-year suspended death sentence. Her Gang of Four accomplices – Zhang Chunqiao, Wang Hongwen and Yao Wenyuan – are given death or life imprisonment.

1983   Jiang Qing's death sentence moderated to life imprisonment. She is kept in Beijing's Qin Cheng prison initially, then placed under house imprisonment in the mid-1980s, rumoured to be undergoing treatment for cancer.

1984   Mao's second wife, He Zizhen, dies aged seventy-five in Shanghai.

1986   On the tenth anniversary of Mao's death, Deng Xiaoping refers to his contribution to the Chinese Revolution as immortal and his mistakes secondary. Memorial rooms for Zhou Enlai, Zhu De and Liu Shaoqi are opened within the Memorial Hall of Mao Zedong.

1989   Students and workers active in the pro-democracy movement paralysing urban China, most notably Beijing and Shanghai, use portraits and quotations of Mao to criticise CCP corruption.

1991   Jiang Qing commits suicide by hanging.

1993   Centenary of Mao's birth. Mao is survived by one child from each of his three marriages: Mao Anqing, Li Min and Li Na.

Glossary of Mandarin Words

bai jiu – rice liquor
bei – north
Beida – Beijing University

Chang Zheng – Long March
cheongsam – (Cantonese) slender high collared dress

Da chuanlian – revolutionary travels by Red Guards
danwei – work unit
Da Xue Shan – Great Snowy Mountains
Da zi bao – big character poster (usually of protest)
Dongbei – northeastern
Dong Fang Hong – the East is Red, an opera and song

fandian – rice house, i.e. restaurant
feng shui – wind and water; feeling, atmosphere
fushiben – ration book

gao bie – last viewing of the deceased by mourners
Gong An Ju – Public Security Bureau, i.e. police
Gong Chan Dang – Share Property Party, i.e. Communist Party
gong she – commune

Hanzu – Han nationality people
He – river
Hong Jun – Red Army
Hong Qi – Red Flag (car)
Hong wei bin – Red Guard
Hu – lake
Huangtu Gaoyuan – Yellow earth (loess) plateau
hua quan – a rowdy drinking game
hukou – citizenship

Jiang – River
Jiangxi hua – Jiangxi Province local language
Jiefang – Liberation (truck)
jin – unit of weight equal to 500 grammes
Jing Lao Yuan – old folk's home

Kang – bed platform that can be heated
Kuomintang – Nationalists

laoban – patron, boss
Lao Ren Jia – respected elder title
lao wai – old foreigner
li – unit of distance, equal to half a kilometre
liang – unit of weight, equal to fifty grammes
liang piao – crop tickets

mao – unit of currency, one tenth of one yuan
mao niu – yak
Mao Zhu Xi – Chairman Mao
mu – unit of area, equal to one sixth of an acre

oushi – shoo

Putonghua – Mandarin

qiao – bridge
qing ke jiu – highland barley liquor

rendan – a medicine, Chinese sal volatile
renkou – 'people's mouths', i.e. population
Renminbi – literally 'people's money' i.e. yuan (see below)
Ribao – Daily, newspaper

sampan – (Cantonese) boat of three bamboos
sha – kill
shan – mountains
Sichuan hua – Sichuan Province local language

tongzhi – comrade

Wan Sui – Long Life
wei ji – crisis
Wenhua da geming – Great Proletarian Cultural Revolution
Wu Jing – armed police
wu shu – kung fu martial arts
wupan – (Cantonese) boat of five bamboos

xiao lu – footpath
Xibei – northwestern
Xinhua – New China (News Agency, bookstores)
Xin Min Xue Hui – New People's Study Society
xiu xi – siesta

yamen – a Tibetan fortress
yaodong – cave dwelling hewn into loess
Yizu – Yi nationality
yuan – Chinese currency (1993, 10 yuan = 1 pound)

zanba – a staple food of roast barley flour dough
Zangzu – Tibetan nationality
zhong – loyalty

Index